Credit Markets and the
Distribution of Income

To Zaverben

Credit Markets and the Distribution of Income

Anup Shah

Department of Economics
The University of Newcastle Upon Tyne
Newcastle Upon Tyne
NE1 7RU

ACADEMIC PRESS
Harcourt Brace Jovanovich, Publishers
London   San Diego   New York   Boston   Sydney   Tokyo   Toronto

This book is printed on acid-free paper

ACADEMIC PRESS LIMITED
24–28 Oval Road
LONDON NW1 7DX

United States Edition published by
ACADEMIC PRESS INC.
San Diego, CA92101

A catalogue
record for this
book is available
from the British
Library

ISBN 0-12-638130-5

Typeset by Mathematical Composition Setters Ltd
Salisbury, Wiltshire, UK

Printed in Great Britain by
Hartnolls Limited, Bodmin, Cornwall

Contents

Preface ix

Chapter 1   Introduction 1

  The credit market in the Arrow–Debreu economy 2
  A theoretical model with credit constraints 3
  Arrow–Debreu equilibrium with credit constraints 9
  Temporary equilibrium with credit constraints 9
  Extension of the Jaffee–Russell model to earnings
    uncertainty 9
  Distribution of credit constraints over borrowers 10
  Implications for the model of this monograph 11
  The plan 12
  Mathematical methods 15
  Notes on background literature 17

Chapter 2   Life-cycle theory with credit constraints ... 20

  The individual's problem 21

A formal solution 23
Lifetime plan with a constrained phase 28
The size of the lifetimes excess burden of a tax 34
Unexpected temporary income change: an illustration of the
    importance of spreading the burden of reduced income 41
Windfall income 43
Intertemporal income transfer 44
Implications for the aggregate consumption function 45
Conclusion 46
Appendix to Chapter 2 46

**Chapter 3   Distributional implications of credit
              constraints** 50

Welfare and choice of earnings profile 51
Choice of earnings profile 54
Distributional implications 60
Conclusion 62

Chapter 4   Differing borrowing and lending rates 63

Analysis of the solution to the choice problem 65
Individuals who never borrow 68

**Chapter 5   Intergenerational implications of credit
              constraints** 71

The model and its formal solution 72
Analysis of the optimal plan 73
Choice of earnings profile 78
Optimal bequests with a non-concave utility-from-bequests
    function 79
Characterization of dynasties 82
The role of wealth 83
Conclusion 83

**Chapter 6   Credit constraints and work–leisure
              choice** 85

The statement of the problem 86
The formal solution 88

Analysis of optimal plans 88
Work constraints 95
A review 97
Appendix to Chapter 6 98

Chapter 7   Labour market structure 102

Job choice 103
Labour market structures 110
Assessment 116
Dynasties and dual labour markets 117
Implications for the unexpectedly unemployed 118
Conclusion 122

Chapter 8   Housing tenure choice 124

The statement of the problem 125
The solution 128
Analysis 131
Evidence 142
Conclusion 145
Appendix to Chapter 8 147

Chapter 9   Extensions and implications 150

Consumption efficiency 151
Famines and starvation 154
Self-employment 158
Relative deprivation 164
Conclusion 168

Chapter 10   Conclusion 170

Mathematical method 170
The argument 171
Insights 174
A final word 178

Bibliography 180

Author Index 187

Subject Index 189

Preface

The late 1970s and the 1980s saw a great deal of research on the life-cycle theory of consumption and labour supply. One impression of this work is that of high-calibre research coming to terms with the realization that a significant proportion of individuals do not behave according to the life-cycle theory and that the most important reason seems to be the presence of binding liquidity constraints.

Advances in techniques and technology have concentrated the research minds on what is 'do-able', for example, the appropriate specifications of the consumption and the labour supply functions. The driving force behind the research appears to be a laudable search for precision in estimates. But there are costs of a single-minded focus on obtaining precision: the turning of a blind eye to the broader picture and the neglect of other harder questions which are nevertheless important and interesting.

One such subject is the consequences of liquidity constraints for consumers, and when one thinks through the consequences, they turn out to be diverse, widespread and long-lasting. This is precisely what this monograph sets out to do and it is hoped that the reader will find a reasoned case for thinking that the consequences are far-reaching and therefore deserving of greater attention. Indeed, it would be gratifying if more economists became aware of the consequences of credit constraints for consumer behaviour as a result of reading and thinking about the argument of this monograph.

A lot of economists and their writings have influenced and shaped this monograph. But equally, I have also benefited from talking to non-economists and observing people going about their business of living.

However, at crucial stages, three economists did point my head in the right direction in a significant way: Lord Desai made me look at conventional economics from unconventional viewpoints, Jim Mirrlees made me aware of the importance of rigour in economic thinking, and Steve Nickell showed me how to think clearly. As usual, no one, apart from myself, is responsible for any errors.

CHAPTER 1

Introduction

This is a monograph on economic theory. That may sound daunting but it is not hard theory. In fact, because it concentrates on individual behaviour, it is easy-to-understand theory. The model is therefore familiar and simple. One states the individual's problem by writing down the objective function and specifying the constraints. The problem is then solved and the solution interpreted. The solution may also generate further results.

However, matters are a little bit more complicated. This is because, in order to analyse individual behaviour in relation to credit markets, one needs an intertemporal perspective instead of an atemporal one – an individual borrower may borrow in the present and pay off the loan in the future. As a result one writes down the objective function and specifies the constraints taking time explicitly into account.

Of course, as is usual, the statement of the problem normally generates a lot of discussion. The discussion may be divided into that which surrounds the objective function and that which concerns the constraints. When dealing with the individual's problem, the objective is usually to optimize, and in our case, it is the maximization of an intertemporal utility function. Such a function is defined over consumption at various dates and is usually assumed to be concave, with the consequence that the necessary conditions

for optimality are also sufficient. It is also often necessary, in order to proceed further with the analysis, to adopt a specific class of utility functions.
But the idea of individuals maximizing over time is not generally agreed
upon. In particular, those who view rational behaviour with cynicism are
bemused by far-sightedness, cannot accept individuals as capable of calcu-
lating complicated problems, and believe in unselfish behaviour, would reject
such an objective function. But the disagreement is well defined and it
would appear that there is an agreement to disagree without generating any
new controversies. All it remains for a researcher to do is to make a subjective choice of either working with such an objective function or discarding
it and looking for something else. In fact, in this monograph we shall be
concerned with maximization of an individual's intertemporal utility function. The chief reason for making this orthodox assumption is that we wish
to demonstrate that our model is consistent with orthodox analysis yet can
give rise to some unorthodox and interesting economic outcomes.

The discussion surrounding the constraints is less settled and more
interesting. Partly this is because many economists think that the specification of constraints can capture the essence of reality and so make economic theory relevant. Now the standard constraint in the intertemporal
consumer theory is the overall budget constraint – lifetime consumption
plus any bequests should not exceed lifetime income plus any inheritance.
Since such a constraint implies that during the lifetime the individual can
borrow freely, it is thought that the constraint is unrealistic. For, in reality,
many individuals cannot borrow freely. If so, it is important to know the
reasons why. It is, of course, impressive if the reasons have the persuasion
of sound logic or, equivalently, good theory. It is therefore important to
investigate whether or not imperfect credit markets can arise in theory. But
the theory has to be widely accepted and this means neoclassical theory.
Such a presumption is likely to raise protest. But the protest is likely to
question the usefulness of neoclassical theory not the fact that it is more
widely accepted than other theories. To be sure, neoclassical theory, as it
stands, is limited in scope. However, we wish to show that it can be enlarged
in scope to yield interesting insights.

We now proceed to show that the constraint of restricted borrowing, or
a borrowing constraint, in the intertemporal utility-maximization problem
is not arbitrary. That is, it arises from conventional theory. If so, then the
problem of this monograph will seem to be consistent with conventional
theory as well.

The Credit Market in the Arrow–Debreu Economy

In an equilibrium model without time (i.e. an atemporal equilibrium model there is no problem of credit because there is no borrowing and lending. The problem of credit is therefore best analysed within an intertemporal setting. Here, in order to assume that the individual's choice is constrained only by the requirement that terminal wealth be non-negative, we also need to assume that there is a perfect personal credit market. According to Bliss, 'a perfect market is one in which the individual transactor is anonymous; it matters not who he is, what he plans to do with his purchase or how he has produced his output. Nor need the market concern itself with the actor's complete plan of action. It is enough that he wants a can of baked beans and that he has the means to pay for it' (Bliss, 1975, pp. 9–10). At first sight it may appear that imperfect credit markets must exist outside the realms of an Arrow-Debreu intertemporal economy. This is because the lender knows the present value of the borrower's wealth with certainty. Then it would seem that provided that the lender is satisfied with the borrower's ability to pay off his debts, the borrower may borrow as much as he likes provided that he satisfies his intertemporal budget constraint. But even here there is a problem because even if both the lender and the borrower agree on the borrower's intertemporal budget constraint, there is no institution to guarantee the operation of credit trustworthiness. The lender can never be certain that his loans will be honoured; if the borrower so chooses, he may default. It is worth pursuing this in some detail.

A Theoretical Model with Credit Constraints

Consider a two-period intertemporal model. Individuals who plan to borrow in the first period can be grouped into honest borrowers who never default and dishonest borrowers who default whenever it is in their interest to do so. All borrowers have identical preferences defined over consumption in two periods and identical earnings profile.

Demand for loans

Honest borrowers
All honest borrowers are identical in all respects. The honest borrower solves the following problem:

$$\text{Maximize } U(c_1, c_2)$$
$$c_1, c_2$$

subject to

$$c_2 = y_2 - (1 + r)L, \qquad L = c_1 - y_1,$$

where c_i denotes consumption in period i, $i = 1, 2$; y_i denotes exogenously given earnings in period i; r is the one-period interest rate; L is the size of the loan which is taken out at the beginning of the first period and repaid with interest at the beginning of the second period. Since the constraint is satisfied, the borrower is ensured to be honest.

The first-order condition is

$$\frac{U_1}{U_2} = R, \qquad R \equiv (1 + r),$$

where U_i is the partial derivative of U with respect to its ith argument. Assuming that the utility function is strictly quasi-concave, a unique interior maximum exists. We can then write:

$$c_1 = c_1(R, y_1, y_2).$$

If

$$\frac{\partial c_1}{\partial R} < 0,$$

then

$$L = c_1(R, y_1, y_2) - y_1 = L(R, y_1, y_2), \qquad \frac{\partial L}{\partial R} < 0$$

is the loan demand function.

Dishonest borrowers
Dishonest borrowers are identical to honest borrowers except that they may or may not default. The decision to default depends on which course of action yields greater utility. Hence, the dishonest borrower will

$$\text{Maximize } U(c_1, c_2)$$

subject to $c_1 = y_1 + L$
and $c_2 = y_2 - RL$, i.e. does not default,
or $c_2 = y_2 - z$, i.e. defaults,

where z is the cost of default. Because dishonest borrowers do not wish to be detected, L is the same as that for honest borrowers. But this means that first-period consumption, c_1, is chosen to be the same as that for the honest borrowers. Since $U_2 > 0$, the dishonest borrower will default if c_2 under default is greater than that under no default, i.e. if

$$[c_2 = y_2 - RL] < [c_2 = y_2 - z] \Rightarrow RL > z,$$

that is, whenever the contract repayment, RL, is greater than the penalty of default, z.

Supply of loans

Lenders, being risk-neutral, maximize expected profits. In order to work out expected revenue, the lenders need to guess the proportion of individuals who do not default. It is assumed that the cost of default differs among dishonest individuals. This results in a probability-of-repayment relationship: $\lambda(RL)$ which denotes the expected proportion of contracts of size RL that are not defaulted upon. For required repayments below a certain minimum cost of default, i.e. $RL < Z_{MIN}$, no one defaults and dishonest individuals display honest behaviour. For contract sizes above the maximum cost of default possessed by an individual, i.e. $RL > Z_{MAX}$, all dishonest individuals default. Therefore,

$$\lambda(RL) = 1 \quad \text{whenever} \quad Z_{MIN} > RL,$$

and it is plausible to postulate that

$$\lambda'(RL) < 0 \quad \text{whenever} \quad Z_{MIN} < RL < Z_{MAX}.$$

Expected revenue is given by $\lambda(RL)RL$, that is, contracted repayment times the likelihood of repayment. Lenders obtain their funds in a perfect capital market at the constant one-period interest rate i with no other costs. The profit expression is then:

$$\Pi = \lambda(RL)RL - IL, \quad I \equiv 1 + i.$$

A competitive loan market and free entry implies a zero profit condition so that the supply function of loans is given by:

$$\lambda(RL)R = I$$

clearly when

$$RL < Z_{MIN} \Rightarrow \lambda = 1 \quad \text{and} \quad R = I$$

and when

$$RL > Z_{MIN} \Rightarrow \lambda < 1 \quad \text{and} \quad R > I.$$

Equilibrium

Substituting demand, $L(R, y_1, y_2)$, into supply, $\lambda(RL)R = I$, we obtain:

$$\lambda(RL(R, y_1, y_2))R = I.$$

Given y_1, y_2 and I, the equilibrium condition yields R and, from $L(R, y_1, y_2)$, the equilibrium size of loans.

The above model is essentially that which was first presented by Jaffee and Russell (1976). They went on to show that either the market reaches a multiple-contract equilibrium in which lenders enter the market and make short-run profits but are forced to leave in the long run or a stable single-contract equilibrium.

Single-contract equilibrium
The single-contract equilibrium solution which dominates is not at the intersection of supply and demand for loans. It is where the volume of credit demanded by the borrower is greater than that supplied by the lender. The reasoning is interesting and is worth pursuing with the help of diagrams.

Figure 1.1(a) shows the iso-utility curves of the borrower in the (L, R)

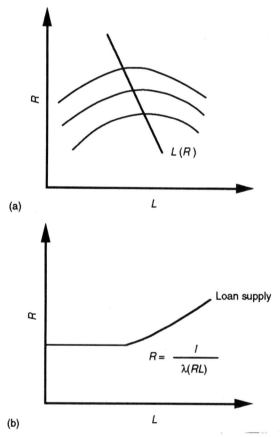

Figure 1.1 *(a) Borrower's iso-utility curve. (b) Supply curve for loans.*

space. These are obtained as follows. Using the budget, write $U(c_1, c_2) = U(L + y_1, y_2 - RL)$ and set:

$$U(L + y_1, y_2 - RL) = \text{constant}.$$

Totally differentiating yields:

$$\frac{dR}{dL} = \frac{U_1/U_2 - R}{L}.$$

At the demand curve, since $U_1 = RU_2$, $dR/dL = 0$. In addition, it can be shown that around this point $d^2R/dL^2 < 0$. Furthermore, the slope of the iso-utility curve can change sign only at the point of intersection with the demand curve, so the iso-utility curves rise monotonically until they reach the demand function and fall monotonically thereafter.

Figure 1.1(b) shows the supply curve for loans in the (L, R) space. It is a plot of $R = I/\lambda(RL)$. The slope of the supply function depends on the properties of the λ function. Up to the point $L = Z_{\text{MIN}}/I$ the supply curve is flat, for between $L = 0$ and $L = Z_{\text{MIN}}/I$ no one defaults so that $\lambda = 1$, and $R = I$ satisfies the supply-function equation. Beyond the point $L = Z_{\text{MIN}}/I$, the supply function is either positively sloped or backward-bending. Jaffee and Russell show that if λ has the Pareto distribution and the mean of the distribution does not exist then the supply curve will be positively sloped; if λ has the exponential distribution then the supply curve will be backward-bending.

The obvious candidate for equilibrium is the point at which the demand curve intersects the supply curve. However, this point is inefficient because there exists another point at which the zero-profit condition is satisfied and the borrower is better off. This point lies on the supply curve since along

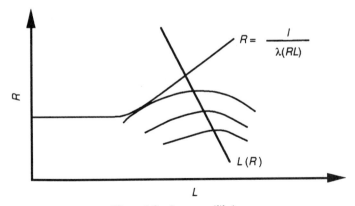

Figure 1.2 *Loan equilibrium.*

it the zero-profit condition is satisfied, but it is off the demand curve. In Figure 1.2 it is at the point of tangency of an iso-utility curve and the supply curve. But at this point the volume of credit demanded is greater than that supplied at the equilibrium contract rate. This is because of the upward sloping nature of the supply curve, caused by greater expectations of default at higher loan volumes, and the downward concavity of the iso-utility function of the borrower. The advantage of rationing is that fewer individuals default at the smaller loan size, and under competition these gains are passed on to the honest borrowers.

A Summary of the Jaffee–Russell Model

The Jaffee–Russell model is an attempt to provide an economic rationale for the allocation of credit by means other than the interest rate. The explanation, based on moral hazard and asymmetric information, may be summarised as follows.

Even in a world of certainty, honesty cannot be guaranteed. Then the possibility exists that some borrowers may intentionally default. Moreover, borrowers can have differing default propensities. Since lenders are unable to distinguish between the borrowers on an *a priori* basis, borrowers have more information about the likelihood of default than do lenders. The lenders can only know the aggregate average default propensity and therefore treat each borrower as if he has the average propensity. Premised on this information asymmetry between the borrower and the lender, the Jaffee-Russell paper shows that in a competitive loan market, a single-contract equilibrium will occur at a point of rationing. That is, it will occur at a point where the volume of credit demanded by the borrower is greater than that supplied by the lender. Since borrowers default if default costs are less than the loan and interest payments combined, rationing works as it stops some borrowers from defaulting. A feature of the rationing equilibrium is that at the equilibrium point borrowers who do not default pay a premium above the opportunity cost of loan funds to support those indistinguishable borrowers who do default. It all depends on the distribution of the costs of default because if it is such that when all demands for loans are met, some borrowers default, then in order for lenders to recover their opportunity costs, honest borrowers who repay their loans must subsidize the defaulters. Credit rationing makes honest borrowers better off because fewer people default so that the subsidy they have to pay to lenders to recoup their opportunity cost is reduced. In normal markets, of course, excess demand would induce an increase in the interest rate. Here, an increase in the interest rate would attract more dishonest borrowers and drive out the honest borrowers.

Arrow–Debreu Equilibrium with Credit Constraints

Returning to the scenario of an Arrow-Debreu economy with honest and dishonest individuals, we can either assume that somehow all contracts are honoured and proceed to show that equilibrium exists or admit borrowing constraints and consider the existence of equilibrium with such constraints. In fact, provided that Walras's law holds and we can also assert the continuity of excess demand schedules, equilibrium can be shown to exist and *a priori* there is no reason to suppose that these requirements will not be met. All that really happens is that in addition to the overall budget constraint there is a continuous sequence of debt-holding conditions which must be met.

Temporary Equilibrium with Credit Constraints

The problem of imperfect credit markets is much more prevalent within a sequence economy than an Arrow-Debreu economy because then there is the possibility of the individual choosing to meet his obligations but being unable to do so because his expectations turn out to be incorrect. Within a temporary equilibrium framework, agents' expectations about the future differ; in particular those of the lender and the borrower. This means that as soon as we introduce, say, income uncertainty, the nature of personal loans is such that it makes it impossible for the borrower to be anonymous so that perfect credit markets cannot exist and the individual may not be able to transact just as he would like.

Extension of the Jaffee–Russell Model to Earnings Uncertainty

So long as the lending behaviour and the demand functions remain unchanged, the analysis goes through when the honest–dishonest distinction is replaced by the lucky–unlucky distinction. Lucky individuals are honest and with a propitious second-period income whereas unlucky individuals are also honest but have impropitious second-period income. Under the following characterization of the problem, the only thing that changes is the default condition so that the analysis does, indeed, go through.

All individuals have the same utility function and the same period 1 income as before. However, period 2 income, $\tilde{y}_2$, is stochastic with y_2 denoting its mean. Individuals treat y_2 as the certainty equivalent of $\tilde{y}_2$. Then the individuals will display the same loan-demand behaviour as in the honest–dishonest case.

Ex post, however, individuals may experience actual incomes sufficiently below y_2 to cause the necessity of default. Default occurs whenever the cost of default, $z = \tilde{y}_2 - y_2$, is less than the difference between the required repayment level and period 2 income:

$$z < (RL - y_2).$$

Recall that in the honest–dishonest case, dishonest individuals defaulted when

$$z < RL.$$

Hence the two conditions for default are identical except for the constant displacement of y_2.

It is reasonable that z will be distributed across the population, with 'lucky' individuals receiving high z and 'unlucky' individuals receiving low z. The result, therefore, is that the distribution of z will determine a default function $\lambda(RL)$ in the same manner as in the honest–dishonest case. But the $\lambda(RL)$ function is the critical input from the demand side into the lender behaviour. Hence the analysis goes through. But there are points of difference and it is worth noting them.

First, honest–dishonest individuals are assumed to know their future default states *ex ante*; lucky–unlucky individuals do not. One implication is that in the honest–dishonest case the lender loses on defaults, but gains only the contracted amount otherwise. In the lucky–unlucky case, the lender loses on unlucky borrowers, but does not share in the gain of lucky borrowers beyond the contracted amount.

Second, the case of lucky–unlucky leaves open the possibility of partial default, since default occurs whenever $z < (RL - y_2)$ but total default must occur only when $\tilde{y}_2 = 0$.

Finally, note that although individuals all act on the assumption that they will not default, there is a fallacy in that *ex post* unlucky borrowers will default.

Distribution of Credit Constraints over Borrowers

The analysis carried out so far yields the result that all borrowers face the same credit constraint. But the model can be extended such that some borrowers face a more stringent credit constraint than others.

Consider the situation in which lenders face individuals with different propensities to default but they have no knowledge of individual default propensities. But suppose that individuals have some other observable characteristics. Then lenders may attempt to sort them into different risk classes on the basis of the observable characteristics. For this to work, individual characteristics and risk classes should be correlated and the lenders should have knowledge of such correlation, perhaps based on past data.

Suppose, then, lenders divide borrowers into two − high and low − risk classes. Given the same value of debt to repay, the probability of not observing default for the high-risk group is lower than for the low-risk group. That is,

$$\lambda_h(R_h L_h) < \lambda_l(R_l L_l), \qquad R_h L_h = R_l L_l.$$

These default functions are constructed in the same way as before.

Although some borrowers have been classified as high risk and others as low risk, all borrowers have the same demand function for loans. The supply functions for loans to the two classes are defined by the zero profit conditions:

$$\lambda_h(R_h L_h) R_h L_h = I L_h,$$
$$\lambda_l(R_l L_l) R_l L_l = I L_l.$$

Given the foregoing analysis, it can be shown that in equilibrium $L_h < L_l$ and $R_h > R_l$. Therefore, there can exist a credit-market equilibrium with two types of loan contracts and in which the high-risk borrowers are more severely credit-constrained than low-risk borrowers.

The analysis of the Jaffee−Russell model is based on the implications of the fundamental notions of moral hazard and imperfect information. It is a theoretical model which shows that in equilibrium the loan market clears by rationing. Therefore, individual borrowers are credit-constrained. Thus the problem of an individual maximizing a two-period utility function subject to an overall budget constraint and a credit constraint is consistent with an equilibrium model which is grounded in sound theory. But the Jaffee−Russell model itself can be embedded within a general equilibrium framework. Although this has not been demonstrated formally, conceptually there does not appear to be a problem.

Implications for the Model of this Monograph

So credit constraints can arise in a model in which there is competition between lenders, there are many borrowers, and all agents optimize. The individual borrower then typically maximizes intertemporal utility subject to an overall budget constraint and a credit constraint. Now, in part, a lot of discussion in economics surrounds constraints because it is thought that a great deal of interesting economics is contained in the constraints. If so,

rich analysis can arise from the specification of constraints. But there is a
need for a word of caution here, and it concerns the number of constraints.
Too many constraints can strangle theory thereby making the problem
uninteresting, at least intellectually. But in this monograph, we shall be analysing a model of individual behaviour in which the utility function is
defined over multi-period consumption and the maximization is carried out
subject to an overall budget constraint and a sequence of debt limits which
may or may not bind. As a result, we are able to extend the theory of intertemporal consumer behaviour and go a great deal further in tracing out the
consequences of credit constraints for behaviour. We are able to do this
partly because the specification of the constraints has, indeed, made the
problem richer but partly also because the conventional methods of
analysis, such as comparative statics, can be employed easily.

Because our setting is a multi-period one whereas that of Jaffee and
Russell is of two periods, there is a difference between the two which is
worth noting. Consider the Jaffee–Russell individual who borrows. He
faces a given credit limit. As we have seen, the model can be extended such
that the credit limit can vary over individual characteristics. Now when we
go from two periods to many periods, there is an interesting consequence.
In a two-period model, the first-period loan must be repaid in full in the
second period. In a multi-period model, the repayment can be staggered
over many periods. Thus, over time, the size of the loan can be adjusted
and the lender can learn about the borrower's credit-worthiness. By monitoring repayments, the lender can also learn about the borrower's earnings
profile. This works as follows: if repayments are related to earnings and if
they are regularly made then they will trace out the earnings profile. This
point is worth bearing in mind when we examine the mathematical
specification of the problem in the next chapter.

The Plan

The task of this monograph can be stated quite simply. It is to derive the
theoretical implications for consumer behaviour of credit constraints
arising from consumer loan markets (as opposed to commercial loan
markets). One way of looking at the structure of the monograph is to view
it as an analysis of degree of choice in individual plans. This structure can
be brought out by briefly considering the contents of each chapter.

In the standard problem, the individual maximises an intertemporal
utility function subject to an overall budget constraint. The result is that
consumption then depends on income but only to the extent that income
affects lifetime resources. Reanalysing the problem in the next chapter with

the possibility of a credit constraint binding sometime in life not only changes the result, but it is also shown that the changes matter as they imply some interesting consequences for many policy issues. All this makes up Chapter 2.

Chapter 3 investigates the effects on plans of greater choice, that is, the consumer chooses a consumption plan and an investment-in-human-capital plan. Given concavity, in order to raise welfare, one would have thought that the consequences of credit limits would be spread over all choices and this, in fact, turns out to be so. However, the upshot is rather interesting since it is shown that, unlike the traditional result in which initial assets do not matter for choices, credit constraints make initial assets important. In fact, we can identify a threshold level of initial assets which has a crucial bearing on choice. Finally, we derive results for the distribution of income which are at total variance with the standard results.

The above summary of Chapter 3 suggests that it should be worth considering bequest choice since bequests made by one generation of a dynasty form the inheritance of the next generation of the same dynasty. It would then be interesting to see if a credit-constrained generation which starts with initial assets which are less than the threshold level can bequeath such that the inheritance for the next generation is greater than the threshold level. For there is an intriguing question here, which is can, with the help of parents, children break out of a low-wealth, low-earnings situation? Alternatively, can a whole dynasty be locked into such a situation by choice conditioned on credit constraints? Although Chapter 5 concentrates on the intergenerational consequences of credit constraints, it also advances one of the monograph's themes of the effect of greater choice on the influence of credit constraints on an individual's plans.

Persevering with this theme, work is introduced as a choice variable in Chapter 6. This chapter examines the possibility of the individual increasing welfare by spreading the burden of credit constraints on work as well as consumption over life. The chapter also takes on board the possibility that work may be job-entailed. Though Chapter 6 concentrates on a work–leisure trade-off, in a lifetime context it is hard to ignore a work–training trade-off. One important difference between the trade-offs is that whereas the work–leisure trade-off assumes a given wage profile, the work–training trade-off implies that the wage profile changes. This is because the wage rate reflects productivity which is determined by training which takes time. The upshot is that work choice is best viewed as job choice, each job being characterized by a job-entailed work and wage profile. Chapter 7, then, analyses such job choices. It finds that job choice can be significantly influenced by credit constraints that an individual may face. In particular, if jobs can be divided into primary-sector jobs and secondary-sector jobs then, *ceteris paribus*, an individual who faces greater effective credit-rationing is more likely to choose a secondary-sector job. Although the marginal individual is indifferent between the two job types since his welfare is the same in either sector, the present-value lifetime earnings are smaller in the secondary sector. Then there results a labour market structure which has empirical and logical consistency.

In Chapter 8, the model is extended to trace out further consequences of credit constraints. The extension allows for portfolio choice as the individual may hold housing equity in addition to financial assets. It is shown that in equilibrium owned housing is cheaper than rental housing. As a result, those who hold a portfolio of financial and housing assets consume the same housing services more cheaply than those who hold financial assets only. The possibility then exists that those who are severely credit-constrained earn low lifetime income and rent expensive housing. In particular, those with low assets are more likely to be locked into such a situation.

Chapter 9 explores the effects of credit constraints in other areas of economics. The idea is to show that credit constraints can have a wide-ranging influence. The chapter is organized around four topics. In the first topic of consumption efficiency, the idea that if human capital affects an individual's work productivity then it should also affect his consumption efficiency is taken on board. The second topic deals with famines and shows that if famines result from a relative price change then binding credit constraints lead to a redistribution of productive agricultural assets from the poor to the rich. The third topic deals with self-employment. Becoming self-employed typically requires set-up capital. This requirement acts like an entrance fee to a club. Then access to capital becomes an important determinant of self-employment. The final topic is that of relative deprivation. We develop the concept of a relative deprivation threshold and show how an individual can be deprived for part of his life if credit constraints bind. The concluding chapter consists of a 37-step argument of the monograph. It also takes an overview of the subject and ends by articulating the major themes and insights of the monograph.

It is worth emphasizing that the outcomes arise from choices made in non-credit markets conditioned on credit constraints. Since choices extend over many markets, the consequences of credit constraints extend widely as well. In addition, the consequences are markedly different from standard ones. For instance, consider labour-market structure. A dual labour market is characterized by two sectors: the primary sector which is characterized by good pay, training, promotion and job security, and the secondary sector which has low pay, little training, poor promotion prospects and little job security. Our analysis isolates the threshold level of initial assets and connects this with the segmentation of the labour market. The analysis also shows that, all other things being equal, those with initial assets below the threshold level choose the secondary-sector jobs whereas those with initial assets above the threshold level choose the primary-sector jobs. Furthermore, our intergenerational analysis shows that it can be a steady-state feature for a whole dynasty to be locked into the secondary sector. Since the allocation of individuals to the sectors is by choice, our model provides a choice-theoretic basis for the dual labour-market structure. This is interesting for it means that individuals choose an outcome which is best for themselves given the constraints but which may be viewed as undesirable by policy makers.

Mathematical Methods

The life-cycle theory of consumer behaviour analyses the problem of allocation of consumption over time, subject to an overall lifetime budget constraint. In this monograph, the problem is analysed subject to additional constraints. Since these are inequality constraints, optimal control theory is used as a tool of analysis. It is useful to compare the advantages and disadvantages of employing it for analysis with its close rival, the classical calculus of variations.

(i) The modern version of the calculus of variations is often called 'optimal control theory'. This theory resulted from the problems arising from optimally controlling the behaviour through time of some system such as a spacecraft, but it is now used to solve problems in many fields including that of economics.

The theory of optimal control was developed by Pontryagin and his associates (1962) in the late 1950s. Although Hestenes (1966) wrote on similar lines in the late 1940s, and work by Bellman and Dreyfus (1962) in dynamic programming is closely related to Pontryagin's work, it is the work of Pontryagin and his associates that is chiefly responsible for the modern approach to calculus of variations, for the renewed interest in variational problems and for its widespread use.

(ii) In a variational problem, the task is to characterize the trajectories of the state variables of the system under consideration so as to obtain a local extreme value of the integral objective function, a task for which the classical calculus of variations is suited. Optimal control theory solves the same problems by means of a 'closed loop' control. If u is the optimal control and x is the present state then we have $x \rightarrow u \rightarrow \dot{x} \rightarrow x$. In contrast, traditional variational analysis has to solve the problem each time for a different initial state. Optimal control analysis solves a family of an infinite number of problems simultaneously, because it tells us what to do whatever the value of x, by means of the policy function, $u(x)$. The end product of optimal control analysis is, therefore, synthesis and this recursive aspect has been recognized by Arrow (1968). On the investment decision facing a firm in economic theory, he writes (1968, p. 1): 'in continuous time analysis the basic production relation is between the stocks of capital goods and the flows of current inputs and outputs; the earlier part is controlling only in that the stock of capital goods is a cumulation of past flows'. On the technique he employs, he writes (1968, pp. 1–2); 'The Russian mathematician Pontryagin and his associates have developed an elegant theory of control of recursive processes related both to Bellman's work and the classical calculus of variations'.

It must be emphasized that the classical calculus of variations is well equipped to handle cases where interior optimal trajectories exist which satisfy the appropriate end-point or boundary conditions and many economists prefer calculus of variations to optimal control. To quote Mirrlees (1971, p. 179): 'The use of the Maximum Principle has a number of serious disadvantages. It does not show us how to obtain certain important supplementary conditions on the optimum. The analysis provides no hint as to how it could be made more rigorous. It does not provide any insight into the kind of maximization that is going on'. Such comments justifiably arise because the methods of calculus of variations are more explicit and yield an explicit variational analysis.

(iii) In many problems in economics, inequality constraints on both control and state variables are present. Therefore, it could easily turn out that in certain problems one of the optimal trajectories will not be interior to all the constraints. In such a situation, it is possible to obtain the optimal trajectories by some appropriate extensions of the classical calculus of variations method. But although in principle traditional methods can be adapted to handle such problems, the modern optimal control theory yields, rather naturally, the necessary conditions for optimal trajectory, whenever the trajectory alternates between lying in the interior and on the boundary of the constraints. This point has been emphasized by Hadley and Kemp (1971, p. 238); 'the new theory allows for inequalities in the constraints: and, technically, this is the most important advance beyond the classical theory'. In fact, to quote Karl Shell (1967, footnote p. vi): 'Roughly the maximum principle is to the ordinary calculus of variations as the Kuhn–Tucker conditions are to the (ordinary) first-order conditions of the differential calculus'.

(iv) Perhaps the most fundamental innovation of the optimal control method is in its treatment of the control variables. It is in fact because the control variables need not be continuous that the Pontryagin derivation of the necessary conditions takes a different form from that of the traditional methods. This is an important advantage, as stressed by Wan (1971, p. 416): 'When the control variable is restricted to take values in a given set, the maximum principle provides a method of solution both convenient and illuminating'.

(v) It must be emphasized, however, that the two approaches are essentially equivalent. The calculus of variations arrives at the solution by treating the problem as a 'problem of Bolza' by applying the Euler–Lagrange equations to a Lagrangean expression involving the integrand and the differential side constraints. The method of Pontryagin *et al.* arrives at the solution by treating the problem as a problem in optimal control by applying the maximum principle to the Hamiltonian function. An extension along these lines to the situation where there are two differing types of inequality constraints, is contained in Bruno (1967) which gives the two formulations of the same problem, both formulations yielding the same answers. Bruno is an example of an author starting his work within an explicit calculus of variations framework and later being persuaded to adopt the more direct optimal control version. Quite a number of other such cases are to be found in the literature. Often the author starts by adopting one method and ends up utilizing the other, sometimes having been persuaded to do so by anonymous referees.

(vi) On the whole, the optimal control approach is the more versatile. It can handle a wide variety of problems with relative ease. Not surprisingly, the rather widespread use of optimal control methods in economics is explained largely by the directness with which results are arrived at. Furthermore, according to Arrow (1968, p. 2), 'the Pontryagin principle has the great advantage of yielding economically interesting results very naturally'. Besides it has an enormous advantage in that it yields as a by-product costate variables which serve as shadow prices in economics. In addition, this often provides a more convenient way of obtaining a phase diagram.

Notes on Background Literature

The conceptual apparatus for analysing consumer behaviour over time in economic theory was laid down by Fisher (1930) in his theory of saving and interest and much of the modern consumer savings theory is a reformulation and extension of Fisher's work. His study shows how an individual with a fluctuating lifetime stream of income can even out his consumption by alternately lending and borrowing, and how his decisions depend on the market rate of interest. Fisher's general equilibrium approach also shows how these savings decisions interact with investment decisions to determine market interest rates. Essentially Fisher's work rests on three basic assumptions. First, the consumer possesses perfect foresight so that in order to plan his current consumption he is able to forecast accurately future prices and wage rates. Fisher's second assumption is that the consumer faces a perfect credit market and implies that any consumer may borrow against his future earnings at a given rate of interest and lend his savings at the same rate. Finally, it is assumed that the consumer chooses a consumption–savings path so as to maximize a discounted intertemporal utility function. Together with these three assumptions it is also presupposed that the planning horizon is finite. In this monograph we shall be mainly concerned with the consequences of discarding the second assumption.

The life-cycle hypothesis, developed and tested by Brumberg (1956), Modigliani and Ando (1957, 1963) and Modigliani and Brumberg (1954) in the Fisherian tradition, stresses the assumption that the consumer maximizes an intertemporal utility function subject to a lifetime resource constraint. As a result, the demand for current consumption is a function of lifetime resources, the rate of interest and other parameters which depend on age. This original version of the life-cycle theory is in many ways similar to Friedman's permanent-income theory (1957). However, the life-cycle theory lays greater stress on the underlying utility function, family size and non-human capital. The two theories also differ in their choice of framework for empirical verification. Finally, another important difference is in the relation between consumption and age; for example, in the life-cycle theory, current consumption out of windfall income depends on age, as all lifetime resources must be used up, whereas this is not the case for the permanent-income theory in which a household lives for ever.

The models of Atkinson (1971), Blinder (1974, Chap. 2) and Yaari (1964) can be thought of as the modern reformulation of the Fisher consumer problem, albeit with a bequest motive, and they usefully serve as a point of departure for Chapters 2 and 3 of this monograph. Atkinson (1971) can be thought of as an extension of the Yaari formulation to incorporate wealth taxation. However, his is an extremely valuable piece of analysis since it lays down methods for effecting comparative statics. Deaton (1972), too, carries out a comparative statics exercise to examine the effects of a change in the rate of interest on current consumption.

Ramsey (1928) was the first to consider an intertemporal model of consumption and work. He assumed both intertemporal and contemporaneous additive separability of the utility function in goods and leisure, constant wages and a perfect credit market. A modern reformulation is that of Weiss (1972). Under the Ramsey assumptions, consumption moves independently of wages whereas the supply of work follows wages. Blinder (1974, Chap. 3) analyses a model similar in formulation to that of Weiss but concentrates on retirement periods. The retirement period occurs when leisure, defined as a proportion of the time period, takes the value of unity. Heckman (1974) extends Ramsey's work to the case where the instantaneous utility function is not separable. The studies mentioned in this paragraph should prove to be useful additional background material for Chapter 6.

CHAPTER 2

Life-Cycle Theory with Credit Constraints

Suppose credit constraints exist and persist. Does this matter? It is one thing to assert that they do and quite another convincingly to demonstrate that they matter. In order to present the argument for credit constraints mattering, we shall begin with a model, that of consumer intertemporal optimization. Not all microeconomists would accept that such a model is the best one for the task at hand; this is particularly so for those not of a neoclassical bent. But since neoclassical methods are understood by the majority of economists, it appears that this route should at least have the largest audience.

Having taken the model on board, we incorporate credit constraints and work out the solution. The solution generates further analysis and such analysis forms the bulk of this chapter and the subsequent chapters. Although this chapter is largely analytical, some quantitative feel is provided and some existing evidence referred to. When checking whether the analytical implications matter or not, the reader should also bear in mind that we have eschewed the macro implications. The econometric formulation and testing of the consumption function and the like have undergone a big revival recently and at the centre of the debate here is the role played by credit constraints. It is simply not possible to do justice to the debate in this monograph. Therefore, we have confined ourselves to micro and distributional implications of credit constraints.

The Individual's Problem

Consider an individual at time $t = 0$. He plans consumption over the interval $[0, T]$ so as to maximize lifetime utility. Since problems arising from uncertainty are not dealt with here, T is assumed to be known with certainty. Let $c(t)$ be the rate of consumption at time t. It is assumed that the instantaneous utility function, $U(c(t))$, is strictly concave and differentiable and also that $U_c(c)$ tends to zero as c tends to ∞, and $U_c(c)$ tends to ∞ as c tends to zero. It is also assumed that utility is additively separable so that the individual maximizes the integral of the instantaneous utility function. The implication of this assumption is that it makes $U(c(t_1))$ independent of $c(t_2)$, $t_1 \neq t_2$ and is, therefore, somewhat restrictive as it rules out intertemporal complementarities. But the advantage of analytical tractability is considerable. Thus the individual is assumed to maximize

$$J = \int_0^T e^{-\rho t} U(c(t)) \, dt, \qquad 0 \leqslant t \leqslant T, \tag{2.1}$$

where ρ is the constant subjective rate of time discount.

Turning to the constraints facing the individual, let $A(t)$ denote the asset holdings of the individual at time t so that $A(0)$ stands for initial assets and $A(T)$ for terminal assets. Initially it is assumed that both $A(0) = A_0$ and $A(T) = A_T$ are given. This assumption will be relaxed later on once some results arising from the simpler model have been derived. Let $r(t)$ denote the rate of interest at time t and $y(t)$ the wage income. Then savings are governed by the differential equation:

$$\dot{A} = r(t)A(t) + y(t) - c(t), \qquad 0 \leqslant t \leqslant T. \tag{2.2}$$

Given (2.2) and the end points,

$$A(0) = A_0 \qquad \text{and} \qquad A(T) = A_T, \tag{2.3}$$

the lifetime budget constraint can be specified as

$$A_0 + \int_0^T e^{-rt} y(t) \, dt - e^{-rt} A_T = \int_0^T e^{-rt} c(t) \, dt. \tag{2.4}$$

One implication of the specified lifetime budget constraint is that provided it is satisfied, the individual can borrow and lend freely. But this is contrary to the analysis of the previous chapter which implies a credit limit of the form,

$$A \geqslant \bar{A}, \qquad 0 \leqslant t \leqslant T. \tag{2.5}$$

However, the reasons for (2.5) were based on a two-period model. When this model is extended to a multi-period setting, there results one significant modification to the credit limit specification in (2.5).

The reasoning is as follows. When (2.5) binds, i.e. $A = \bar{A}$ over some interval in life, it implies that $y = c - r\bar{A}$. This means that the individual has to meet current consumption expenditure and current interest payments from current earnings. If he cannot pay the interest charges then (2.5) is violated. Obviously, this can happen if $y < -r\bar{A}$. But also, he may not be able to meet interest charges if $(y + r\bar{A}) > 0$ but such that it is low relative to marginal utility of consumption. The essential point is a simple one: the individual may be honest and not want to default, but has no choice. Therefore, in order to prevent a violation of (2.5) the lender has to ensure that debt can be serviced in addition to there being no incentive to default. To accomplish this, the lender can make use of the observation that both debt service payments and consumption must come out of current earnings on a debt-constrained phase. Let us consider this. For a given change in y, although $r\bar{A}$ and hence the pecuniary value of defaulting is unchanged, the utility value will change (see Shah (1990) for a proof). Intuitively, a given change in y has more impact on utility when the change occurs on a debt-constrained phase as opposed to an unconstrained phase.

Thus the probability of default will come to depend on earnings: the greater the earnings, the smaller the probability of default. Under such conditions, the credit limit can be written as

$$\bar{A} = \bar{A}(y), \qquad \bar{A}'(y) < 0.$$

A linear approximation of this is

$$\bar{A} = \alpha_2 y, \qquad \alpha_2 \leqslant 0. \tag{2.5a}$$

In assessing the risk of default, the lender can make use of other observable characteristics of the individual and the relationship between these and group statistical information. Then, on the basis of this observation, the lender can divide borrowers into risk classes. Then if a borrower is considered low risk — a white married male, say — he will be assigned a low α_2. This obviously means, according to (2.5a), that such a borrower will be able to run up a larger debt, compared to a black unmarried female, say, with the same wage income. In general, then, α_2 will vary with individual characteristics other than wage income.

The rule in (2.5a) is imposed by the lender and therefore may not be satisfactory to the borrower. This is because the individual borrows to supplement current consumption in anticipation of higher future earnings, but the amount he can borrow depends on his current earnings. In other words, he can borrow the maximum amount when he probably least needs it and the minimum amount when his needs are the greatest. Therefore, this rule has myopic characteristics.

Before turning to the implications of the credit-rationing rule (2.5a) when taken together with equations (2.1)–(2.4), let us consider an extension to the rule. Thus far, two other major sources of credit have been ignored. Building society lending is considered later on when housing is introduced as a separate good and therefore it is ignored for now.

Secondly, lending by those such as parents is usually income independent so that (2.5a) may be simply written as:

$$A(t) \geqslant \bar{A}(t) \, \forall t \qquad \bar{A}(t) = \alpha_1 + \alpha_2 y(t), \qquad (2.5b)$$

where $\alpha_1 \leqslant 0$, depends on the wealth of the individual's parents. α_1 may also depend on time but we shall avoid this complication.

Having specified the equations of the model and discussed them individually it is worth considering the implications of the equations taken together. Assuming that α_1 and α_2 are known and fixed, all that the individual needs to do in order to anticipate future debt limits is to correctly predict future earnings. Therefore, if there are no unforeseen changes in earnings, the planning problem allows the individual to correctly anticipate the earnings path, and therefore, the sequence of debt limits. He can thus take appropriate actions beforehand so that (2.5b) is always satisfied. A further implication of (2.2) and (2.5b) is that until the individual reaches the credit limit, he can obtain additional credit without difficulty. Moreover, the additional credit may be used for repayment instalments, consumption purposes, and on whatever consumption goods the individual chooses as he is not directed to buy specific goods which can serve as collateral. The individual is also free to choose the rate of consumption, provided $A > \bar{A}$.

Finally, note that a single rate of interest is used for both lending and borrowing. There is the further complication that the borrowing rate is usually higher than the lending rate. A discussion of this and subsequent analysis is postponed but it does turn out that if certain conditions are imposed on $\dot{y}/y$, then working with two rates of interest does not add significantly to the analysis of credit rationing.

From here on, t will be suppressed whenever the meaning is clear.

A Formal Solution

The Lagrangian for the problem is:

$$L = U(c) + \lambda(rA + y - c) + \mu(A - \bar{A}),$$

maximization of which yields the following necessary conditions:

$$U_c = \lambda, \qquad 0 \leqslant t \leqslant T, \tag{2.6a}$$

$$\dot{\lambda} = \lambda(\rho - r) - \mu \qquad 0 \leqslant t \leqslant T, \tag{2.6b}$$

where μ is such that,

$$\mu \geqslant 0, \qquad \mu(A - \bar{A}) = 0.$$

Furthermore, at the junction point of the phases characterized by $A > \bar{A}$ (henceforth called the unconstrained phases), and the phases characterized by $A = \bar{A}$ (henceforth called the constrained phases), the equation

$$c = r\bar{A} + y - \dot{\bar{A}}$$
$$= y\left(1 - \alpha_2\left(\frac{\dot{y}}{y} - r\right)\right) + r\alpha_1 \tag{2.6c}$$

must be satisfied since then the equality $A = \bar{A}$ holds. Note that in order to ensure that c is positive we need to assume that $(1 - \alpha_2(\dot{y}/y - r)) > 0$ as $r\alpha_1 \leqslant 0$. The necessary conditions imply that along the unconstrained phase,

$$\dot{c} = \frac{U_c}{U_{cc}}(\rho - r), \tag{2.6d}$$

so that during this phase consumption changes are independent of income changes. Along the constrained phase, if $\dot{y}/y$, r, α_1 and α_2 are constant over time,

$$\dot{c} = \dot{y}\left(1 - \alpha_2\left(\frac{\dot{y}}{y} - r\right)\right),$$

so that along this phase consumption follows income. As (2.6c) must be satisfied at the junction points by the phases entering and leaving a constrained phase and also throughout a constrained phase, and as c is continuous during each of the phases, it must follow that c is continuous throughout the lifetime. Then, from (2.6a), it follows that λ is continuous too. Thus, although in general λ need not be continuous in optimal control problems with inequality constraints on the state variables, here we have a case where λ is, in fact, continuous. Had we known this initially, then the continuity of c could also have been established by employing the strict concavity of L in c. Note that the complete set of necessary conditions, (2.2), (2.5b), (2.6a)–(2.6c), are also by the concavity of L, sufficient.

Determinants of the occurrence of a constrained phase

For any given individual a constrained phase need not occur and therefore the first task is to examine the factors responsible for its occurrence and duration. In order to identify the key individual parameters it is best to consider a simple example in which the optimal consumption path under the assumption of perfect credit markets is first derived and then examined for the reasons of its possible characterization, in part, by negative holding of assets.

Accordingly assume that:

$$U(c) = \ln c + \text{constant} \qquad (2.7)$$

and $r(t) = r$, a constant. Let $y(t) = y(0)e^{\gamma t}$, where γ is a positive constant, and $A(0) = A_0 = 0$ and $A(T) = A_T = 0$. Then using the lifetime budget constraint:

$$\int_0^T c(t)e^{-rt}\, dt = \int_0^T y(0)e^{(\gamma - r)t}\, dt,$$

and the equation:

$$c(t) = c(0)e^{(r - \rho)t}, \qquad (2.8)$$

obtained by utilizing the first-order conditions, (2.6b) and (2.6c), it can be written that:

$$c(0) = \frac{\rho}{r - \gamma} \frac{[1 - e^{-(r - \gamma)T}]}{[1 - e^{-\rho T}]}\, y(0).$$

Finally, by employing an elementary mathematical proposition that $(1/z)[1 - e^{-zT}]$ is a decreasing function of z with value 1 at $z = 0$ for given T, it can be stated that

$$c(0) \gtreqless y(0) \qquad \text{as} \qquad \rho \gtreqless (r - \gamma). \qquad (2.9)$$

Therefore, the subjective discount rate, the market interest rate and the earnings growth rate are the parameters whose relative magnitudes determine whether the individual will borrow or not. But in order to obtain the rather simple result in (2.9) some simplifying assumptions were made and it is proper that the consequences of relaxing them be examined next.

(a) A less restrictive utility function to employ is

$$U(c) = \frac{1}{1 - \varepsilon}\, c^{1 - \varepsilon} + \text{constant}, \qquad \varepsilon > 0, \qquad \varepsilon \neq 1; \qquad (2.7a)$$

a special case of this when $\varepsilon = 1$ is (2.7). $-\varepsilon = cU''(c)/U'(c)$ and is the elasticity of marginal utility with respect to consumption. Repeating the previous exercise, it can be easily shown that the condition (2.9) is modified to:

$$c(0) \gtreqqless y(0) \text{ as } \frac{r(\varepsilon - 1) + \rho}{\varepsilon} \gtreqqless (r - \gamma). \qquad (2.9a)$$

(b) It is clear from (2.9a) that the time profile of earnings has an important bearing on saving and dissaving decisions and the assumption of $y(t) = y(0)e^{\gamma t}$ was made in an attempt to capture a simple relationship between savings and earnings. However, at best this assumption is a crude first approximation for it ignores biological and institutional factors that affect an individual's earnings path. Within a life-cycle model it is more realistic to assume that earnings increase initially as the productivity of the individual increases, reach a peak, and then decrease with productivity. There may be variations among different groups of workers and this is illustrated in Figure 2.1 for manual and non-manual workers. The consequences for current asset stocks and savings will then depend on the location of the peak and the skewness of the distribution. Among individuals who are characterized by zero values of A_0 and A_t and high ρ, an individual whose earnings peak later on in life will currently dissave more than an individual whose earnings peak earlier on in life, their present values of earnings being equal.

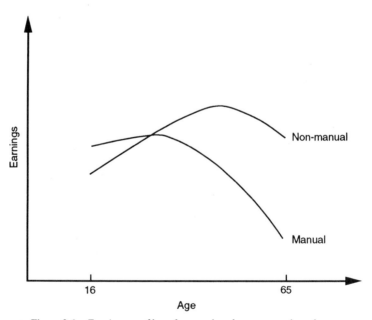

Figure 2.1 *Earnings profiles of manual and non-manual workers.*

(c) The assumption of a constant rate of interest is strong, but retaining this assumption with a single peak in the earnings profile has the analytical advantage of at most one constrained consumption phase occurring within a lifetime.

(d) Thus far inheritance and bequests have been side-stepped. The way bequests can be introduced into the model depends on the interesting but unresolved motives for making bequests. Usually, economic theorists treat bequests either as a substitute for planned consumption of heirs or as a transfer which is determined according to the preferences of the individual. But Varian (1974) has suggested that parents make bequests to ensure that their children will be placed away from the lower regions of the income distribution. Bequests are also a means whereby parents may use the prospect of such gifts to control the behaviour of their children. Quite apart from the motives for making bequests it appears to be correct to say that inheritance and bequests are particularly important stocks via which intergenerational dynamics of wealth distribution may be traced out. In fact, this is something that we shall turn to when considering the extent to which the conclusions of the simple model that we are currently pursuing can be pushed. But to return to the task at hand, recall that we are concerned with the effect of the mere presence of such an arrangement on individual life-cycle plans. Therefore assume that the individual receives $A(0) = A_0$ at the beginning of the life and leaves $A(T) = A_T$ at the end, where A_0 and A_T are given. Also, in order to isolate the influence of

$$A(0, T; r) = (A_0 - A_T e^{-rT}) \neq 0,$$

i.e. a non-zero value of the difference between the initial assets and the present value of terminal assets, revert momentarily to the assumption $y(t) = y(0)e^{\gamma t}$. Then restricting $A(0, T; r)$ such that it can be ensured that $c(0) > 0$, current consumption is derived in the usual way. Thus,

$$c(0) = \rho \, \frac{A(0, T; r)}{(1 - e^{-\rho T})} + \frac{\rho}{r - \gamma} \, \frac{(1 - e^{-(r-\gamma)T})}{(1 - e^{-\rho T})} \, y(0). \qquad (2.10)$$

Notice that whereas r, ρ and γ affect the proportionality relationship between $c(0)$ and $y(0)$, the presence of $A(0, T; r)$ yields an intercept term. To proceed a little further, take the case $A(0, T; r) > 0$. Then the presence of the term $A(0, T; r)$ encourages a higher level of initial consumption (there is a positive intercept) but $dc(0)/dy(0)$ is unaffected (the slope remains unchanged). Furthermore, $\dot{c}/c$ is unaltered. The obvious implication of saving or dissaving decisions not being solely dependent on the parameter set $\{\rho, r, \gamma\}$ is that the individual may dissave throughout his lifetime yet not borrow; the two paths depicted in Figure 2.2 are possible.

The preceding analysis should alert us to the type of individual who is

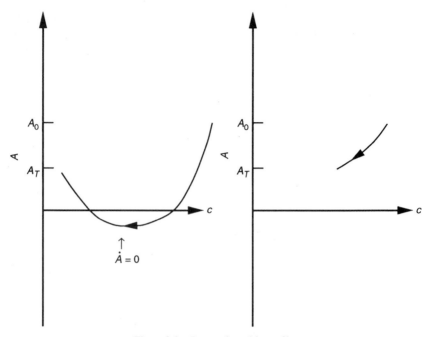

Figure 2.2 *Personal wealth profiles.*

likely to be credit-rationed − those facing high-earning growth rates and subjective discount rates, receiving little inheritance and so on are more likely to be credit-rationed. Thus prepared, we can now spend some time on characterizing the lifetime plan of an individual more formally and then carry out a few comparative statics exercises. This should bring out the essential differences between plans with and without credit-rationing. Thus armed, we should then be able to trace out the implications of credit-rationing in full.

Lifetime Plan with a Constrained Phase

Given perfect credit markets, the conditions under which an individual will borrow have been examined. It has transpired that whether or not an individual will borrow, and thereby possibly incur a credit-constrained phase, will depend on the specification of A_0, $A_T, r, \rho, \varepsilon$ and the time-shape of the earnings profile. In general, with a single-peaked earnings profile,

$$(2.7a), \ r(t) = r, \ r < \rho, \ A(0) = A_0, \ A(T) = A_T \text{ and } (2.5b). \quad (2.11)$$

A lifetime plan will consist of three phases: A first unconstrained phase

will be followed by a constrained phase which, in turn, will be followed by
a last unconstrained phase. Employing additional notation, it can be stated
that the constrained phase will last from $t = \bar{t}_1$ to $t = \bar{t}_2$ where both $\bar{t}_1$ and
$\bar{t}_2 \in [0, T]$ and $\bar{t}_1 \leqslant \bar{t}_2$. Formally, the three phases are characterized as
follows.

Phase 1 $[0, \bar{t}_1]$

$$\dot{A} < 0, \tag{2.12}$$

$$\frac{\dot{c}}{c} = \frac{r - \rho}{\varepsilon} \quad \text{for all } t \in [0, \bar{t}_1[, \tag{2.13}$$

$$c(t) = c(0) \, \exp\left[\left(\frac{r - \rho}{\varepsilon}\right)t\right], \quad 0 \leqslant t \leqslant \bar{t}_1, \tag{2.14}$$

$$\int_0^{\bar{t}_1} c(t)e^{-rt}\, dt = \int_0^{\bar{t}_1} y(t)e^{-rt}\, dt + A_0 - \bar{A}(\bar{t}_1)e^{-r\bar{t}_1}. \tag{2.15}$$

Phase 2 $[\bar{t}_1, \bar{t}_2)$

$$\dot{A} = \alpha_2 \dot{y}, \tag{2.16}$$

$$\dot{c} = \dot{y}\left(1 - \alpha_2\left(\frac{\dot{y}}{y} - r\right)\right), \tag{2.17}$$

$$c(t) = y\left(1 - \alpha_2\left(1 - \alpha_2\left(\frac{\dot{y}}{y} - r\right)\right)\right) + \alpha_1 r \quad \text{for all } t \in [\bar{t}_1, \bar{t}_2), \tag{2.18}$$

$$\int_{\bar{t}_1}^{\bar{t}_2} c(t)e^{-rt}\, dt = \int_{\bar{t}_1}^{\bar{t}_2} y(t)e^{-rt}\, dt + \bar{A}(\bar{t}_1)e^{-r\bar{t}_1} - \bar{A}(\bar{t}_2)e^{-r\bar{t}_2}. \tag{2.19}$$

Phase 3 $[\bar{t}_2, T]$

$$\dot{A} > 0, \tag{2.20}$$

$$\frac{\dot{c}}{c} = \frac{r - \rho}{\varepsilon} \quad \text{for all } t \in [\bar{t}_2, T], \tag{2.21}$$

$$c(t) = c(\bar{t}_2) \, \exp\left[\left(\frac{r - \rho}{\varepsilon}\right)(t - t_2)\right], \quad t_2 \leqslant t \leqslant T, \tag{2.22}$$

$$\int_{\bar{t}_2}^{T} c(t)e^{-rt}\, dt = \int_{\bar{t}_2}^{T} y(t)e^{-rt}\, dt + \bar{A}(\bar{t}_2)e^{-r\bar{t}_2} - A_T e^{-rT}. \tag{2.23}$$

Thus on the constrained phase, consumption is equal to earnings plus
change in the debt limit minus interest payment. On the unconstrained

phases consumption has an exponential path. At the junction points between the constrained and unconstrained phases, consumption is continuous but not differentiable.

In a lifetime plan such as the one characterized above, the junction points $\bar{t}_1$ and $\bar{t}_2$ are determined together with initial consumption $c(0)$ such that the overall budget constraint is satisfied with consumption being continuous at the junction points. In order to see what is involved in their determination consider the following. The individual faces a debt limit $\bar{A}(t)$. His choice of initial consumption under a perfect credit market would have entailed reducing $A(t)$ beyond $\bar{A}(t)$. On the other hand his choice of $c(0)$ under an imperfect credit market is such that when he is about to stop dissaving, the debt outstanding is exactly $\bar{A}$. The implication, proved in Proposition 2.1 below, is that he consumes less than he would under a perfect credit market. He then stays on the constrained phase and leaves it only when he can just accumulate enough savings to pay off his debt given his optimal consumption and savings trajectories. The junction points and the initial consumption are thus determined endogenously and the overall budget constraint is exactly satisfied. The implied paths of consumption and saving are optimal because a higher initial consumption would entail a discontinuity in consumption at the junction point $\bar{t}_1$ which is clearly not optimal given strict concavity of the utility function and a lower initial consumption would imply that there is income which is unspent.

For the individual who is not credit-rationed, there is only one phase in which consumption is characterized by

$$\frac{\dot{c}}{c} = \frac{r - \rho}{\varepsilon} \ \forall \, t \in [0, T], \tag{2.24}$$

$$c(t) = c(0) \, \exp\left[\frac{(r - \rho)}{\varepsilon} t\right], \qquad 0 \leqslant t \leqslant T, \tag{2.25}$$

and the individual dissaves in the beginning and saves later on to satisfy the overall lifetime budget constraint:

$$\int_0^T c(t)\mathrm{e}^{-rt} \, \mathrm{d}t = \int_0^T y(t)\mathrm{e}^{-rt} \, \mathrm{d}t + A_0 - A(T)^{-rT}. \tag{2.26}$$

Clearly, the lifetime plans under the two regimes differ. But the differences are large because two individuals with large differences in credit limits have been considered. It is worth examining the differences between two individuals with small differences in credit limits. This is because it brings out more clearly and rigorously the effects of credit limitations and the means of doing this – comparative statics – is a valuable tool for analysis of lifetime plans. In order to simplify the technicalities we will conform to the generally accepted view of the shape of the earnings profile but impose a few minor restrictions. Thus it will be assumed that earnings grow at a constant rate and continue to grow for some time after the individual leaves the constrained phase to begin discharging his debt and save for old age. When earnings start declining they continue to do so rapidly thereafter and very little is earned during the final part of life.

Proposition 2.1. Given the assumption set (2.11), if c is continuous and differentiable in α_2, then as a result of a slight increase in α_2:

  (i)   consumption decreases throughout the first phase,
 (ii)   during the second phase the change in consumption depends on $(r - \dot{y}/y)$,
(iii)   consumption increases throughout the third phase,
 (iv)   the duration of the first phase does not increase,
  (v)   the duration of the third phase decreases, and
 (vi)   the duration of the second phase increases.

Proposition 2.2. Given the assumption set (2.11), if c is continuous and differentiable in α_1, then, as a result of a slight increase in α_1, (i), (ii), (iii), (v) and (vi) as in Proposition 2.1 hold and, (iv) the duration of the first phase decreases.

Proposition 2.3. Given the assumption set (2.11), if c is continuous and differentiable in A_0, then as a result of a slight decrease in A_0,

  (i)   consumption decreases throughout the first phase,
 (ii)   the duration of the first phase decreases,
(iii)   the duration of the second phase increases.

It is worth illustrating the above propositions, which are essentially comparative statics results, and this is accomplished by simulation methods. A great deal of simplification results when the simple expression, $y(t) = y(0)e^{\gamma t}$, $\gamma \geqslant 0 \,\forall t$, for the earnings profile is employed. In fact Blinder (1974), Wise (1975), Zbalza (1979), Willis and Rosen (1979) and many others have used and fitted such a profile in their empirical studies. Nevertheless the assumption is a strong one and is employed here only for illustrative purposes. Reasonable values of various other parameters were chosen and the ranges of the values are given in Tables 2.1–3. The usefulness of the tables lies more in uncovering patterns than in bringing out the magnitudes of the individual numbers.

Reading up and down any of the three tables illustrates Proposition 2.1. The tables show that the constrained phase, $[\bar{t}_1, \bar{t}_2]$, increases with α_2 and

Table 2.1　Simulations of the effects of a change in initial assets.

		$A_0 = 2000$	$A_0 = 4000$	$A_0 = 6000$
$\alpha_2 = 0$	t_1	4.84	6.80	8.29
	t_2	50.00	50.00	50.00
	$c(0)$	6360	6745	7052
	J	197.641	197.945	198.236
$\alpha_2 = -0.5$	t_1	7.41	8.79	9.97
	t_2	44.10	44.10	44.10
	$c(0)$	6835	7124	7380
	J	197.874	198.161	198.436
$\alpha_2 = -1$	t_1	9.28	10.40	11.40
	t_2	41.57	41.57	41.57
	$c(0)$	7192	7438	7665
	J	198.076	198.35	198.615
$\alpha_2 = -1.5$	t_1	10.81	11.78	12.66
	t_2	39.59	39.59	39.59
	$c(0)$	7493	7713	7920
	J	198.255	198.518	198.774
$\alpha_2 = -2$	t_1	12.14	13.00	13.80
	t_2	37.89	37.89	37.89
	$c(0)$	7759	7962	8154
	J	198.415	198.67	198.918

$T = 50$, $r = 0.04$, $\varepsilon = 1$, $y(0) = 5500$, $\gamma = 0.03$, $\rho = 0.04$, $\alpha_1 = 0$.

Table 2.2　Simulations of the effects of a change in initial assets.

		$A_0 = 2000$	$A_0 = 4000$	$A_0 = 6000$
$\alpha_2 = 0$	t_1	8.52	12.05	14.76
	t_2	50.00	50.00	50.00
	$c(0)$	5989	6204	6375
	J	292.369	292.696	293.014
$\alpha_2 = -0.5$	t_1	13.16	15.69	17.86
	t_2	39.98	39.98	39.98
	$c(0)$	6242	6402	6542
	J	292.464	292.781	293.089
$\alpha_2 = -1$	t_1	16.58	18.65	20.52
	t_2	35.80	35.80	35.80
	$c(0)$	6427	6562	6685
	J	292.533	292.841	293.143
$\alpha_2 = -1.5$	t_1	19.42	21.23	22.88
	t_2	32.57	32.57	32.57
	$c(0)$	6579	6699	6811
	J	292.581	292.883	293.179
$\alpha_2 = -2$	t_1	21.92	23.54	25.05
	t_2	29.83	29.83	29.83
	$c(0)$	6711	6820	6924
	J	292.613	292.909	293.200

$T = 50$, $r = 0.04$, $\varepsilon = 1$, $y(0) = 5500$, $\gamma = 0.03$, $\rho = 0.02$, $\alpha_1 = 0$.

Table 2.3 Simulations of the effects of a change in initial assets.

		$A_0 = 2000$	$A_0 = 4000$	$A_0 = 6000$
$\alpha_2 = 0$	t_1	3.72	5.20	6.32
	t_2	50.00	50.00	50.00
	$c(0)$	6624	7135	7545
	J	143.39	143.681	143.953
$\alpha_2 = -0.5$	t_1	5.67	6.70	7.58
	t_2	45.38	45.38	45.38
	$c(0)$	7265	7652	7996
	J	143.68	143.947	144.203
$\alpha_2 = -1$	t_1	7.07	7.90	8.65
	t_2	43.37	43.37	43.37
	$c(0)$	7752	8084	8390
	J	143.936	144.189	144.431
$\alpha_2 = -1.5$	t_1	8.21	8.93	9.58
	t_2	41.78	41.78	41.78
	$c(0)$	8168	8466	8748
	J	144.17	144.41	144.643
$\alpha_2 = -2$	t_1	9.20	9.84	10.43
	t_2	40.41	40.41	40.41
	$c(0)$	8539	8815	9079
	J	144.385	144.615	144.839

$T = 50$, $r = 0.04$, $\varepsilon = 1$, $y(0) = 5500$, $\gamma = 0.03$, $\rho = 0.06$, $\alpha_1 = 0$.

hence with $\bar{A}$. Since $\bar{t}_1$ decreases and $\bar{t}_2$ increases, both the unconstrained phases become shorter. The changes in the durations of the phases are accompanied by a decrease in consumption during the first phase. Reading across the three tables illustrates the pattern implied by Proposition 2.3. As initial assets fall, consumption throughout the first phase decreases as well. $\bar{t}_1$ also decreases so that the constrained phase becomes longer at the expense of the initial unconstrained phase. The duration of the last phase is unchanged. Lifetime utility can also be worked out and the row marked J gives this value. As expected with diminishing marginal utility, each gain in lifetime utility as a result of every 2000-unit increase in A_0 decreases as credit-rationing becomes weaker. Finally, each of the three tables has differing values of the subjective time discount rate. The pattern here is that a higher value of ρ is accompanied by a longer constrained phase, greater initial consumption, and less lifetime utility.

Drawing upon the preceding analysis and simulations, the prominent features of plans with and without credit rationing are presented in Figure 2.3.

Under perfect credit markets, the individual is able to smooth out lifetime income freely and this results in the consumption path labelled c^1. Then $c^1(0)$ is reckoned with reference to lifetime income only so that $c(t)$ is locally independent of $y(t)$ and c depends only on r, ε and ρ. As a result,

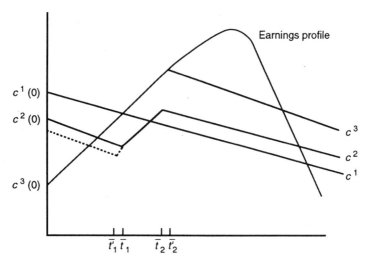

Figure 2.3 *Lifetime consumption with and without credit constraints.*

the sketch of c^1 in the diagram bears no relation to the shape followed by the income profile.

When the debt limit is effective during the early part of life, the individual bases his choice of initial consumption on the discounted value of the net earnings over the interval $[0, t_1]$ instead of $[0, T]$. This reduces his ability to smooth out consumption during the early part of life. Hence the path labelled c^2 results and this is independent of the shape of the earnings profile initially but later on, over the interval $[\bar{t}_1, \bar{t}_2]$, follows the profile as shown in the figure. Furthermore, as the bulk of the lifetime income occurs midway through life, $c(0)$ is reduced. But the diagram shows that consumption is higher later on in life because all income must eventually be consumed. The broken consumption path shows the effect of a decrease in A_0 on path c^2. Current consumption is lowered and the rationed phase becomes longer, $[\bar{t}_1'', \bar{t}_2]$. Finally, path c^3 corresponds to the case in which $A_0 = 0$, $\alpha_1 = 0$ and $\alpha_2 = 0$. Here $c^3(0) = y(0)$.

Having shown that there are differences in lifetime consumption plans between those who are credit-rationed and those who are not the task is to demonstrate that these differences matter. One way in which this can be done is by applying the analysis to policy issues.

The Size of the Lifetimes Excess Burden of a Tax

It is well known that certain types of tax have distortionary effects on behaviour, leading to a loss of consumer's surplus. The lump-sum compensation required to hold the consumer's welfare constant in such instances has been developed by Harberger (1964) within an atemporal context. Levhari and Sheshinski (1972) have extended the formulation of lump-sum compensation to an intertemporal framework. Basically, they consider a lifetime-utility-maximizing individual who pays an interest tax and they then derive an expression for the lifetime excess burden of such a tax. The excess burden is positive because the tax distorts the individual's intertemporal consumption plans. The chief reason for feeling uneasy here is that for many individuals the principal source of income is earned income. But, as we have shown, an important implication of an earned income profile is that its shape over life often induces a person to borrow and, furthermore, the individual's lifetime plan may be characterized, in part, by a constrained phase during which he neither saves nor dissaves. But this implies that the distortion caused by an interest tax is not relevant during the constrained phase. Thus lifetime excess burden of an interest tax can shrink to a smaller value when earned income is taken into account (see Shah, 1983).

In order to lay all this out properly, consider the problem in which lifetime utility (2.1) is maximized subject to:

$$\dot{A}(t) = (1 - \tau)(r(t)A(t) + y(t)) + v(t) - c(t), \qquad 0 \leqslant t \leqslant T, \quad (2.2a)$$

the end-point conditions, (2.3), and the debt constraint (2.5b). Here $r(t)A(t) + y(t)$ is the pre-tax income, a sum of interest and labour earnings; τ is the constant tax rate, and hence $(1 - \tau)$ times $(r(t)A(t) + y(t))$ is the post-tax income; $v(t)$ denotes the tax proceeds which are returned to the individual.

The current-value Lagrangian for the problem can be written as

$$L = U(c) + \lambda((1 - \tau)(rA + y) + v - c) + \mu(A - \bar{A}),$$

maximization of which for all t yields:

$$U_c = \lambda, \qquad 0 \leqslant t \leqslant T,$$

$$\dot{\lambda} = \lambda(\rho - (1 - \tau)r) - \mu, \qquad 0 \leqslant t \leqslant T,$$

where μ is such that

$$\mu \geqslant 0, \qquad \mu(A - \bar{A}) = 0.$$

The necessary conditions (which by the concavity of L are also sufficient) imply that along the unconstrained $(A > \bar{A})$ phases,

$$\dot{c} = \frac{U_c}{U_{cc}} (\rho - (1 - \tau)r),$$

and along the constrained $(A = \bar{A})$ phases,

$$c = r\alpha_1 + y\left(1 - \alpha_2\left(\frac{\dot{y}}{y} - r\right)\right).$$

It is readily apparent that while the tax distorts the consumption plan during the unconstrained phases, it leaves it unaffected during the constrained phase. This is because during the constrained phase the individual is really optimizing subject to an instantaneous budget according to which he neither desires to save nor to dissave with the future in mind. And since tax proceeds are returned to him, his plans are unaffected during this phase. Note that it is the tax on interest income which is distortionary as the tax on earned income does not affect the time-shape of the consumption plan.

In order to assess the magnitude of the lifetime excess burden of the tax and the variation over individual characteristics some simulations were carried out. The first set is presented in Table 2.4, the top row of which shows the parameter values which are held fixed. These are the same values used in the previous simulations. The column under $\tau = 0$ gives the durations of the constrained interval and the values of initial consumption for differing α_2. The column under $\tau = 0.3$ gives the same information when a tax of 30% is imposed. One effect of the tax is to increase the duration of the constrained interval. Initial consumption also increases and since the tax proceeds are instantaneously returned to the individual, this reveals that the intertemporal substitution effect works such that initial consumption increases at the expense of future consumption. When τ was increased to 0.5 and 0.7, the respective $c(0)$ values increased further.

The values of the column $\tau = 0.3$, J constant, were derived as follows. The lifetime utility, J, of column $\tau = 0$ was noted. Then with $\tau = 0.3$, A_0 was increased until the same lifetime utility was achieved. The difference between the respective A_0's, denoted by ΔA_0, is the lifetime excess burden of tax. Since each unit increase of A_0 raised utility only minutely, utility was rounded up to 3 decimal points since this permitted us to search with A_0 taking values of multiples of 5 and thereby speed up the convergence process. Examining Table 2.4 it is immediately apparent that A_0 increases as α_2 decreases. To appreciate the speed with which this happens, the information is transferred to Figure 2.4. For high values of α_2, or with stringent debt limits, the lifetime excess burden is negligible. As debt limits are lifted and the constrained phase shrinks, lifetime excess burden becomes significantly larger. The acceleration in lifetime excess burden can be better understood by looking at the values of J given in Table 2.5. Notice that under the column $\tau = 0.3$, as α_2 decreases J first increases and then starts decreasing. There are two forces at work here. Firstly, as α_2 decreases, lifetime utility increases since greater smoothing out of consumption is

Table 2.4 Simulations of effects of changes in the tax rate and the credit constraint.

	$\tau = 0$		$\tau = 0.3$		$\tau = 0.3$, J constant			$\tau = 0.5$, J constant	$\tau = 0.7$, J constant
α_2	(t_1, t_2)	$c(0)$	(t_1, t_2)	$c(0)$	(t_1, t_2)	$c(0)$	ΔA_0	ΔA_0	ΔA_0
0	6.80, 50.00	6,745	5.70, 50.00	6,988	5.71, 50.00	6,989	5	15	30
−1	10.40, 41.57	7,438	8.68, 42.80	7,841	8.70, 42.80	7,846	35	75	130
−2	13.00, 37.89	7,962	10.82, 39.62	8,492	10.85, 39.62	8,501	70	160	265
−3	15.15, 34.96	8,406	12.58, 37.06	9,050	12.62, 37.06	9,064	115	270	450
−4	17.03, 32.42	8,800	14.11, 34.84	9,550	14.16, 34.84	9,568	180	400	680
−5	18.71, 30.12	9,160	15.48, 32.00	10,010	15.53, 32.80	10,033	240	560	940
−6	20.26, 27.99	9,495	16.73, 30.91	10,439	16.80, 30.91	10,468	315	740	1,250
−7	21.70, 25.98	9,809	17.89, 29.12	10,845	17.97, 29.12	10,879	405	950	1,605
−8	23.06, 24.05	10,106	18.98, 27.40	11,230	19.07, 27.40	11,272	505	1,175	1,995
−9	$t_1, t_2 \notin [0, T]$	10,192	20.01, 25.74	11,600	20.13, 25.74	11,657	720	1,545	2,555
−10		10,192	20.99, 24.12	11,955	21.21, 24.12	12,062	1,370	2,375	3,615
−11		10,192	21.93, 22.54	12,298	22.30, 22.54	12,489	2,515	3,740	5,240
−12		10,192	$t_1, t_2 \notin [0, T]$	12,382	$t_1, t_2 \notin [0, T]$	12,530	2,650	5,700	7,510
−13		10,192		12,382		12,530	2,650	7,260[a]	10,475
−14		10,192		12,382		12,530	2,650	7,260	14,025[b]

$T = 50$, $\varepsilon = 1$, $\rho = 0.04$, $y(0) = 5500$, $\gamma = 0.03$, $A_0 = 4000$, $\alpha_1 = 0$, $r = 0.04$.
[a] The debt constraint ceases to bind at $\alpha_2 = -12.63$.
[b] The debt constraint ceases to bind at $\alpha_2 = -13.95$.

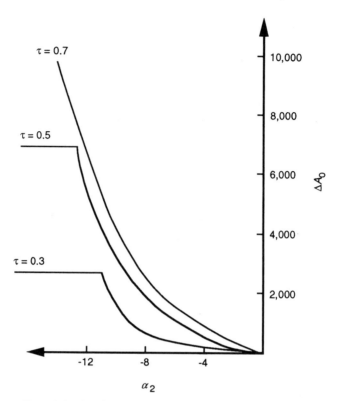

Figure 2.4 *Graphic representation of simulations in Table 2.4.*

Table 2.5 Values   of J corresponding to differing values of α_2
and τ.

α_2	$\tau = 0$	$\tau = 0.3$
0	197.495	197.944
-1	198.350	198.345
-2	198.670	198.661
-3	198.928	198.914
-4	199.134	199.114
-5	199.293	199.267
-6	199.408	199.375
-7	199.482	199.441
-8	199.514	199.465
-9	199.516	199.448
-10	199.516	199.390
-11	199.516	199.289
-12	199.516	199.257
-13	199.516	199.257

possible. But secondly, as α_2 decreases, the distortionary effect of τ begins to have impact and, given concavity of the utility function, the first factor eventually gives way to the second.

Table 2.4 also presents ΔA_0 for $\tau = 0.5$ and $\tau = 0.7$, each column being computed in the same manner. These values are plotted in Figure 2.4. While higher values of τ imply greater excess burden, this is most telling for low values of α_2. For example, $(\Delta A_0 / \tau = 0.5, \alpha_2 = 0) - (\Delta A_0 / \tau = 0.3, \alpha_2 = 0) = 10$, but

$$(\Delta A_0 \mid \tau = 0.5, \alpha_2 = -6) - (\Delta A_0 \mid \tau = 0.3, \alpha_2 = -6) = 425,$$

and

$$(\Delta A_0 \mid \tau = 0.5, \alpha_2 = -12) - (\Delta A_0 \mid \tau = 0.3, \alpha_2 = -12) = 3050.$$

Therefore, it does seem that for low values of α_2, lifetime excess burden is very sensitive to τ.

To see how lifetime excess burden varies with the rate of interest, we carried out the simulations which are reported in Tables 2.6 and 2.7 together with Table 2.4. (Note that, since lifetime excess burden is meagre for $r = 0.02$, Table 2.5 was computed with ΔA_0 taking on unrestricted values.) Two features stand out upon examination: one is that ΔA_0 is very sensitive to r and the second is that, because of the acceleration in ΔA_0 as α_2

Table 2.6 Simulations with the parameters set as in Table 2.4 except that $r = 0.02$.

α_2	$\tau = 0$		$\tau = 0.3$		$\tau = 0.3$, J constant		
	(t_1, t_2)	$c(0)$	(t_1, t_2)	$c(0)$	(t_1, t_2)	$c(0)$	ΔA_0
0	5.12, 50.00	7,105	4.83, 50.00	7,208	4.83, 50.00	7,209	3
-1	7.65, 43.28	8,143	7.21, 43.63	8,316	7.21, 43.63	8,317	4
-2	9.39, 40.26	8,972	8.84, 40.77	9,203	8.84, 40.77	9,205	12
-3	10.77, 37.86	9,705	10.13, 38.48	9,990	10.13, 38.48	9,992	18
-4	11.92, 35.78	10,380	11.21, 36.49	10,715	11.21, 36.49	10,718	23
-5	12.92, 33.91	11,016	12.14, 34.70	11,400	12.15, 34.70	11,403	34
-6	13.80, 32.18	11,624	12.97, 33.04	12,053	12.98, 33.04	12,058	47
-7	14.60, 30.56	12,201	13.71, 31.49	12,684	13.72, 31.49	12,690	62
-8	15.32, 29.03	12,776	14.39, 30.02	13,295	14.40, 30.02	13,303	78
-9	15.98, 27.58	13,329	15.01, 28.63	13,892	15.02, 28.63	13,900	96
-10	16.59, 26.18	13,870	15.58, 27.28	14,475	15.59, 27.28	14,486	116
-11	17.16, 24.84	14,400	16.11, 25.99	15,048	16.12, 25.99	15,060	138
-12	17.70, 23.55	14,922	16.61, 24.75	15,611	16.62, 24.75	15,625	162
-13	18.19, 22.30	15,436	17.07, 23.54	16,167	17.09, 23.54	16,183	188
-14	18.67, 21.08	15,943	17.51, 22.36	16,715	17.53, 22.36	16,733	216
-15	19.11, 19.90	16,444	17.92, 21.22	17,257	17.94, 21.22	17,277	246
-16	$t_1, t_2 \notin [0, T]^*$	16,693	18.32, 20.11	17,793	18.34, 20.11	17,821	350

$T = 50$, $\varepsilon = 1$, $\rho = 0.04$, $y(0) = 5500$, $\gamma = 0.03$, $A_0 = 4000$, $\alpha_1 = 0$, $r = 0.02$.
*The debt limit ceases to bind at $\alpha_2 = -15.5$.

Table 2.7 Simulations with the parameters set as in Table 2.4 except that $r = 0.06$.

	$\tau = 0$		$\tau = 0.3$		$\tau = 0.3$, J constant		
α_2	(t_1, t_2)	$c(0)$	(t_1, t_2)	$c(0)$	(t_1, t_2)	$c(0)$	ΔA_0
0	12.54, 50.00	6,235	7.21, 50.00	6,731	7.25, 50.00	6,738	45
-1	20.03, 36.33	6,518	11.27, 41.46	7,314	11.37, 41.46	7,336	175
-2	25.96, 30.78	6,702	14.36, 37.79	7,729	14.54, 37.79	7,767	370
-3		6,744	17.03, 34.85	8,063	17.29, 34.85	8,122	645
-4		6,744	19.46, 32.28	8,345	19.88, 32.28	8,445	1,170
-5	$t_1, t_2 \notin [0, T]$	6,744	21.74, 29.92	8,592	22.39, 29.92	8,751	1,980
-6		6,744	23.92, 27.70	8,812	24.87, 27.70	9,048	3,085
-7		6,744	$t_1, t_2 \notin [0, T]^a$	8,986	$t_1, t_2 \notin [0, T]^b$	9,226	3,905

$T = 50$, $\varepsilon = 1$, $\rho = 0.04$, $y(0) = 5500$, $\gamma = 0.03$, $A_0 = 4000$, $\alpha_1 = 0$, $r = 0.06$.
[a] The debt constraint ceases to bind at $\alpha_2 = -6.88$.
[b] The debt constraint ceases to bind at $\alpha_2 = -6.61$.

decreases, this sensitivity is more apparent as the constrained phase nears complete shrinkage. Therefore, at this stage it is safe to conclude that the excess burden of tax is the greater when τ and r are high, provided that the consumer is able to borrow more or less freely. However, if debt limits are stringent then even a combination of high τ and r elicits only scanty ΔA_0.

For those who have greater initial wealth, the constrained phases are of correspondingly shorter duration. It therefore seems worthwhile to examine how lifetime excess burden varies with A_0. The simulations for this are reported in Tables 2.8 and 2.9 together with Table 2.4 and it is really apparent that ΔA_0 is rather insensitive to variations in A_0. The reason

Table 2.8 Simulations with the parameters set as in Table 2.4 except that $A_0 = 2000$.

	$\tau = 0$		$\tau = 0.3$		$\tau = 0.3$, J constant		
α_2	(t_1, t_2)	$c(0)$	(t_1, t_2)	$c(0)$	(t_1, t_2)	$c(0)$	ΔA_0
0	4.84, 50.00	6,360	4.07, 50.00	6,525	4.08, 50.00	6,527	5
-1	9.28, 41.57	7,192	7.76, 42.80	7,542	7.77, 42.80	7,545	25
-2	12.14, 37.89	7,759	10.12, 39.62	8,245	10.14, 39.62	8,252	55
-3	14.44, 34.96	8,226	12.00, 37.06	8,830	12.03, 37.06	8,841	100
-4	16.40, 32.42	8,636	13.60, 34.84	9,348	13.64, 34.84	9,364	155
-5	18.15, 30.12	9,007	15.02, 32.80	9,820	15.08, 32.80	9,842	225
-6	19.75, 27.99	9,350	16.32, 30.91	10,259	16.38, 30.91	10,286	300
-7	21.23, 25.98	9,670	17.51, 29.12	10,672	17.58, 29.12	10,705	380
-8	22.62, 24.05	9,972	18.63, 27.40	11,064	18.71, 27.40	11,104	480
-9		10,104	19.68, 25.74	11,438	19.79, 25.74	11,491	650
-10		10,104	20.68, 24.12	11,798	20.88, 24.12	11,895	1,240
-11		10,104	21.64, 22.54	12,145	21.98, 22.54	12,323	2,330

$T = 50$, $\varepsilon = 1$, $\rho = 0.04$, $y(0) = 5500$, $\gamma = 0.03$, $A_0 = 2000$, $\alpha_1 = 0$, $r = 0.04$.

Table 2.9 Simulations with the parameters set as in Table 2.4 except that $A_0 = 6000$.

α_2	$\tau = 0$		$\tau = 0.3$		$\tau = 0.3$, J constant		
	(t_1, t_2)	$c(0)$	(t_1, t_2)	$c(0)$	(t_1, t_2)	$c(0)$	ΔA_0
0	8.29, 50.00	7,052	6.94, 50.00	7,360	6.94, 50.00	7,363	15
-1	11.40, 41.57	7,665	9.50, 42.80	8,117	9.52, 42.80	8,123	45
-2	13.80, 37.89	8,154	11.48, 39.62	8,729	11.52, 39.62	8,739	85
-3	15.83, 34.96	8,579	13.14, 37.06	9,264	13.17, 37.06	9,277	130
-4	17.63, 32.42	8,960	14.60, 34.84	9,748	14.64, 34.84	9,767	190
-5	19.26, 30.12	9,311	15.92, 32.80	10,196	15.97, 32.80	10,220	250
-6	20.76, 27.99	9,638	17.13, 30.91	10,617	17.20, 30.91	10,646	330
-7	22.17, 25.98	9,946	18.26, 29.12	11,015	18.34, 29.12	11,051	420
-8	23.49, 24.05	10,238	19.38, 27.40	11,395	19.42, 27.40	11,438	525
-9		10,238	20.34, 25.74	11,760	20.47, 25.74	11,823	790
-10	$t_1, t_2 \notin [0, T]$	10,238	21.30, 24.12	12,111	21.53, 24.12	12,227	1,500
-11		10,238	22.23, 22.54	12,450	$t_1, t_2 \notin [0, T]^*$	12,643	2,675

$T = 50$, $\varepsilon = 1$, $\rho = 0.04$, $y(0) = 5500$, $\gamma = 0.03$, $A_0 = 6000$, $\alpha_1 = 0$, $r = 0.04$.
*The debt constraint ceases to bind at $\alpha_2 = -10.97$.

for this may be due to the fact that the duration of the constrained phase responds rather sluggishly to changes in A_0. And, of course, it is only $\bar{t}_1$ that responds to changes in A_0, $\bar{t}_2$ being unaffected.

The above exercise demonstrates that constrained phases, and therefore credit limits, have a significant quantitative influence on the size of the lifetime excess burden of a tax. In fact, even with a high interest rate and a high tax rate, the excess burden is insignificant if the credit limits bind in a stringent manner. Of course, to the extent that earnings do fall towards the end of life, credit limits will be less binding and excess burden will increase. However, it still remains true that it is the initial steep segment of the earnings profile which provides the motive for borrowing early in life even if the earnings profile changes slope later on in life. For a sufficiently steep initial segment, the individual's life-plan consists of dissaving and borrowing, followed by neither saving nor dissaving, then saving to pay off the debt, followed by saving for old age and finally dissaving. As long as there is a first stage of dissaving and potential borrowing to which an initial steep segment is a causal factor, debt limits can imply constrained phases and hence reduced excess burden.

Unexpected Temporary Income Change: An Illustration of the Importance of Spreading the Burden of Reduced Income

The previous exercise showed that constrained phases matter since there intertemporal substitution of consumption is not carried out. Now we wish to demonstrate that the existence of effective credit-rationing influences consumption during unconstrained phases and that this matters for certain kinds of policy. Consider, therefore, two individuals at the beginning of their lives and who are differentiated from each other by debt limits only. Then an equal small decrease in $y(0)$ will produce differing changes in $c(0)$'s.

(a) The individual who is never credit-rationed contemplates a slightly smaller lifetime income with reference to which $c(0)$ is reckoned. Since

$$c(t) = c(0) \, \exp\left[\left(\frac{r-\rho}{\varepsilon}\right)t\right] \quad \forall\, t \in [0, T],$$

he is able to 'spread' the burden of reduced income on all $c(t)$, and thereby mitigate the decrease in $c(0)$.

(b) The individual who expects to be credit-rationed from time $\bar{t}_1$ onwards plans consumption according to

$$c(t) = c(0) \, \exp\left[\left(\frac{r-\rho}{\varepsilon}\right)t\right] \quad \forall\, t \in [0, \bar{t}_1],$$

implying that he is able to 'spread' the burden of reduced income on all $c(t) \, \forall\, t \in [0, \bar{t}_1]$ so that initial consumption will be more greatly reduced by the temporary income fall. In fact, for the individual who has little initial assets and virtually cannot borrow, $dc(0)/dy(0)$ is very close to one. This is because $c(0)$ is now reckoned with respect to

$$\int_0^{\bar{t}_1} y(t) e^{-rt} \, dt,$$

where $\bar{t}_1 = 0 + \varepsilon$, and ε is very small. In effect, credit limits prevent the individual from planning consumption over a long period of time. Finally note that if another, older, individual who is currently on a constrained phase is considered then

$$\frac{\partial c}{\partial y} = \left[1 - \alpha_2\left(\frac{\dot{y}}{y} - r\right)\right] > 0. \tag{2.27}$$

In fact,

$$\frac{\partial c}{\partial y} \geqslant 1 \quad \text{if} \quad \left(\frac{\dot{y}}{y} - r\right) \geqslant 0.$$

Therefore, an unexpected temporary income change can have a non-negligible effect on aggregate current consumption in an economy consisting of individuals facing differing debt limits and who are of differing ages. In an economy without debt limits, the effect is negligible. A temporary income change can arise from a temporary tax change. But when thinking about income change in terms of a tax change it is worth bearing in mind that the temporary tax change is assumed not to be mistaken for a permanent change. In other words, the future income expectations are unaltered or inelastic. If not, then such a change will also have a non-negligible effect on consumption under perfect credit markets.

Windfall Income

In the previous application, the result that credit-rationing prevents long-term planning was exploited and the example of a small income change was employed. In this section we exploit the result (see Proposition 3) that access to greater inherited wealth allows consumption to be planned over a longer period.

Therefore consider the following exercise. Split the optimal consumption path over the interval $[0, T]$ at some point $\hat{t} \in [0, T]$. Corresponding to t will be the stock of assets $A(\hat{t})$. Given $A(\hat{t})$ and unchanged parameters like ε, r, etc., were the individual to re-plan consumption over $[\hat{t}, T]$ then the new plan over $[\hat{t}, T]$ should coincide with the corresponding segment of the old optimal plan. Suppose the individual receives a windfall income at $\hat{t}$ so that $A(\hat{t}^+) > A(\hat{t}^-)$. Then the new plan will no longer coincide with the corresponding segment of the old one. The new problem now consists of equations (2.1)–(2.5) with $t = 0$ replaced everywhere by $t = \hat{t}$ and $A(\hat{t})$ given. The formal solution is identical as well, except for the time translation of 0 to $\hat{t}$. It is then relatively easy to show that if $\hat{t}$ lies in the constrained interval of the original optimal plan, then the smaller the windfall, the larger is the effect of the windfall on $c(t)$. In the limit as $A(\hat{t}^+) \to A(\hat{t}^-)$, the effect of the windfall on consumption tends to somewhere near unity. $\hat{t}$ need not be on the constrained phase but restricting it there makes the effect of the size of the windfall on consumption clearer. The reasoning is easy to state: with a large windfall, the individual is able to carry out some degree of intertemporal substitution between present and future consumption. As the windfall becomes smaller across identical individuals, in the limit it can be thought of as a slight increase in y at $\hat{t}$. Then:

$$c(\hat{t}) = y(\hat{t})\left(1 - \alpha_2\left(\frac{\dot{y}}{y} - r\right)\right)$$

and

$$\frac{\partial c(\hat{t})}{\partial y(\hat{t})} \geq 1 \quad \text{if} \quad \left(\frac{\dot{y}}{y} - r\right) \geq 0.$$

The above reasoning can be used to test for the presence of credit-rationing. At the very least, the micro data should have observations on the consumption of the individuals in a given year and windfall in that year (e.g. in 1950 and 1956 US war veterans received unanticipated national-service life-insurance dividend handouts). In fact work using such data suggests that the marginal propensity to consume out of such windfalls is very high (see Bodkin (1959) and Wiseman (1975)) but the data, methods and results have been subject to dispute (see Friedman (1960), Bird and Bodkin (1965) and Lee (1975)). Finally, Deaton (1987) has made an interesting observation, which is that when a couple has a first child, consumption falls. Since such an event is usually accompanied by the loss of wife's earnings it suggests another way in which the effectiveness of credit-rationing may be econometrically tested.

Intertemporal Income Transfer

Some institutional arrangements involve a transfer of income over an individual's life, e.g. pensions. The task is to show credit limits matter because changes in such arrangements affect the consumption of credit-rationed individuals differently from those who are not credit-rationed.

Consider a situation in which a slight decrease in current income, $y(0)$, is compensated for by an equal increase in discounted future income, $e^{-rT}y(T)$, so as to leave the present value of lifetime income unchanged.

(a) For the individual who is never credit-rationed and who reckons current and future consumption with respect to lifetime income, such transfer leaves consumption unaltered at every moment in time. The only response of the individual is in a change in the rate of saving.

(b) For the individual who is credit-rationed, the present value of the budget available for the first phase decreases as the individual is unable to lay his hands on increased future income by further borrowing. Therefore, a result similar to that of Proposition 2.3(i) applies so that consumption falls throughout the first phase. Note that for an individual who is actually on the constrained phase (2.27) will apply.

(1) Pensions. One application of the above reasoning is to a situation in which individuals have to increase current pension contributions but receive greater future pension benefits. As a consequence, the current consumption of the individuals who are, or are likely to be, credit-rationed will decrease whereas that of the individuals who are never credit-rationed will be unchanged. Of course, in reality, increasing pension contributions results in income decreasing throughout the working life, not just at $t = 0$, and

increasing throughout the retirement period, not just at $t = T$. Moreover, the increased contributions may not match up with increased benefits. But the thrust of the reasoning of the previous paragraph goes through.

(2) Income tax progressivity. Another application is to a situation in which the income tax becomes less progressive, the total tax payment being held constant. The immediate implication is that less tax is paid later on in life, more currently, so that the income profile becomes steeper. As a consequence, the current consumption of the individuals who are likely to be credit-rationed will decrease whereas that of the individuals who are never credit-rationed will be unchanged.

Implications for the Aggregate Consumption Function

In order to obtain implications of credit-rationing for aggregate behaviour based on individual behaviour the conditions for aggregation have to be derived and met. Such a task is by no means easy and will not be undertaken here. Instead, we will simply isolate the expected qualitative effects of credit-rationing on aggregate behaviour.

(a) In aggregate, with credit-rationing, there will be a higher savings ratio. This is because credit limitations will prevent dissaving by some borrowers.
(b) The aggregate marginal propensity to save will depend on the proportion of individuals who face credit-rationing (see Shah (1980) for a demonstration). This proportion will depend on the distribution of assets, credit limits, age, subjective discount rates and the like.
(c) The aggregate marginal propensity to consume will rise with the proportion of the population that faces credit-rationing.

In fact, much of the recent empirical work on rational expectations life-cycle hypothesis, stimulated by Hall's (1978) pioneering work, could be picking up the effects of credit constraints. Consider time-series studies first. Muellbauer (1983) thinks that in his empirical work on surprises in the consumption function there is evidence to suggest the presence of effective credit-rationing. Flavin (1981, 1985), too, finds that consumption is strongly dependent on current income and only part of this dependency can be explained by possible serial correlation in income. Hayashi (1982) incorporates credit-rationing explicitly in his estimation and finds if consumption is defined to include service flows from consumer durables then there is strong evidence of effective credit-rationing. Bernanke (1985) finds that there is substantial sensitivity of consumer spending to income change in the short run and Campbell (1987) thinks that there is weak evidence supporting insufficient variability of savings. Turning to panel data, Hall and Miskin

(1982) think that 20% of the individuals in their US sample were liquidity-constrained, a result confirmed by Shapiro (1984). (However, note that Altonji and Siow (1987) find that allowing for measurement errors in the data can make a large difference to the results of these two tests). Hayashi (1985b), too, thinks that 15% of his Japanese sample was credit-constrained. Finally, using two sample-year cross-section US data, Hayashi (1985a) detects evidence for the possible presence of liquidity constraints and Mariger (1987) estimates that 15–20% of the sample is liquidity-constrained.

Although the final results are by no means in, there is conformity in the findings using aggregate time-series, panel and cross-section data, namely that about 20% of the population does not behave according to the simple rational-expectations life-cycle hypothesis. The myopic behaviour of approximately 20% of the population could be due to several reasons: high subjective discount rates, non-maximizing behaviour or, very plausibly, liquidity constraints.

Conclusion

In this chapter the model of consumer intertemporal optimization was intro-duced, the idea being to demonstrate that such a model can have interesting and important implications. After working out the solution to the model, and using comparative statics methods, the lifetime plans of those who are credit-constrained and those who are not, an attempt was also made to pro-vide a quantitative 'feel' using simulation methods. It is thought that several interesting and important implications emerged under the headings of: Life-time Excess Burden of a Tax, Unexpected Temporary Income Change, Windfall Income and Intertemporal Income Transfers. Although the impli-cations of the differences in the plans of those who are credit-constrained and those who are not have by no means been exhausted, there should be enough in the preceding analysis to support the argument that credit constraints have interesting implications. It is also worth emphasizing that the above analysis assumed that the earnings profile was given. But an interesting implication of credit constraints emerges when there is choice over earnings profiles and therefore it is to this topic that we turn to in the next chapter.

Appendix to Chapter 2

Proof of Proposition 2.1

(i) During the first phase, upon differentiating (2.6a) and utilizing (2.6b) we obtain:

$$\dot{c} = \left(\frac{r - \rho}{\varepsilon}\right)c, \qquad (2A.1)$$

and

$$\frac{\partial}{\partial t}\frac{c}{\partial \alpha_2} = \left(\frac{r - \rho}{\varepsilon}\right)\frac{\partial c}{\partial \alpha_2}. \qquad (2A.2)$$

From the assumption set (2.11), we can readily see that $\partial c/\partial \alpha_2$ cannot change sign. Given constant ε, all we need to know is the effect on $c(0)$. From the strict concavity of the utility function, $c(0)$ cannot remain unchanged if α_2 changes. If $c(0)$ increases, then from (2A.2) the individual will be decreasing his stock of assets faster, so that, at the new value of α_2,

$$c(\bar{t}_1) > y\left(1 - \alpha_2\left(\frac{\dot{y}}{y} - r\right)\right) + r\alpha_1, \qquad (2A.3)$$

which violates the optimality condition (2.15). Hence $c(0)$ must decrease and therefore consumption decreases throughout the first phase.

This result is straightforward. Since an increase in α_2 decreases the resources available for expenditure during the first phase, $c(0)$ must decrease. From (2A.2) we can state that the reduction in consumption decreases over time.

(ii) During the second phase, (2.15) always holds. Then, during this phase:

$$\frac{\partial c}{\partial \alpha_2} = y\left(r - \frac{\dot{y}}{y}\right),$$

so that the effect on consumption of a change in α_2 depends on the sign of $[r - (\dot{y}/y)]$. Therefore we can write:

$$\left(r - \frac{\dot{y}}{y}\right) \gtreqless 0 \Rightarrow \frac{\partial c}{\partial \alpha_2} \gtreqless 0.$$

(iii) (2A.1) and (2A.2) holds, so that, following the proof of (i), $\partial c/\partial \alpha_2$ cannot change sign during the third phase. If consumption decreases, then the individual will be repaying the smaller debt faster so that, at the new value of α_2,

$$c(\bar{t}_2) < y\left(1 - \alpha_2\left(\frac{\dot{y}}{y} - r\right)\right),$$

which violates the optimality condition (2.15). Hence consumption must increase throughout this phase.

(vi) (a) First consider the case where $[(\dot{y}/y) - r] \leqslant 0$. If $\bar{t}_1$ is unchanged, then at $\bar{t}_1$,

$$\frac{\partial c}{\partial \alpha_2}(\bar{t}_1) = y\left(r - \frac{\dot{y}}{y}\right) > 0,$$

and along this phase

$$\dot{c} = \dot{y}\left(1 - \alpha_2\left(\frac{\dot{y}}{y} - r\right)\right).$$

So, if $\bar{t}_1$ is unchanged or increases, consumption is unchanged or higher. However, as $c(0)$ has decreased, $\dot{c}/c < 0$ and $\dot{c}/c$ is unaltered, it must follow that

$$c(\bar{t}_1) < y\left(1 - \alpha_2\left(\frac{\dot{y}}{y} - r\right)\right) + r\alpha_1,$$

so that we cannot maintain that t_1 is unchanged or has increased. Hence the duration of the first phase must decrease.

(b) Now consider the case where $(\dot{y}/y - r) > 0$. If $\bar{t}_1$ is unchanged, then at $\bar{t}_1$,

$$\frac{\partial c(\bar{t}_1)}{\partial \alpha_2} = y\left(r - \frac{\dot{y}}{y}\right) < 0.$$

This also holds arbitrarily close to $\bar{t}_1$. But along this phase:

$$\dot{c} = \dot{y}\left(1 - \alpha_2\left(\frac{\dot{y}}{y} - r\right)\right).$$

Therefore

$$\dot{c} > \dot{y} \quad \text{as} \quad \left(1 - \alpha_2\left(\frac{\dot{y}}{y} - r\right)\right) > 1.$$

Then, $\partial c/\partial \alpha_2 + \dot{c} > ry > 0$. That is, overall, consumption increases as the duration increases slightly. But as $c(0)$ has decreased, $\dot{c}/c < 0$ and $\dot{c}/c$ is unaltered, it must follow that

$$c(\bar{t}_1) < y\left(1 - \alpha_2\left(\frac{\dot{y}}{y} - r\right)\right) + r\alpha_1,$$

so that we cannot maintain that the duration of the first phase increases. Hence, the duration of the first phase is unchanged or decreases.

(v) (a) First consider the case where $(\dot{y}/y - r) < 0$. If $\bar{t}_2$ is unchanged, then as a result of an increase in α_2, consumption is higher. Then, given that $\dot{c}/c < 0$, and $\dot{c}/c$ is unaltered, savings must be higher in this phase. However, the debt to be discharged has decreased as a result of an increase in α_2. Consequently, the third phase must be of shorter duration.

(b) Now consider the case where $(\dot{y}/y - r) \geqslant 0$. If $\bar{t}_2$ is unchanged then $c(\bar{t}_2)$ is the same or lower. But this implies that consumption is either the same throughout this phase or lower. But from (iii) we know that consumption must increase throughout this phase. But as $\dot{c} = \dot{y}(1 - \alpha_2(\dot{y}/y - r)) \geqslant \dot{y} > 0$, it must follow that the third phase is shorter.

(iv) Since the first phase is unchanged or shorter, and the third phase is shorter as well, the second phase must be longer, given that the $[0, T]$ interval is fixed in duration.

Proof of Proposition 2.2

The proof is quite obvious from the proof of Proposition 2.1 and therefore is omitted.

Proof of Proposition 2.3

(i) As in the proof of Proposition 2.1(i), but with α_2 everywhere replaced by A_0, except in equation (2A.3).

(ii) If $\bar{t}_1$ is unchanged then $c(\bar{t}_1)$ is unchanged as well. Further, we have shown elsewhere that consumption increases along this phase. Hence, if $\bar{t}_1$ is unchanged or increases, consumption does not decrease. But since $c(0)$ has decreased, $\dot{c}/c < 0$ and $\dot{c}/c$ is unaltered, it must follow that:

$$c(\bar{t}_1) < y\left(1 - \alpha_2\left(\frac{\dot{y}}{y} - r\right)\right) + r\alpha_1,$$

so that we cannot maintain that $\bar{t}_1$ is unchanged or has increased. Hence the duration of the first phase must decrease.

(iii) This follows from (ii) and the fact that the third phase is unaltered in duration.

CHAPTER **3**

Distribution Implications of Credit Constraints

In the previous chapter it was shown that credit constraints can affect the individual's lifetime plans in a number of ways. A rational individual should anticipate these effects and may take action to mitigate them. This requires the individual to have an additional choice instrument. The purpose of this chapter then is to analyse the individual's choice of an earnings profile which in the previous chapter was assumed given. So the way in which this chapter and the previous one are linked is that the choice of consumption (topic of the last chapter) can be regarded as a first-step choice in which the earnings profile is assumed given and the choice of the earnings profile (the topic of this chapter) can be viewed as a second-step choice in which the consumption profile solved for an exogenous earnings profile is given. The advantage of such a two-step optimization approach is that it enables us to endogenize the individual's problem systematically and each chapter adds to the previous one, thus making steady progress.

The incentive to exercise earnings-profile choice in a non-trivial way depends on the way in which credit constraints affect welfare via their influence on the shape of the consumption profile. Once this has been analysed we can proceed straightaway to the choice of earnings profile. It is worth noting here that earnings are associated with jobs and jobs are invariably viewed as discrete entities so that a discrete choice approach to the problem is plausible. This leads to some interesting further implications. One is distributional. Thinking in terms of net worth (lifetime earnings plus initial wealth) it is shown that net worth cannot decrease with initial wealth. The other implication is the incentive to gamble. We analyse this in depth and note that it links up with Chapter 5.

Welfare and Choice of Earnings Profile

As increase in the amount of credit that an individual has access to will increase his opportunity set if he is credit-constrained at some interval in life. Such a change, by allowing the individual to allocate his income to consumption more freely, smooths out consumption pattern over life. To the extent that the individual alters his consumption pattern, by a revealed preference argument, his utility increases. We can then write:

$$J = \int_0^T e^{-\rho t} U(c) \, dt = \int_0^T e^{-\rho t} U(c(\bar{A})) \, dt; \quad \frac{\partial J}{\partial \bar{A}} \leqslant 0.$$

The weak inequality above allows for the possibility that an individual who is never credit-constrained will not increase utility when the credit constraint is relaxed.

The result, that a lowering of the debt limit can further prevent the individual from smoothing out his consumption path and result in a decrease in lifetime utility, depends on the assumption that the utility function is strictly concave. This dependence is quite interesting and can be brought out clearly by momentarily simplifying and assuming that $r = \rho = 0$, $A_0 = A_T = 0$ and that the individual receives the same labour income in all periods. Then the optimal consumption in each period is:

$$c(t) = \frac{\int_0^T y(t) \, dt}{T} \quad \text{or} \quad c(t) = y(t).$$

Now let income be received differently such that although the value of

$$\int_0^T y(t) \, dt$$

does not change, $y(0)$ decreases slightly and $y(T)$ increases by the same amount, income for all the other periods remaining unchanged. Then if the individual can lend and borrow freely his optimal consumption will be

$$c(0) > y(0), \qquad c(t) = y(t), \qquad \forall t \in (0, T), \qquad c(T) < y(T).$$

However, if he cannot borrow then the optimal consumption is given by

$$c(t) = y(t), \forall\, t \in [0, T].$$

If $U(c)$ is strictly concave then the loss in utility at $t = 0$ will be greater than the gain in utility at $t = T$ and therefore J will decrease in value. If we assume that $y(t)$ is strictly increasing then we have the situation in Figure 3.1, where the loss in utility (resulting from shaded area 1) will be greater than the gain in utility (resulting from shaded area 2), area of $1 = $ area of 2.

It is possible to obtain a quantitative feel of changes in lifetime utility resulting from changes in credit constraints. Notice that Tables 2.1–2.3 show that either a relaxation of the credit constraint or an increase in initial assets increases utility. This suggests that we can keep utility constant and work out changes in initial assets required as a result of changes in credit constraints.

To illustrate the method, consider the following example. First, certain values are fixed: $T = 50$, $r = 0.04$, $\varepsilon = 1$, $y(0) = 5500$, $\gamma = 0.03$, $\rho = 0.04$, $A_0 = 4000$, $\alpha_1 = 0$, $\alpha_2 = 0$. The program is then run and the value of J is noted at 197.9455. α_2 is then changed to -0.10, and, keeping J constant, a compensating change in A_0 is computed using iterative methods, to obtain a value of 3693. Thus relaxing α_2 from 0 to -0.10 is like giving the consumer 307 extra units of A_0. Using this method, we carried out similar computations for differing values of α_2, A_0 and ρ. To save computing time,

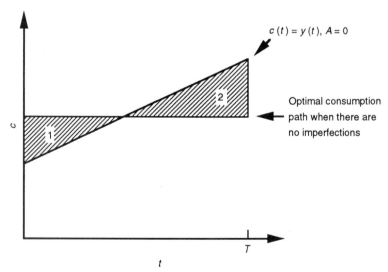

Figure 3.1 *Consumption paths under perfect and imperfect markets.*

A_0 was restricted to take values of multiples of 2. Thus exact convergence to J was not in general possible, but in all cases the error was less than 0.001 units of J, which is acceptable.

The results, presented in Tables 3.1 and 3.2, show that the direction of changes in A_0 when $\bar{A}$ changes and J is held constant conforms to expectations: ΔA_0 falls when one considers either more wealthy individuals or those who have greater credit facilities. Notice from Table 3.1 that given ρ, ΔA_0 changes slowly with α_2; the individual has to be able to borrow

Table 3.1 Simulations of compensation required, holding welfare constant.

	ΔA_0 when $\Delta\alpha_2 = -0.10$, holding J constant		
α_2	$A_0 = 2000$	$A_0 = 4000$	$A_0 = 6000$
0	317	307	293
−0.5	289	279	273
−1.0	265	257	249
−1.5	247	239	231
−2.0	225	219	217
−2.5	207	199	195
−3.0	189	185	181
−4.0	157	147	141
−5.0	121	113	113
−6.0	85	81	73
−7.0	49	39	37
−8.0	9	1	0

$T = 50$, $r = 0.04$, $\varepsilon = 1$, $y(0) = 5500$, $\gamma = 0.03$, $\rho = 0.04$, $\alpha_1 = 0$.

Table 3.2 Simulations of compensation required, holding welfare constant.

	ΔA_0 when $\Delta\alpha_2 = -0.10$, holding J constant		
α_2	$\rho = 0.02$	$\rho = 0.04$	$\rho = 0.06$
0	119	307	395
−0.5	83	279	379
−1.0	59	257	363
−1.5	37	239	351
−2.0	19	219	343
−2.5	0	199	327
−3.0	0	185	317
−4.0	0	147	295
−5.0	0	113	269
−6.0	0	81	243
−7.0	0	39	215
−8.0	0	1	181

$T = 50$, $r = 0.04$, $\varepsilon = 1$, $y(0) = 5500$, $\gamma = 0.03$, $A_0 = 4000$, $\alpha_1 = 0$.

about four times his current income before ΔA_0 decreases by about one-half. Thus wide dispersions in either $\bar{A}$ or A_0 will be consistent with relatively concentrated dispersion of ΔA_0. The interesting implication is that if one starts with rather stringent debt constraints, and it is perceived that lifting these is beneficial, then they can be lifted a considerable way before further relaxation ceases to become worthwhile. However, notice from Table 3.2 that shifts in ρ affect the size of ΔA_0 but do not affect the quantity $(A_0/\alpha_2 = x - \Delta A_0/\alpha_2 = x - 0.5; \; x = 0, \, -0.5, \, -1, \ldots)$ so that the beneficial effects of considerable lifting of debt limits is somewhat restricted to those with greater subjective time discount rates.

Choice of Earnings Profile

The major point arising from the preceding analysis is that when credit constraints bind, the freedom to smooth out consumption over life is restricted and this results in a loss of welfare. The upshot is that since under effective credit constraints it is the shape of the earnings profile which influences the shape of the consumption profile, it will also influence welfare. Of course, the present value of the lifetime earnings associated with earnings profile will also affect welfare. Therefore, the individual will take account of both the shape and the lifetime present-value earnings associated with an earnings profile when making the choice of the earnings profile in the first place. It is worth pursuing this in some depth.

Choice in the absence of credit constraints

Consider the individual who does not face any credit constraints and who faces the following two-stage problem. At the first stage he maximizes (2.1) subject to (2.2) and (2.3), given an earnings profile, y. The solution implies that (2.1) can be written as

$$J = J(y; \rho, r, A_0, \alpha_1, \alpha_2, A_T). \qquad (3.1)$$

The second-stage choice is over earnings profiles that differ in steepness such that a steeper earnings profile implies greater lifetime earnings. The justification for this feature arises from the influence of human-capital investment, education and on-the-job training – on the character of the earnings profile. Since human capital is usually acquired early on in life with the returns deferred to later on in life, a steeper earnings profile represents a greater acquisition of human capital. When the model is closed, it will turn out that such an earnings profile also carries greater present-value life-time earnings. The reason is that credit constraints will prevent individuals from competing away the premium on present-value lifetime earnings associated with steep earnings profiles.

We shall be comparing choice of earnings profiles in the absence of credit constraints with the choice in the presence of credit constraints. It turns out that clear-cut results are very difficult to derive. So from here on we will proceed by way of an example backing it up with simulations.

An example

Let y^1 and y^2 denote two income paths where

$$y^1 = \int_0^T e^{-rt} y_t^1 \, dt, \qquad y_t^1 = y_0^1 e^{\gamma_1 t}$$

and

$$y^2 = \int_0^T e^{-rt} y_t^2 \, dt, \qquad y_t^2 = y_0^2 e^{\gamma_2 t}$$

and where $y^1 < y^2$, $y_0^1 > y_0^2$, $0 \leqslant \gamma_1 \leqslant \gamma_2$, γ_1 and γ_2 being constants. Let

$$J(y^i|A_0, \ldots) = \max \int_0^T e^{-\rho t} \frac{1}{1-\varepsilon} u(c^i)^{1-\varepsilon} \, dt$$

given (2.2), (2.3) and y^i. Then we have the following.

Proposition 3.1. Under the assumption of perfect credit markets, $c_0^1 < c_0^2$ and $J(y^1|A_0, \ldots) < J(y^2|A_0, \ldots)$, where c_0^i is initial consumption associated with income path y^i, $i = 1, 2$.

Proof. Maximizing the objective function subject to the constraints and $y^i = y^1$ yields $c_0^1 = [y^1 + A(0, T; r)] \varepsilon / [r(\varepsilon - 1) + \rho]$ and when $y^i = y^2$, $c_0^2 = [y^2 + A(0, T; r)] \varepsilon / [r(\varepsilon - 1) + \rho]$. Since $y^2 > y^1$, $c_0^2 > c_0^1$. But $c_0^2 > c_0^1 \Rightarrow c_t^2 > c_t^1 \, \forall \, t$. Therefore, since $U_c > 0$ for all finite c, $J(y^2|A_0, \ldots) > J(y^1|A_0, \ldots)$.

In other words, the individual chooses that earnings profile which yields the greatest present-value lifetime earnings since that maximizes consumption at every moment in time and thereby maximizes utility. The choice is made with respect to present-value lifetime earnings only so that the slope of the earnings profile is not an additional separate influence. Hence it is more accurate to write (3.1) as

$$J = J(y; \rho, r, A_0, A_T). \tag{3.2}$$

Choice in the presence of credit constraints

When we consider the choice of an earnings profile under the assumption of imperfect credit markets, however, it is not as clear cut as that of Proposition 3.1. In fact, given the assumptions of Proposition 3.1 and the additional assumption of imperfect credit markets, without further information it is not possible to assert that $c^1(0) < c^2(0)$ and $J(y^1|A_0, ...) < J(y^2|A_0, ...)$. We can show this at once by producing an example. Consider the case where $A_0 = 0$, $\alpha_1 = 0$ and $\alpha_2 = 0$. Then clearly, $c^1(t) = y^1(t)$ and $c^2(t) = y^2(t) \forall t$ so that $c^1(0) = y^1(0)$ and $c^2(0) = y^2(0)$. But as $y^1(0) > y^2(0)$, $c^1(0) > c^2(0)$. Further, since $y^1(t) < y^2(t)$ during the later part of life, we have the situation where $c^1(t) > c^2(t)$ for the earlier part of life and $c^1(t) < c^2(t)$ for the later part of life. Clearly, without even more specific assumptions, it is not possible to assert which of $J(y^2)$ and $J(y^1)$ is greater.

The above is admittedly an extreme example but it serves to make the point that under imperfect credit markets, the consumption path under steep earnings profile does not necessarily dominate the consumption path under a flat earnings profile. The problem is that as the two earnings paths cross, they tend to make the two consumption paths cross as well. If credit-rationing were completely absent, then the crossing of the two earnings paths would not matter as consumption at any time t becomes locally independent of income at time t.

Therefore, it is by no means clear that the individual will choose that feasible earnings profile which has the greatest lifetime present-value earnings. For if such a profile also happens to be steep in shape then it can entail restriction on the individual's ability to smooth out consumption through time. A flatter earnings profile with lower present value earnings but less restriction on smoothing consumption may be preferred.

As initial wealth increases and credit limits are raised, consumption becomes less dependent on income. This implies that the less effectively an individual is credit-constrained, the less incentive there is for him to choose a given flatter earnings profile with lower present-value earnings. It follows that some individuals can be indifferent between the two earnings profiles depending on the degree of credit-rationing they face. For the indifference to occur, this degree and the shape and the present value of earnings must be in some balanced configuration.

It is worth deriving a quantitative feel for this and in order to do so, we proceed as follows. The simulation program is executed with a given set of parameters and the earnings profile and the value of J noted. Holding J constant, the program is re-run with the same parameter set except that $y(0)$ is lowered and γ is set equal to 0.05 (from their sample, Willis and Rosen

(1979) worked out that the sample mean of γ for those with more than high-school education is 0.0535 with a standard deviation of 0.0283). By varying $y(0)$ convergence to J takes place. The present-value lifetime earnings of both the profiles are then compared and the difference recorded. Further results are generated systematically. The results presented below are based on the earnings profile $(y(0) = 5500, \gamma = 0.03)$ which has present-value earnings of 216,408.

Based on Tables 3.3 and 3.4 and Figure 3.2 we can obtain the following impressions. The ratio of present-value compensation to the present-value lifetime earnings of the earnings profile $(y(0) = 5500, \gamma = 0.03)$, call it PVC/PVY, depends on $\bar{A}$, A_0, ρ and γ. Clearly, the ratio decreases as A_0 increases and α_2 decreases. The ratio also decreases with ρ. The spread of the ratio appears to be the least with respect to A_0 and the greatest with respect to $\bar{A}$ and ρ. Moreover, it also appears that if we attempt to explain the dispersion of lifetime earnings over individuals, then small variations in γ together with the presence of binding $\bar{A}$ will produce the greatest dispersion. Variations in ρ together with the presence of binding $\bar{A}$ will also produce sizeable dispersion of lifetime earnings. However, rather large variations of A_0 will be required to produce a moderate dispersion of lifetime earnings.

It is worth tracing out the effects of changes in A_0 in more detail. It has been shown that the present-value compensation for the individual to be

Table 3.3 Simulations of compensation required, holding welfare constant.

α_2	Present-value compensation required when $\gamma = 0.05$		
	$A_0 = 2000$	$A_0 = 4000$	$A_0 = 6000$
0	35,296	34,193	33,220
-1	31,274	30,365	29,457
-2	27,576	26,798	26,019
-3	24,203	23,489	22,840
-4	21,089	20,440	19,856
-5	18,170	17,521	16,937
-6	15,315	14,731	14,212
-7	12,591	12,071	11,553
-8	9,931	9,412	8,958
-9	7,336	6,882	6,493
-10	5,195	4,806	4,483
-11	3,444	3,119	2,860
-12	2,081	1,822	1,627
-13	1,043	914	783
-14	395	265	200
-15	70	5	0

$T = 50$, $r = 0.04$, $\varepsilon = 1$, $y(0) = 5500$, $\gamma = 0.03$, $\rho = 0.04$, $\alpha_1 = 0$.

Table 3.4   Simulations of compensation required, holding welfare constant.

	Present-value compensation required when $\gamma = 0.05$		
α_2	$\rho = 0.02$	$\rho = 0.04$	$\rho = 0.06$
0	16,483	34,193	50,281
−1	12,915	30,365	46,259
−2	9,801	26,798	42,497
−3	7,012	23,489	39,058
−4	4,741	20,440	35,880
−5	2,990	17,521	32,831
−6	1,692	14,731	29,911
−7	784	12,071	27,187
−8	200	9,412	24,397
−9	5	6,882	21,738
−10	0	4,806	19,013
−11	0	3,119	16,353
−12	0	1,822	13,564
−13	0	914	10,774
−14	0	265	8,179
−15	0	5	5,909

$T = 50$, $r = 0.04$, $\varepsilon = 1$, $y(0) = 5500$, $\gamma = 0.03$, $A_0 = 4000$, $\alpha_1 = 0$.

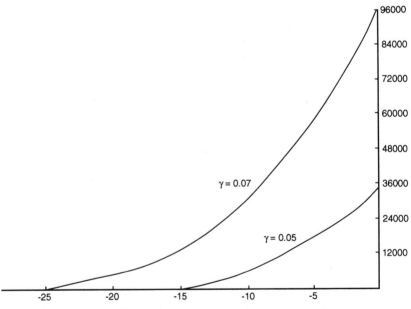

Figure 3.2 *Graphic representation of simulation results.*

indifferent falls with initial assets. Therefore, there is a high enough $A_0 = A_0^*$ at which the individual is indifferent between the two earnings profiles. Call A_0^* the 'threshold level of initial assets'. Now consider the following example which places a numerical value on A_0^*, given the characteristics of the individual. The two earnings profiles are such that the present-value earnings difference is 34 193, (250 601 − 216 408). From Table 3.3, the $A_0 = 2000$ individual needs PVC = 35 296 to be indifferent between the two profiles and therefore chooses the flat one whereas the $A_0 = 6000$ individual chooses the steep one as PVC = 33 220 for him. However, the $A_0 = 4000$ individual is indifferent between the two. Now consider the welfare and the net worth of the individual whose initial assets change from 3999 to 4001. The initial assets and the welfare of the two individuals are virtually equal, but the net worth $(A_0 + \text{PVY})$ is very unequal, at 220 407 and 254 602 respectively.

There is an illuminating way of explaining this result. In Figure 3.3, the indirect utility functions, $J(y^f; A_0)$ and $J(y^s; A_0)$ are plotted against A_0, y^f denoting the flatter earnings profile and y^s the steeper one. They are drawn concave and differentiable. The two curves are shown to intersect so that there is a kink at $A_0 = A_0^*$. The curves also trace out

$$V(A_0) = \max\,[J(y^f; A_0),\ J(y^s; A_0)] \qquad (3.3)$$

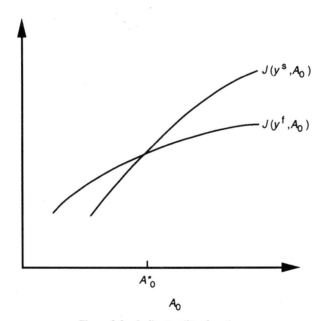

Figure 3.3 *Indirect utility functions.*

and the kink renders $V(A_0)$ non-concave. As long as the two indirect utility functions are concave in A_0 and there is effective credit-rationing, the kink will result.

(a) At very low levels of A_0, to the left of A_0^*, the binding of the credit constraint under the steep-earnings-profile option severely constrains early consumption and so renders $J(y^s) < J(y^f)$.

(b) However, given diminishing marginal utility, a small increase in A_0 yields greater lifetime utility in the steep-earnings option. This is reflected in the steeper slope of $J(y^s)$ at any given value of A_0. Therefore, as $A_0 \rightarrow A_0^*$, $\{J(y^f) - J(y^s)\} \rightarrow 0$.

(c) At A_0^*, the threshold level of initial assets, $J(y^f) = J(y^s)$ so that the individual is indifferent between the two earnings options.

(d) Finally, at high levels of initial assets, to the right of A_0^*, $J(y^s) > J(y^f)$ so that the individual chooses the steep earnings profile.

Distributional Implications

The above analysis, carried out with a choice between only two earnings profiles, served to emphasize that large variations in present-value earnings can result from a small variation in initial assets around some threshold level A_0^*. Further variations in A_0 would not result in variations in present-value earnings. However, suppose that there are many earnings profiles differing in steepness and present-value earnings and ordered such that those with greater present-value earnings are steeper. This ordering perhaps reflects that steeper earnings profiles are associated with greater human-capital investment early on in life. Then it is not too difficult to see that an increase in initial assets will be associated with steep increases in present-value earnings. Thus greater initial assets will be associated with greater present-value earnings implying that net worth,

$$A_0 + \int_0^T e^{-rt} y(t) \, dt - e^{-rT} A_T,$$

increases with A_0. Certainly, absolute inequality will not decrease with A_0; very likely, absolute inequality will be greater.

A comparative-advantage interpretation

The individual who happens to possess A_0^*, his threshold level of initial assets, has no desire to change from the y^s option to the y^f option or vice versa since $J(y^s) = J(y^f)$. The present-value earnings difference just compensates for the uneven consumption over life due to the binding of the credit constraint. If an individual possesses $A_0 > A_0^*$, then present-value earnings difference more than compensates for the uneven consumption path so that he chooses the y^s option. Analogously, $A_0 < A_0^*$ implies that the y^f option is chosen. Since the choice of earnings profile depends on initial wealth, we could say that those who hold wealth in excess of the threshold level possess comparative advantage at the y^s option and those who hold wealth short of the threshold level have comparative advantage at the y^f option.

The incentive to gamble

Upon a first examination, it might be thought that the comparative advantage arises wholly from the imperfections in the credit market. However, this is not quite so, and to see this let us consider an individual who has A_0^*. Suppose he receives a windfall increase ε, where ε can be arbitrarily small, then $A_0 = A_0^* + \varepsilon$ and there results a gain in his utility. An equally small decrease in assets, $A_0 = A_0^* - \varepsilon$, would result in a loss of utility. But the shape of the $V(A_0)$ function around A_0^* implies that the individual's gain in utility exceeds the loss. This implies that the individual would prefer some gambles in A_0 to their expectations. Thus rather than have A_0^* with certainty, the individual prefers a gamble that yields $A_0^* + \varepsilon$ with probability q and $A_0^* - \varepsilon$ with probability $1 - q$ where q satisfies

$$q[A_0^* + \varepsilon] + [1 - q][A_0^* - \varepsilon] = A_0^*. \qquad (3.4)$$

For the individual this gamble is fair since

$$E\{q[A_0^* + \varepsilon - A_0^*] + [1 - q][A_0^* - \varepsilon - A_0^*]\} = 0, \qquad (3.5)$$

making use of (3.4). As shown in Figure 3.3, the gamble improves *ex ante* expected utility.

The individual with A_0^* therefore has an incentive to gamble. If the opportunity to gamble is there and if he loses the gamble then he acquires a comparative advantage at the y^f option. If he wins then he acquires a comparative advantage at the y^s option. However, if the opportunity to gamble is not available then the individual with A_0^* will continue to be indifferent between the two options as he possesses comparative advantage at neither. Therefore, the comparative advantage that an individual possesses reflects the market or opportunities to gamble. This reflection rests on the imperfections in the credit market.

It should not be difficult to see that as A_0 changes, the incentive to gamble also changes. For someone with a very high level of initial wealth the comparative advantage is overwhelmingly at the y^s option, whereas for someone with a very low level of initial wealth it lies with the y^f option. Such individuals miss out the non-concave segment of the $V(A_0)$ function altogether and hence have no incentive to gamble. The incentive to gamble remains for those individuals whose initial wealth places them around A_0^*.

Suppose there is the opportunity to enter into fair gambles. Then it is interesting to consider the effect gambling has on the distribution of wealth. Since at each level of wealth at and around A_0^* there is the incentive to gamble, the incentive will only disappear when such individuals win or lose such that they are placed outside the region of the incentive to gamble. Therefore, no optimizing individual will choose to hold wealth around A_0^* if he has the opportunity to gamble.

The interesting observation here is that markets in fair gambles are rare. In Chapter 5 we shall examine one reason that may explain this feature.

Conclusion

The previous chapter set the stage by analysing the effects of credit constraints on the consumption decision. In this chapter, armed with the consumption decision, we have traced out the effects of credit constraints on the choice of the earnings profile. There are four features worth noting.

First, the view that is unfolding, and the one which we shall be pursuing in the following chapters, is that credit constraints have influences that are far-reaching. The effect of credit constraints do not stop at consumption once we endogenize the problem further. These effects reaching further areas may be much more important.

Second, the role played by wealth is being emphasized. Quite simply, less wealth makes credit-rationing more effective. Wealth thus affects the opportunity set of the individual who makes consumption and investment decisions. The latter's dependence on wealth via credit constraints may be very important.

Third, the distribution of wealth identifies individuals who are most likely to be affected by credit constraints. The individual ceases to be anonymous. Groups of individuals sharing a characteristic may be identified in this way if this characteristic is correlated with wealth.

Fourth, if we allow some discreteness then it has interesting consequences. For instance, effective credit constraints combined with discreteness may provide the individual with an incentive to gamble in which the prize would be an earnings profile carrying greater lifetime income.

CHAPTER 4

Differing Borrowing and Lending Rates

So far, the analysis has assumed a single interest rate and concentrated on quantity constraints on credit. In reality, a whole range of interest rates, consisting of subranges of borrowing and lending rates, is observed to coexist with quantity constraints on credit. But an interesting feature is that almost always the borrowing rates are higher than the corresponding lending rates. It is worth tracing out the implications of this feature to see if it warrants any major modifications to the previous analysis.

For analytical convenience, assume that there is one aggregate borrowing rate, r_2, which is greater than the sole lending rate, r_1 (for previous attempts in this area see Hirshleifer (1958), Tobin and Dolde (1971), Flemming (1973) and Watkins 1977)). In order to isolate the effect of the divergence between the two rates, assume initially that there is no limit on borrowing at the rate r_2. Formally, the basic problem can be restated as:

$$\text{Maximize} \int_0^T e^{-\rho t} \left(\frac{1}{1-\varepsilon} c(t)^{1-\varepsilon} + \text{constant} \right) \, dt, \, \varepsilon > 0,$$

subject to

$$\dot{A} = r_1 A + y - c, \quad A > 0,$$
$$\dot{A} = r_2 A + y - c, \quad A < 0, \quad (4.1)$$
$$\dot{A} = y - c, \quad A = 0;$$

and the end-point conditions,

$$A(0) = A_0, \qquad A(T) = A_T.$$

In purely mathematical terms the optimal control so derived lacks differentiability and cannot be solved using the standard techniques. However, Clarke (1974, 1975a, 1975b) has, in fact, given a formal characterization of necessary conditions for such problems and the adaptation for our economic problem is given below.

The maximum principle can be stated as:

If $A^*(t)$, $C^*(t)$ are optimal then there exists an absolutely continuous $\lambda(t)$ satisfying

$$\dot{A}^*(t), = \frac{\partial H}{\partial \lambda}, \qquad (4.2)$$

$$\dot{\lambda}(t) - \lambda\rho = -\frac{\partial H}{\partial A^*}, \qquad (4.3)$$

and

$$U(c) - \lambda c \leqslant U(c^*) - \lambda c^* \quad \text{for all } c \geqslant 0; \qquad (4.4)$$

where

$$H = U(c) + \lambda f,$$

in which f is the right-hand side of (4.1),

$$\frac{\partial H}{\partial \lambda} = f,$$

and

$$\frac{\partial H}{\partial A^*} \in \begin{cases} \{\lambda r_1\}, & A^* > 0, \\ \{\lambda r_2\}, & A^* < 0, \\ [\lambda r_2, \lambda r_1], & A^* = 0. \end{cases} \qquad (4.5)$$

Clearly the optimal c satisfies

$$U_c = \lambda \qquad (4.6)$$

From (4.2), (4.3), and (4.6) it is clear that the marginal rate of transformation that is equal to the marginal rate of substitution will involve r_1 if the individual is a lender and r_2 if he is a borrower. If he is neither a lender nor a borrower, then his marginal rate of substitution will lie between the above two marginal rates of transformation.

Analysis of the Solution to the Choice Problem

A typical lifetime plan

Our interest lies in characterizing the individual's lifetime plan and the influence of the interest rate differential on it. One way to proceed first to make use of the previous analysis from which it should be evident that the characteristics of a lifetime plan will depend on the values of A_0, ε, ρ, the earnings profile, r_1 and r_2. Then assume that $A_0 > 0$, the earnings profile is flat (an assumption which will later be relaxed), and $\rho > r_2$, so that $(\rho - r_1)/\varepsilon > (\rho - r_2)/\varepsilon > \dot{y}/y = 0$, and hence the following lifetime plan of two phases will result

Phase 1
Phase 1 lasts from $[0, \bar{t})$. During this phase,

$$\dot{\lambda} = \lambda(\rho - r_1).$$
$$\dot{A} = r_1 A + y - c, \ A > 0.$$
$$\dot{A} < 0.$$
$$\text{At } \bar{t}, \ A = 0, \ \dot{A} < 0.$$

Consumption decreases at the rate $(\rho - r_1)/\varepsilon$ during this phase.

Phase 2
Phase 2 lasts from $[\bar{t}, T]$. During this phase,

$$\dot{\lambda} = \lambda(\rho - r_2).$$
$$\dot{A} = r_2 A + y - c, \qquad A < 0.$$
$$\dot{A} < 0 \text{ for all } t, \qquad \bar{t} \leqslant t < \hat{t}.$$
$$\dot{A} = 0 \text{ at } t = \hat{t}.$$
$$\dot{A} > 0 \text{ for all } t, \qquad \hat{t} < t \leqslant T.$$

Consumption decreases at the rate $(\rho - r_2)/\varepsilon$ during this phase and such that

$$c(\bar{t}) > y(\bar{t}),$$
$$c(\hat{t}) = y(\hat{t}) + r_2 A(\hat{t}),$$
$$c(T) < y(T).$$

From the representative lifetime plan, it is obvious that the utility-maximizing individual plans consumption such that he is in debt throughout Phase 2. The timing and extent of this phase depend on A_0, ρ, r_1 and r_2

and this relationship is explored further below by means of comparative statics exercises.

Consider first the effect of a decrease in A_0. Differentiating (4.6) and utilizing (4.2) and 4.(3), we obtain:

$$\frac{\partial}{\partial t}\frac{\partial c}{\partial A_0} = \begin{cases} \left(\dfrac{r_1 - \rho}{\varepsilon}\right)\dfrac{\partial c}{\partial A_0} & A > 0, \\[2ex] \left(\dfrac{r_2 - \rho}{\varepsilon}\right)\dfrac{\partial c}{\partial A_0} & A < 0. \end{cases}$$

Thus $\partial c/\partial A_0$ does not change sign and, from the overall budget constraint, consumption must fall. The reduction in consumption decreases at two rates, $(r_1 - \rho)/\varepsilon$ when $A > 0$ and $(r_2 - \rho)/\varepsilon$ when $A < 0$.

Differentiating,

$$\dot{A} = \begin{cases} r_1 A + y - c, & A > 0, \\ r_2 A + y - c, & A < 0. \end{cases}$$

We can then write

$$\frac{\partial}{\partial t}\frac{\partial A}{\partial A_0} = \begin{cases} r_1 \dfrac{\partial A}{\partial A_0} - \dfrac{\partial c}{\partial A_0}, & A > 0, & (4.7a) \\[2ex] r_2 \dfrac{\partial A}{\partial A_0} - \dfrac{\partial c}{\partial A_0}, & A < 0; & (4.7b) \end{cases}$$

and then draw a phase diagram as in Figure 4.1.

A decrease in A_0 is represented by the line labelled 'initial condition' and it cuts the $\partial A/\partial A_0$ axis at a negative value. Since the terminal assets are unchanged, the line labelled 'terminal condition' cuts the $\partial A/\partial A_0$ axis at value zero. The line labelled r_1 is obtained by setting $\partial/\partial t\ \partial A/\partial A_0$ in (4.7a) equal to zero and the line labelled r_2 is obtained by setting $\partial/\partial t\ \partial A/\partial A_0$ in (4.7b) equal to zero. We have shown that consumption decreases throughout life, that is, $\partial c/\partial A_0 > 0$. We must therefore, begin from a point to the left of P. However, if we were to begin at a point to the right of B, then we would never approach the terminal condition. This means that we must try a path beginning to the left of B. To the left of D, it is clear that $\partial A/\partial A_0 < 0$ but $\partial \dot{A}/\partial A_0 > 0$ so that the fall in A_0 reduces the individual's assets but increases his savings at every point in life. Thus consumption is reduced such that the reduction in interest income is more than cancelled out. This is readily plausible because the individual now has to attain an unchanged level of terminal assets with a reduced level of initial assets.

Between points D and B, the situation is not immediately obvious. However, if the consumer always lends, then he comes under the influence of

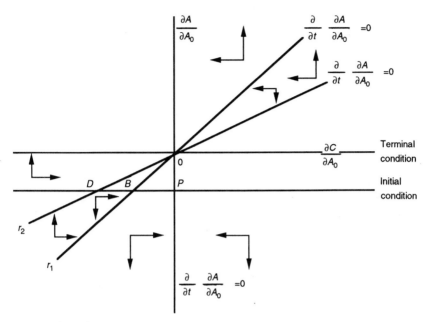

Figure 4.1   *Phase diagram for the effects of a change in initial assets.*

the arrows that carry him to the terminal condition. If he always borrows, then he will come under the influence of the arrows that will take him away from the terminal condition, the implication being that the fall in consumption is not sufficient to outweigh the fall in interest income. For an individual who both lends and borrows, therefore, the reduction in consumption must be such that he will be carried on to the terminal condition, that is, increase his savings throughout life such that the reduction in consumption makes up for the loss in income. In such an instance, starting between B and D will, in fact, carry him to the terminal condition.

Consider the effect of an increase in the borrowing rate.

(a) $A_0 > 0$. We can write, for $A > 0$,

$$\frac{\partial}{\partial t} \frac{\partial c}{\partial r_2} = \left(\frac{r_1 - \rho}{\varepsilon}\right) \frac{\partial c}{\partial r_2}. \tag{4.8}$$

The increase in the borrowing rate will reduce income. If consumption is a normal good, then from (4.8), $c(0)$ must fall. Since r_1 is unchanged, it follows that savings will rise initially. The first phase will now be of a longer duration so that the second phase will be shorter.

(b) $A_0 = 0$. Since they are of the same sign, the income effect together with

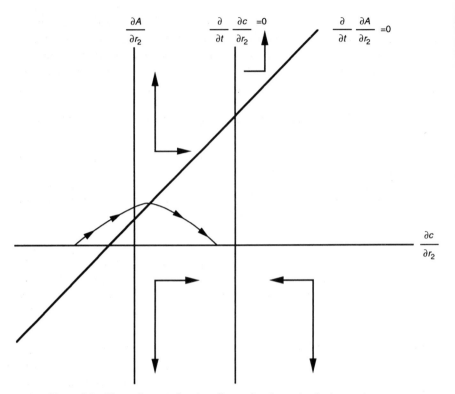

Figure 4.2 *Phase diagram for the effects of a change in the borrowing rate.*

the intertemporal substitution effect implies that $c(0)$ will fall. Differentiating first-order conditions, we have,

$$\frac{\partial}{\partial t}\frac{\partial c}{\partial r_2} = \frac{c}{\varepsilon} + \left(\frac{r_2 - \rho}{\varepsilon}\right)\frac{\partial c}{\partial r_2}, \qquad (4.9a)$$

$$\frac{\partial}{\partial t}\frac{\partial A}{\partial r_2} = r_2\frac{\partial A}{\partial r_2} + A - \frac{\partial c}{\partial r_2}. \qquad (4.96)$$

These two equations imply the situation shown in Figure 4.2. Thus, once again, savings rise initially. Therefore initially the fall in consumption is greater than the extra interest payments. Later on in life, the savings are used to finance the interest payments and the increased consumption.

Individuals Who Never Borrow

Thus an increase in the borrowing rate decreases consumption throughout life and increases savings initially. For the case in which initial assets are positive, it has also been shown that the duration of the first phase increases and that of the second phase decreases. As the borrowing rate continues to increase, however, the relation $(\rho - r_1)/\varepsilon > (\rho - r_2)/\varepsilon > \dot{y}/y = 0$ must be modified to read $(\rho - r_1)/\varepsilon > \dot{y}/y = 0 \geqslant (\rho - r_2)/\varepsilon$. In such a case, the following proposition can be proved.

Proposition 4.1. Given the basic assumptions made in this section, and in addition, if

$$\left(\frac{\rho - r_1}{\varepsilon}\right) > \frac{\dot{y}}{y} = 0 \geqslant \left(\frac{\rho - r_2}{\varepsilon}\right),$$

then the individual will never borrow and his consumption in the second phase will always be equal to income.

Proof. Suppose, contrary to the proposition, $c(\bar{t}) > y(\bar{t})$. Then, from (4.1) and $\dot{c}/c = (r_2 - \rho)/\varepsilon > 0$, the overall budget can never be satisfied as $A(t) = 0$, and $\dot{c}/c > \dot{y}/y$. Hence $c(\bar{t})$ cannot be greater than $y(\bar{t})$. If $c(\bar{t}) < y(\bar{t})$, then $\dot{c}/c = (r_1 - \rho)/\varepsilon < 0$ so that at $t = T$, from (4.1), there will be resources left over, unspent. Therefore, $c(\bar{t}) = y(\bar{t})$ and $c(t) = y(t) \, \forall \, t > \bar{t}$.

Although the relation $(\rho - r_1)/\varepsilon > 0 > (\rho - r_2)/\varepsilon$ is not necessary (though it is sufficient) to prevent borrowing it does serve to isolate the factors responsible for the assertion in the proposition. Intuitively, the individual dissaves because he places greater weight on consuming earlier on in life. But in so doing, he is prevented from borrowing in order to finance this consumption as the high borrowing rate implies that his consumption grows faster than wage income.

Therefore individuals who face relatively high borrowing rates will never borrow, even if $\rho > r_1$, and for part of their lives consumption will equal earnings and no savings or dissavings will be taking place. It is then natural to enquire about individuals for whom $c = y$ and $\dot{A} = 0$ throughout life. Therefore consider the individual with zero initial assets. For him, at any time t, if $c(t) > y(t)$ then the overall budget constraint will be violated and if $c(t) < y(t)$ then there will be positive assets left over at time $t = T$. Hence $c(t) = y(t)$ and $\dot{A} = 0$ for all t is the optimal policy for an individual with $A_0 = 0$. For non-zero values of A_0 close to $A_0 = 0$, the results of the comparative statics exercise of a decrease in A_0 can be utilized. For an individual whose first phase consists of decumulating assets and whose second phase is characterized by $c = y$ and $A = 0$, a decrease in A_0 decreases consumption during the first phase (during which $c > y$) and also decreased dissavings ($\dot{A} < 0$ in this phase). Thus as $A_0 \to 0$, $C \to y$ and $A \to 0$. Hence for less wealthy individuals, high borrowing rates mean longer phases characterized by $c = y$ and $\dot{A} = 0$.

Thus far, it has been assumed that $\dot{y}/y = 0$. If $\dot{y}/y = \gamma > 0$ then Proposition 4.1 can be extended to state that if $(r_2 - \rho)/\varepsilon > \gamma > (r_1 - \rho)/\varepsilon$, then the individual will never borrow. The proof is straightforward and derives from the observation that if $c(\bar{t}) > y(\bar{t})$, then $\dot{c}/c = (r_2 - \rho)/\varepsilon \geqslant \gamma$, which violates the overall budget.

We can now assess the differences, if any, that the analysis of this section makes to the previous sections. If the borrowing rate is high relative to the sum of the subjective discount rate and the earnings growth rate then the additional presence of a credit constraint does not matter since the individual never plans to borrow. But there results a phase during which current consumption depends strongly on current earnings which is similar to the constrained phase that results under an effective credit constraint. The analysis of the previous sections can therefore be considered relevant to situations in which although the borrowing rate is greater than the lending rate it is nevertheless lower than the sum of the subjective discount rate and the earnings growth rate. In fact, as long as there are intervals in the individual's life during which the sum of ρ and γ is high enough, as during the early part of the working career, the analysis will be of relevance. Moreover, as we shall see, for a great proportion of the individual's borrowing, r_2 is, in fact, surprisingly low, so that the analysis continues to be of relevance. Therefore, this section has identified the situations for which it is relevant. Finally, for wider implications of the model of this section, the reader can refer to Shah (1981).

CHAPTER 5

Intergenerational Implications of Credit Constraints

This chapter traces out the intergenerational consequences of credit constraints. The reason for pursuing this course of analysis is to investigate the ways, if any, in which the previously obtained intragenerational results change in any important manner. It is, however, expected that the analysis of this chapter will demonstrate that all the intragenerational consequences of credit constraints will be affected. For recall that one immediate consequence of credit constraints is that the individual is prevented from smoothing out his lifetime consumption profile, the extent depending on the given level of initial assets or inheritance. The level of inheritance received by the $(i + 1)$th generation, of course, depends on the bequests made by the ith generation. Consequently, if bequests are choice-determined by the ith generation so will the inheritance received by the $(i + 1)$th generation and hence the extent to which the $(i + 1)$th-generation individual can smooth out his lifetime consumption profile. The decision on the level of bequests should take these consequences into account so that bequests made by the ith generation will be determined by the extent of credit constraint faced by the $(i + 1)$th generation.

Of course, this course of action implies that we are pursuing the theme of the effect of greater choice on the influence of credit constraints on an individual's plans. The result is likely to show that credit constraints have far-reaching consequences. We shall analyse the effect of bequest choice in two stages. First, it will be assumed that the earnings profile is given. Second, the earnings profile will also be a choice variable. This second stage ties in neatly with the second half of Chapter 3 in which the individual chose the earnings profile but bequest choice was not allowed for.

The Model and its Formal Solution

The model is the same as that of Chapter 2 except that $A(T)$ is now a choice variable. The individual is assumed to maximize

$$\int_0^T e^{-\rho t} U(c(t))\, \mathrm{d}t + e^{-\rho T} B(A(T)), \qquad 0 \leqslant t \leqslant T, \qquad (5.1)$$

where B is an increasing, strictly concave and differentiable function in $A(T)$, subject to the differential equation

$$\dot{A} = rA + y - c, \qquad 0 \leqslant t \leqslant T, \qquad (5.2)$$

where $A(0) = A_0$ is given, and subject to the debt constraint

$$A(t) \geqslant \bar{A} = \alpha_1 + \alpha_2 y(t), \qquad 0 \leqslant t \leqslant T. \qquad (5.3)$$

Stated this way, the objective function in (5.1) is easily reconciled with the new view on transmission of wealth. According to this view, there is an extended life-cycle model in which utilities of unborn generations of the same dynasty are taken explicitly into account (see Becker and Tomes (1979), Bevan (1979), Flemming (1979), Laitner (1979) and Shorrocks (1979)). However, if utility of each generation depends on its resources and if resources (and preferences) are invariant across generations, then the new-view objective function can be collapsed to (5.1). Given the assumption made above and given that we shall be mainly concerned with analysing steady-state equilibrium in which resources and preferences are constant over generations of the same dynasty, (5.1) will be seen to be consistent with the new view.

There is nothing in the assumptions to ensure positive bequests. In a growing economy, heirs are likely to be wealthier than parents and heirs may bequeath more to old-age parents than parents do to their young heirs. This is potentially an interesting problem but needs a great deal of consideration and is not pursued here. Instead, it will simply be assumed that $B'(A(T)) \to \infty$ as $A(T) \to 0$ so that bequests are always ensured to be positive.

The Hamiltonian for the problem is as before and its maximization yields the following necessary conditions:

$$U'(c) = \lambda, \qquad\qquad 0 \leqslant t \leqslant T, \qquad\qquad (5.4)$$

$$\dot{\lambda} = \lambda(\rho - r) - \mu, \qquad 0 \leqslant t \leqslant T, \qquad (5.5)$$

where μ is such that

$$\mu \geqslant 0, \qquad \mu(A - \bar{A}) = 0.$$

The above conditions are the same as before. However, there is also a new one, namely,

$$\lambda(T) = B'(A(T)), \qquad\qquad (5.6)$$

so that, using (3.4),

$$U'(c(T)) = B'(A(T)), \qquad\qquad (5.7)$$

which states that at death-bed the value of the last resource should be such that its utility from consumption is equal to its utility in bequests.

Our task now is to examine the difference that the presence of bequest choice makes to an individual's consumption plan. In addition, we should want to examine the determinants of bequests more closely. In order to do all this, we first need to work out an optimal life-cycle plan.

Analysis of the Optimal Plan

In order to proceed further, it will be assumed as before that $U(c) = c^{1-\varepsilon}/(1-\varepsilon) + \text{constant}$, $\rho > r$, $y(t) = y(0)e^{\gamma t}$ and also that $B(A) = b/(1-\pi)A^{1-\pi}$, $b > 0$, $\pi > 0$. And, as before, given that A_0 and $A(T)$ are non-negative and that $\dot{c}/c$ and c are continuous in time, a lifetime plan consisting of at most three phases will result, the middle constrained phase lying between the two unconstrained phases.

Next, consider the effect of an increase in A_0 on the plans of the individual.

Proposition 5.1. If c and $A(T)$ are continuous and differentiable in A_0, then as a result of an increase in A_0,

(i) consumption increases throughout the first phase;
(ii) the duration of the first phase increases;
(iii) consumption and bequests are unchanged in the third phase;
(iv) the duration of the second phase decreases; and
(v) the duration of the third phase is unchanged.

The result of a slight decrease in either α_1 or α_2 is the following.

Proposition 5.2. If c and $A(T)$ are continuous and differentiable in α_1 and α_2, then as a result of a slight decrease in either α_1 or α_2:

  (i) consumption increases throughout the first phase;
 (ii) the duration of the first phase increases;
(iii) consumption increases and bequests decrease in the third phase;
 (iv) the duration of the second phase decreases; and
  (v) the duration of the third phase increases.

Since the proofs of these propositions follow along the lines of the proofs of the previous Propositions 2.1, 2.2 and 2.3, they are omitted here, but it is instructive to illustrate them and the simulations for these are reported in Table 5.1. Reading across the table illustrates Proposition 5.1 and reading down illustrates Proposition 5.2. The following points arising from the propositions are worth emphasizing.

(a) Changes in A_0 leave bequests unchanged; an increase in A_0 is absorbed into consumption during the first phase and is not passed on, in whole or part, to the next generation. The reason is that the effective credit constraint prevents the individual from freely smoothing out his consumption so that any increase in A_0 is immediately absorbed into consumption and not spread over the entire life.
(b) A slight decrease in $\bar{A}$ results in fewer bequests. The reason is that as a result of the relaxation of the credit limit, the individual is able to smooth out consumption more freely during the later part of life which increases the marginal utility of consumption and decreases the marginal utility of bequests and hence fewer bequests are made.

The implications of points (a) and (b) above when taken together are quite interesting and best brought out when examined in a steady state situation. Therefore, we now turn to a derivation of the steady-state distribution of bequests. First of all, we need to derive the relationship between bequests made by parents and inheritance received by children. Assume that when each individual is aged H he has e^{nH} children and that when he dies $T - H$ years later his estate is divided equally between them. (In order both to keep the analysis simple and facilitate simulations, it is assumed that children are begotten late in life. Thus when childhood lasts from 0 to 15 ($=$ economic age 0) and working span is 50 years, $T = 50$, children are born 15 years from death or at economic age 35. The theoretical analysis can be extended to an earlier birth date for children and it would most likely involve two constrained phases rather than one. The likely consequence is that it would put additional strain on consumption plans of both the children and the parents. Using the superscript i for the ith generation of a

Table 5.1 Simulations illustrating Propositions 5.1 and 5.2.

Initial assets of first generation		$A_0 = 0$	$A_0 = 2000$	$A_0 = 4000$	$A_0 = 6000$	$A_0 = 8000$	$A_0 = 10\,000$
$\alpha_2 = 0$	t_1	0	6.45	9.19	11.32	13.13	14.73
	t_2	41.14	41.14	41.14	41.14	41.14	41.14
	$c(0)$	5101	5688	6009	6270	6501	6713
	$A(T)$	4188	4188	4188	4188	4188	4188
	J	135.264	135.621	135.963	136.288	136.602	136.904
$\alpha_2 = -0.5$	t_1	7.30	9.87	11.92	13.69	15.27	16.71
	t_2	39.01	39.01	39.01	39.01	39.01	39.01
	$c(0)$	5671	5969	6219	6443	6650	6844
	$A(T)$	3933	3933	3933	3933	3933	3933
	J	135.366	135.709	136.037	136.353	136.658	136.955
$\alpha_2 = -1$	t_1	10.53	12.51	14.25	15.81	17.23	18.56
	t_2	37.17	37.17	37.17	37.17	37.17	37.17
	$c(0)$	5925	6165	6383	6585	6775	6958
	$A(T)$	3714	3714	3714	3714	3714	3714
	J	135.448	135.779	136.098	136.405	136.406	136.997
$\alpha_2 = -1.5$	t_1	13.11	14.81	16.35	17.77	19.09	20.33
	t_2	35.53	35.53	35.53	35.53	35.53	35.53
	$c(0)$	6109	6321	6518	6705	6885	7058
	$A(T)$	3519	3519	3519	3519	3519	3519
	J	135.515	135.837	136.148	136.45	136.475	137.032
$\alpha_2 = -2$	t_1	15.38	16.90	18.31	19.62	20.86	22.03
	t_2	34.02	34.02	34.02	34.02	34.02	34.02
	$c(0)$	6257	6450	6634	6811	6981	7147
	$A(T)$	3341	3341	3341	3341	3341	3341
	J	135.569	135.883	136.189	136.487	136.776	137.06
$\alpha_2 = -2.5$	t_1	17.46	18.86	20.17	21.40	22.57	23.69
	t_2	32.60	32.60	32.60	32.60	32.60	32.60
	$c(0)$	6381	6562	6736	6904	7068	7228
	$A(T)$	3177	3177	3177	3177	3177	3177
	J	135.612	135.921	136.222	136.515	136.801	137.081
$\alpha_2 = -3$	t_1	19.42	20.72	21.96	23.13	24.25	25.32
	t_2	31.25	31.25	31.25	31.25	31.25	31.25
	$c(0)$	6488	6660	6826	6988	7146	7301
	$A(T)$	3024	3024	3024	3024	3024	3024
	J	135.646	135.95	136.247	136.537	136.82	137.096

$T = 50$, $r = 0.04$, $\rho = 0.06$, $\varepsilon = 1$, $\pi = 1$, $b = 1$, $\alpha_1 = 0$, $\gamma = 0$, $y(0) = 5000$, $\text{PVY}(^*) = 108\,083$.
$(^*)\,\text{PVY} \equiv \text{present-value earned income, } \int_0^T e^{-rt} y(t)\, dt.$

given dynasty, $i = 1, 2, \ldots$, we can then write:

$$A_0^{i+1} = A^i(T)e^{-r(T-H)}e^{-nH} = G(A^i(T)), \tag{5.8}$$

or, inverting the function:

$$A^i(T) = G^{-1}(A_0^{i+1}). \tag{5.9}$$

To avoid taxonomic proliferation, it will be assumed that $r > n$.

From Proposition 5.1 we know that $A^i(T)$ is independent of A_0^i. In fact, $A^i(T)$ depends on the given value of $\bar{A}$. Furthermore, Proposition 5.2 implies that

$$A^i(T) = M(\bar{A}), \qquad M'(\bar{A}) > 0; \tag{5.10}$$

substituting (5.10) into (5.8),

$$A_0^{i+1} = A_0^{i+2} = A_0^{i+3} = \cdots. \tag{5.11}$$

Inserting this value of A_0^{i+1} in (5.9) then gives $A_i(T)$. Denote this equilibrium value of bequests by $A^*(T)$. The following proposition is then obtained readily.

Proposition 5.3

(a) The equilibrium level of bequests of all dynasties facing the same $\bar{A}$ but having differing A_0^i at $i = 1$ and being effectively credit-constrained during the first two generations is equal to $A^*(T)$.

(b) Using (5.10) it also follows that the bequests of those dynasties that face higher $\bar{A}$ will converge to higher level of bequests, that is, if $\bar{A}_1 > \bar{A}_2 > \bar{A}_3 \ldots$, then $A_1^*(T) > A_2^*(T) > A_3^*(T) \ldots$, where the subscript j on A_j and $A_j^*(T)$ denotes the jth dynasty, $j = 1, 2, 3, \ldots$.

Consider now, the steady-state level of bequests for dynasties that are never credit-constrained. The ith generation's overall budget can be written as

$$A^i(T)e^{-rT} = A_0^i + \int_0^T (y^i - c^i)e^{-rt}\, dt.$$

Using the optimality conditions with μ set equal to zero and following Atkinson (1971, p. 211), the following relation is easily derived;

$$A^i(T) = F^i(A^i(0)) > 0$$

and F is concave when $\varepsilon \leqslant \pi$ and convex when $\varepsilon > \pi$. When $\varepsilon \leqslant \pi$, the G^{-1} curve of (5.9) cuts the concave curve F from below when plotted on the $(A(T), A_0)$ plane and we then have a globally stable equilibrium level of bequests, $A^{**}(T)$, to which bequests of all families that are not credit-constrained converge.

Table 5.2 Simulations illustrating Propositions 5.3 and 5.4.

Initial assets of the second generation	$A(0) = 4188$	$A(0) = 3933$	$A(0) = 3714$	$A(0) = 3519$	$A(0) = 3341$	$A(0) = 3177$	$A(0) = 3024$	$A(0)$
α_2	0	−0.5	−1	−1.5	−2	−2.5	−3	α_2 does not bind
t_1	9.41	11.86	14.01	15.09	17.86	19.64	21.36	—
t_2	41.14	39.01	37.17	35.53	34.02	32.60	31.25	—
$c(0)$	6036	6211	6353	6472	6575	6665	6745	6965
$A(T)$	4188	3933	3714	3519	3341	3177	3024	2562
J	135.994	136.026	136.053	136.074	136.089	136.099	136.103	137.01

$T = 50$, $r = 0.04$, $\rho = 0.06$, $\varepsilon = 1$, $\pi = 1$, $b = 1$, $\alpha_1 = 0$, $\gamma = 0$, $y(0) = 5000$, PVY $= 108\,083$.

Proposition 5.4. In an economy with a constant population growth and stable age distribution where every individual has identical preferences and faces the same r and earnings profile, there may exist $n + 1$ equilibrium levels of bequests, $A_1^*(T), A_2^*(T), ..., A^{**}(T)$, such that all non-credit-constrained dynasties converge to $A^{**}(T)$ whereas the jth dynasty facing $\bar{A}_j$ and being effectively credit-constrained converges to $A_j^*(T), j = 1, ..., n$. Further, if $\bar{A}_1 > \bar{A}_2 > \cdots > \bar{A}_n$ then $A_1^*(T) > A_2^*(T) > \cdots > A_n^*(T) > A^{**}(T)$.

Propositions 5.3 and 5.4 are illustrated in Table 5.2 where the values of $A(T)$ of Table 5.1 are used as initial $A(0)$ values. Reading across the table, as α_2 decreases from 0, $A^*(T)$ decreases from 4188 and sticks at 2562 when there are no effective credit constraints. Notice that lifetime utility J increases as α_2 decreases. Using Propositions 5.3 and 5.4 there follows the next proposition.

Proposition 5.5. If two dynasties, starting as wealthy and less wealthy, face the same credit limit $\bar{A}$ and if only the less wealthy is credit-constrained from the first generation onwards, then the wealthy dynasty will also be credit-constrained from some future generation onwards.

Proposition 5.5 is easily proved once it is noted that in steady-state equilibrium $A^*(T) > A^{**}(T)$.

It is clear in steady-state equilibrium both that credit-constrained individuals are less well off and that they bequeath more. The former result is evidently due to the fact that credit limits are an additional constraint in the optimization problem. As for the latter, effective credit constraints restrict the smoothing out of consumption in early life with the consequences that the resultant extra saving is allocated to later life, thereby implying larger bequests. And more stringent credit constraints imply more resources for later life.

Choice of Earnings Profile

In Chapter 3 it was reasoned that if individuals are differentiated by credit limits only, then those who face more stringent credit limits are more likely to choose a flatter earnings profile carrying less present-value earnings. The implications for the distribution of net worth were also worked out. The effectiveness of credit limits, however, depends on the level of initial assets but if we allow individuals to be differentiated also by initial wealth then one might plausibly think that those who face more stringent credit limits also have lower initial wealth.

The purpose of this chapter has been, of course, to endogenize initial wealth or inheritance. It might be thought that allowing for such greater choice might weaken the above result. Indeed, the analysis carried out thus far in this chapter shows that the more credit-constrained bequeath more. Hence, one would have thought that this should weaken the effectiveness of credit constraints for the generation that receives the bequests and thereby possibly reverses the previous result on the choice of earnings profile and the distribution of net worth.

Unfortunately, once earnings-profile choice is allowed for, it is by no means evident that the more credit-constrained would, in fact, bequeath more. To see this, consider the individuals of the ith generation having the same initial assets but facing differing credit limits. The individual chooses an earnings profile $(y(0), \gamma)$ from a given set. From the analysis of Chapter 3 it is clear that a credit-constrained individual has less incentive for choosing a steeper (lower $y(0)$, greater γ) earnings profile with greater lifetime earnings than a non-constrained individual. But for those who are never credit-constrained, it is easy to show that if consumption and bequests are normal goods then $\partial A(T)/\partial$ (lifetime earnings) > 0. It then immediately follows that once we admit choice over earnings profiles the bequests of credit-constrained individuals in steady state are not necessarily greater than those of non-constrained individuals.

There is now enough intuitive background to carry out a more formal analysis of simultaneous bequest and earnings-profile choice. We shall work with two earnings profiles and therefore be able to invoke the notion of threshold level of wealth, A_0^*, introduced in Chapter 3. In fact, this present section links in neatly with Chapter 3 once parents are assumed to recognize the role played by A_0^* in the decision making of their heirs. The first step is to reformulate the objective function so as to recognize the discrete alternatives faced by the heirs.

Optimal Bequests with a Non-Concave Utility-from-Bequests Function

In Chapter 3 it was shown that the indirect utility functional is non-concave when the individual chooses between two earnings profiles that differ in steepness and present value earnings. A parent, considering the decision to bequeath, will take into account this feature of the heir's welfare. As a result, the objective function is now

$$\text{Maximize} \int_0^T e^{-\rho t} U(c(t)) \, dt + B(A(T)),$$

where $B(A(T))$ is non-concave. Consequently, there should be two levels of bequests at which the first-order condition

$$U'(c(T)) = B'(A(T))$$

is satisfied. At the lower level of bequests, the heir chooses the flat earnings profile whereas at the higher level the steep profile is chosen. In order to proceed more formally, it is best to break up the problem into two separate problems, consider the optimal solution to each, and then draw a comparison between the two maxima in order to obtain the global maximum.

Thus let $B(A(T); y^f)$ reflect the welfare of the heir under the flat earnings profile and $B(A(T); y^s)$ under the steep profile. Since the heir faces discrete alternatives, the parent will consider two alternative maximands:

$$\int_0^T e^{-\rho t} U(c(t)) \, dt + B(A(T); y^f)) \text{ and } \int_0^T e^{-\rho t} U(c(t)) \, dt + B(A(T); y^s).$$

If the parent solves the problem under the assumption that the heir chooses a steep earnings profile and bequeaths wealth which falls short of the threshold level, then the parent's problem will have been incorrectly formulated. Clearly, a constraint which requires the heirs to choose the steep profile must be incorporated in the formulation. Thus;

$$\text{Maximize} \int_0^T e^{-\rho t} U(c(t)) \, dt + B(A(T); y^s)$$

subject to

$$\dot{A} = rA + y - c,$$
$$A_0 \text{ given},$$
$$A \geqslant \bar{A}$$

and

$$A(T) \geqslant A(T)^*,$$

where $A(T)^*$ translates into the threshold level of inheritance for the heirs. The last inequality constraint, therefore, ensures consistent decision making. The first-order condition which is of interest is

$$U'(c(T)) = B'(A(T); y^s) + \theta^s, \qquad \theta^s(A(T) - A(T)^*) = 0,$$
$$\theta^s \geqslant 0, \qquad (A(T) - A(T)^*) \geqslant 0,$$

where θ^s is a non-negative Kuhn–Tucker multiplier. Thus,

$$U'(c(T)) = B'(A(T); y^s) \text{ whenever } A(T) > A(T)^* \qquad (5.12)$$

and

$$U'(c(T)) > B'(A(T); y^s) \text{ whenever } A(T) = A(T)^*. \qquad (5.13)$$

The optimizing problem under the assumption that the heir chooses a flat earnings profile can be similarly formulated. Thus:

$$\text{Maximize} \int_0^T e^{-\rho t} U(c(t)) \, dt + B(A(T); y^f)$$

subject to

$$\dot{A} = rA = y - c,$$
$$A_0 \text{ given,}$$
$$A \geqslant \bar{A}$$

and

$$A(T) \leqslant A(T^*).$$

The first-order condition of interest in this case is

$$U'(c(T)) = B'(A(T); y^f) - \theta^f, \qquad \theta^f(A(T)^* - A(T)) = 0,$$
$$\theta^f \geqslant 0, \qquad (A(T)^* - A(T)) \geqslant 0,$$

where θ^f is a non-negative Kuhn–Tucker multiplier. Thus,

$$U'(c(T)) = B'(A(T); y^f) \text{ whenever } A(T) < A(T)^* \qquad (5.14)$$

and

$$U'(c(T)) < B'(A(T); y^f) \text{ whenever } A(T) = A(T)^*. \qquad (5.15)$$

Our task now is a discussion of the global optimum level of bequests and the first step is to show that it is never $A(T)^*$. Suppose to the contrary that the heir inherits A_0^*. He will be indifferent between the y^f and y^s options, but suppose that he chooses the y^s option by flipping a coin. From (5.12) and (5.13) the parent's optimal choice of bequests implies that $U'(c(T)) \geqslant B'(A(T)^*; y^s)$. But at $A(T)^*, B'(A(T)^*; y^s) > B'(A(T)^*; y^f)$. Then it follows that $U'(c(T)) > B'(A(T)^*; y^f)$. If the heir were to choose y^f instead of y^s then his utility would be unchanged because A_0 is, by assumption, the level of assets at which he is indifferent between y^s and y^f. The utility of the parent would be unchanged as well since, in addition, the whole of the consumption profile is unchanged. But since $U'(c(T)) > B'(A(T)^*, y^f)$, a slight reduction in $A(T)$ would raise total welfare,

$$\int_0^T e^{-\rho t} U(c(t)) \, dt + B,$$

until $U'(c(T)) = B'(A(T); y^f)$. Hence bequesting $A < A^*$ is a Pareto improvement. A similar argument shows that bequeathing $A > A^*$ is also a Pareto improvement.

Therefore, the outcome is just two levels of $A(T)$ defined by $U'(c(T)) = B'(A(T); y^s)$ and $U'(c(T)) = B'(A(T); y^f)$ and such that the level of bequests under the former first-order condition is strictly greater than the threshold level which in turn is strictly greater that the level of bequests under the latter first-order condition. The question then is which of the two levels of bequests is the global maximum level. To answer it, consider the trade-off involved in moving from the lower level to the higher level of bequests. As the level of bequests increases

(a) Initially total utility falls as the increase in bequests cannot fully compensate for the decrease in consumption necessary to finance the increase in bequests.

(b) Once past the threshold level, however, the increase in the bequest level more than compensates for the decrease in consumption necessary to finance the increase in bequests. The total gain in utility under (b) is more likely to outweigh the total loss in utility under (a) if, for instance, the present-value earnings differential between the two earnings profiles is large. In other words, *a priori*, it is difficult to identify the global maximum level of bequests; all that can be said is that it depends on the unspecified factors such as the present-value earnings differential, the parameters of the utility function and so on.

Characterization of Dynasties

Consider a dynasty. If the parameters facing a given dynasty are unchanged then the dynasty is characterized by every generation either (i) opting for the y^s option and passing on wealth which is greater than the threshold level or (ii) opting for y^f and passing on wealth which is less than the threshold level.

To see this, suppose that a dynasty does not fall in either of the above categories. Then suppose the parent chooses y^f and the heir chooses y^s. Then the parent must bequeath $A(T) > A^*(T)$. As a result, the heir chooses the y^s option and earns more. If bequests and consumption are normal goods then bequests under y^s will be greater than y^f. Hence the heir will not bequeath less than the parent and so less than the threshold level. Since all parameters facing the dynasty are unchanged by assumption, the inheritance is greater than the threshold level for all, so that every generation chooses the y^s option.

An analogous argument is easily spelt out to show that if the parent chooses a y^s option and the heir chooses a y^f option then the dynasty will become characterized by every generation going for the y^f option. One implication of the analysis is that if two dynasties start with very similar initial wealth holdings, say one with $A_0^* - \varepsilon$ and another with $A_0^* + \varepsilon$ where ε is arbitrarily small, then they will end up bequeathing differing amounts.

The Role of Wealth

The analysis of the previous sections points to the possibility of a dynasty being locked into a flat earnings profile. This locking-in is most likely to occur to a dynasty that starts with low initial wealth. The blacks in the Unites States are a good example since if one traces their history to the point in time when the emancipation of slaves took place, one finds that the majority of black families had zero wealth and today the majority of blacks have jobs that are characterized by flat earnings profiles. The y^f earnings profile is characterized by less present-value lifetime earnings and the blacks are certainly the poorest of all groups in the USA.

A dynasty may start with low wealth but can bequeath its way out of y^f profile into y^s profile. That is, parents with wealth less than the threshold level can bequeath more than the threshold level. Such a situation can arise if the parent places greater weight on the welfare of the heir relative to his own consumption. Note that the transition can be very rapid, reflecting the discrete nature of earnings-profile choice. A good illustration here is the experience of the Japanese and Chinese Americans who started as poorly paid unskilled workers in Hawaii's sugar plantations. The heirs of these plantation workers are today over-represented in the professional workers class. It is thought that the Chinese and Japanese parents invested heavily in their children's human capital.

Although a dynasty may be able to bequeath its way out of y^f option, the dynasty which cannot is, in the absence of any exogenous shocks, in fact firmly locked into such an option. The tight lock is caused by low wealth allied to credit constraints and discrete alternatives. It is really low wealth that gives great effectiveness to credit constraints and it is discrete alternatives that make the transition difficult, although it is rapid if it happens. Wealth impinges on lifetime earnings. Inequality of lifetime earnings is a relatively neglected but not unimportant subject. What we have shown is that poverty of wealth, credit and lifetime earnings can go together.

Conclusion

The analysis of this chapter may be pulled together as follows. If earnings are assumed to be given and if all the individuals of a given generation are identical except for the credit limits they face, the parents of a dynasty facing more severe credit constraints bequeath more, thereby weakening the effectiveness of credit limits for their heirs. However, if earnings choice is allowed for, then it is possible that such parents bequeath less. As a result, the heirs will choose the flat earnings profile with less present-value earnings.

The choice of discrete alternatives also creates an incentive for the heir to gamble at certain levels (see Chapter 3). The parent will shrewdly perceive the incentive for the heir to gamble and bequeath accordingly. Thus when the heir's gain in utility in opting for a steep earnings profile outweighs the loss in utility of the parent in providing more bequests, more bequests will in fact be planned for. And when the heir chooses the flat earnings profile, less bequests will be planned for. Hence by internalizing initial wealth, total welfare is raised and the incentive to gamble recedes as the incentive to bequeath obviates a market for gambles. It then turns out that there is a rapid convergence to the steady state in which a given dynasty is characterized by every generation either (i) opting for the y^s option and passing on wealth which is greater than the threshold level or (ii) opting for y^f and passing on wealth which is less than the threshold level. Thus poverty of wealth, credit and lifetime earnings can go together.

In the previous chapters, the consequences of credit constraints were fully analysed. In this chapter, we have explored one way in which the consequences may be mitigated. By introducing concern for heirs' welfare, we have shown that the consequences may be weakened for heirs by parents making bequests. But without making further specific assumptions, it is not possible to state anything definite so that it is possible that parental bequeathing may not be enough to overcome the major effects of credit constraints on heirs' plans. However, what we have been able to show is the importance of wealth allied to credit constraints. It is very likely for a dynasty with low wealth to get locked into poverty.

CHAPTER **6**

Credit Constraints and Work–Leisure Choice

In this chapter, the model is extended to allow for work–leisure choice although, in order to make the exposition easier, the bequest motive is dropped. This is in keeping with the methodology pursued so far which is to examine the effects of greater choice on the results first obtained in Chapters 2 and 3. One reason for allowing for work–leisure choice is that when the individual anticipates credit constraints he can take evasive action to reduce the burden on his current consumption. This can work in two ways. One is that the individual can work harder in order to reduce his borrowings. The other is that if credit limits depend on earnings then greater work implies a higher credit limit.

While the model with the work–leisure choice incorporated can be worked out, there must have been reasons for ignoring such choice in the first place. One reason is that of methodology: simple analysis is presented in the beginning to bring out the essential points while extensions are brought in later on to see how far the essential insights survive. The other reason is that the work–leisure choice may not be a real one. We explore this in two stages: in this chapter we note that there is evidence of work being job-entailed and incorporate this feature into the model as work constraints. Thus we allow for the possibility that work on constraints may bind at some intervals in life. In the next chapter we take on board the concept of work being entirely job-entailed. The idea we work with is that in making job choices individuals are aware of its two dimensions: a lifetime wage profile and a lifetime work (and training) profile.

Returning to the present chapter, we begin by looking at evidence on work constraints and then formulate the individual's choice problem. We then look at the solution and concentrate on an analysis of the phases in the individual's optimal plan. Finally, we make the connection with the next chapter.

The Statement of the Problem

The basic model which underpins the analysis of this chapter and most of the next is stated below, and a major alteration is incorporated and analysed towards the end of the next chapter. Once again, we are concerned with an individual who plans over a lifetime of given length T. Let h denote the proportion of time spent at work at age t and, as before, let $c(t)$ denote the flow of consumption at age t. Utility at age t is given by an additive separable utility function, $U(c(t)) - V(h(t))$, which is such that $U_c > 0$, $U_{cc} < 0$, $V_h > 0$ and $V_{hh} < 0$ so that the marginal utility of consumption is positive and decreasing while the marginal disutility of work is positive and increasing.

Constraints on work

If labour markets are competitive and always clear by wage adjustment then the individual will be able to make unconstrained choices about labour supply. But unemployment and other constraints on labour supply are characteristic of modern labour markets. It appears that the work decision that generates unemployment and hours variation are usually delegated to employers placing individuals off their supply curves. Within this framework, differences in technology and characteristics of demand will generate differences in unemployment and hours worked even among observationally identical workers. For example, Murphy and Topel (1987) analyse current Population Survey data for the USA (1977–84) and find that

jobs differ widely in the average amounts of unemployment borne by workers and cyclical risks in hours and income are much higher in some industries than in others. The amounts of income and employment variation borne by the typical worker are striking. Adjusting for measurement error, a conservative estimate of the average year-to-year variation in individual earnings is nearly 18% of average annual income. The typical year-to-year variation in hours worked is nearly six full-time weeks of employment   (p. 104)

Since these estimates are much larger than fluctuations in average earnings and hours at either the industry or aggregate level, the main components of income and employment variation faced by workers would appear to be idiosyncratic (firm- or individual-specific) rather than tied to fluctuations in industry or aggregate economic activity. The hypothesis that workers are free to choose their level of labour supply at each t and thus equate their marginal rate of substitution between leisure and consumption to an exogeneously determined wage rate has been subjected to econometric tests by various researchers (e.g. Wales and Woodland, 1976; Ham, 1982, 1986; Moffitt, 1984; Lundberg, 1985), and they all conclude that individuals are often off their labour-supply curves so that they do not in general equate their marginal rate of substitution to the exogeneously given wage on a period-by-period basis. In other words, labour supply often does not represent individuals' labour supply preferences.

The above discussion suggests an upper limit, $\bar{h}(t)$, on $h(t)$. In fact it will be assumed that $h(t) < \min(E, \bar{h}(t))$ where $0 \leqslant E < 1$ and $0 < \bar{h}(t) \leqslant 1$ and where E represents an intolerable proportion of time spent at work so that $\lim_{h \to E} V_h(h) \to \infty$ and h is always less than E. Further, since $h < 0$ is meaningless, the optimization has to be carried out subject to the non-negativity constraint, $0 \leqslant h(t)$. Collecting the two constraint specifications on h, we have

$$0 \leqslant h < \min(E, \bar{h}). \tag{6.1}$$

The individual earns real wage $w(t)$ per unit of time spent at work at age t and as a first approximation it is assumed independent of his choices. But we shall have more to say on this matter at the appropriate stage in the development of the analysis. The individual starts life with assets A_0 and operates in an environment of perfect certainty. The interest rate is r, the rate of time preference is ρ and there are no costs of adjustment associated with changing the level of consumption and work.

Formally, the individual's problem is to choose c and h at each age so as to maximize lifetime utility:

$$\int_0^T e^{-\rho t}\{U(c) - V(h)\} \, dt \tag{6.2}$$

subject to

(a) the lifetime budget constraint:

$$A_0 + \int_0^T e^{-rt}(w(t)h(t)) \, dt - e^{-rt}A(T) \geqslant 0, \tag{6.3}$$

which can be rewritten as an assets accumulation equation,

$$\dot{A}(t) = rA(t) + w(t)h(t) - c(t), \text{ given} \tag{6.4}$$

(b) the constraints on h, (6.1), and
(c) the credit constraint:

$$A(t) \geqslant \bar{A}(t), \quad \bar{A}(t) = \alpha_1 + \alpha_2 w(t)h(t), \quad \alpha_1 \leqslant 0, \quad \alpha_2 \leqslant 0, \tag{6.5}$$

which was extensively discussed in the early chapters.

The Formal Solution

The Lagrangian, L, for the problem is

$$L = U(c) - V(h) + \lambda(rA + wh - c) + q_1(\bar{h} - h) + q_2(h) + \mu(A - \bar{A}). \tag{6.6}$$

The necessary conditions are:

$$U_c = \lambda, \tag{6.7}$$

$$V_h = \lambda w - q_1 + q_2 - \mu \alpha_2 w, \tag{6.8}$$

$$\dot{\lambda} = \lambda(\rho - r) - \mu, \tag{6.9}$$

$$\dot{A} = rA + wh - c, \tag{6.10}$$

where q_1, q_2 and μ are such that

$$q_1 \geqslant 0, \quad q_1(\bar{h} - h) = 0,$$
$$q_2 \geqslant 0, \quad q_2 h = 0,$$
$$\mu \geqslant 0, \quad \mu(A - \bar{A}) = 0.$$

Note that, by the concavity of L, these necessary conditions are also sufficient.

Recall that in previous chapters the focus of attention had been on the lifetime plans of the individual. Given the above analysis, it is therefore appropriate to draw up a parallel set of plans. However, the above first-order conditions are too general to enable us to draw up an analytically manageable lifetime plan. Hence, a few simplifying assumptions are in order.

Analysis of Optimal Plans

Simplifying assumptions

The choice of assumptions is dictated by a trade-off between analytical tractability and realism. First, it will be assumed that the instantaneous utility function takes the following form:

$$U_c = c^{-\varepsilon}, \quad V_h = \zeta h^{\eta}, \quad \text{where} \quad \zeta > 0,$$

$$\frac{-U_{cc}c}{U_c} = \varepsilon > 0 \quad \text{and} \quad \frac{V_{hh}h}{V_h} = \eta > 0.$$

ζ is a taste parameter which is of a relatively high value for those who, *ceteris paribus*, dislike supplying a given increase of work. The specific forms are particularly useful when it comes to carrying out comparative statics exercises.

The wage profile is specified as

$$\frac{\dot{w}}{w} = \theta(t), \quad w(t) = w(0) \, \exp\left[\int_0^T \theta(\tau) \, d\tau\right].$$

The growth rate of the wage, θ, is assumed to vary over time, being positive at the beginning of life and negative towards the end. This is quite consistent with stylized evidence on the time-shape of wage rates. However, it will simplify matters a great deal if it is assumed that when $\dot{w}/w > 0$, $\theta(t) = \bar{\theta}$, a constant. This is an innocuous assumption but it helps us to omit a few tedious technical steps when consumption during the phase in which credit constraints bind is analysed. It will also be assumed that when $\dot{w}/w < 0$, the wage declines rapidly. This is another convenient, but harmless, assumption that ensures that the credit-constrained phase lies entirely on the first slope of the wage profile instead of straddling it over both slopes. It is worth noting at this stage that the path of the wage over life will vary between groups of workers. Further assumptions on θ to reflect differences between groups of workers will be made at a later stage.

Finally, it will be assumed that $\rho > r$. Of course, ρ will vary over individuals but the analysis can be readily extended to allow for this. As long as the individual desires to borrow against anticipated earnings, it does not matter whether $\rho > r$ or $\rho < r$. It is best to stick to the $\rho > r$ case so as to minimize taxonomic proliferation.

It should be interesting to compare lifetime phases with the inclusion of the work variable with the phases without work that were derived earlier on. To carry out the comparison in logical steps we should begin by comparing the lifetime plan in which work is always a choice variable and then bring in work constraints. Then it is in order to digress a little and ask if and when work constraints bind.

The time-path of work

Using the first-order conditions ((6.7)–(6.9)) with $\mu = 0$ the following path of c and h are obtained:

$$\frac{\dot{c}}{c} = \frac{r - \rho}{\varepsilon},\tag{6.11}$$

$$\frac{\dot{h}}{h} = 0 \text{ whenever } h = 0,\tag{6.12}$$

$$\frac{\dot{h}}{h} = 0 \text{ whenever } h = \bar{h},\tag{6.13}$$

$$\frac{\dot{h}}{h} = \frac{\rho - r + \theta}{\eta} \text{ whenever } 0 < h < \bar{h}.\tag{6.14}$$

With the help of (6.11)–(6.14) the time-path of the first-order conditions (6.7) and (6.8) during the early part of life are illustrated in Figure 6.1. Here, the wU_c curve shifts upward with age and at an interior solution, $wU_c = V_h$, intersects with the V_h curve. As illustrated, the individual plans increasing work over time once he has entered the labour force so that the work constraint, $h \leqslant \bar{h}$, may eventually bind.

It is clear from the diagram that the binding of the constraint will depend on the level at which $\bar{h}$ is set. The diagram has a time-invariant $\bar{h}$. When we arrive at the stage at which $\bar{h}$ is incorporated in the phases, a time-varying work constraint will be considered.

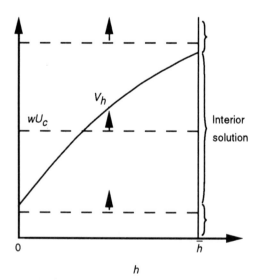

Figure 6.1 *The time path of the first order conditions.*

The phases of the lifetime plan without work constraints

We now examine the optimal lifetime plan with work as an unconstrained choice variable and first consider the intervals in life during which the individual is most likely to borrow. In order to identify these, we first need to know the time-shape of the earnings profile. From (6.11), (6.12), (6.14) and the assumption made on the wage profile, it is easy to deduce that earnings are likely to increase initially and decrease towards the end of life. But, given strict concavity of the utility function, the individual will attempt to smooth out the consumption path over life. Therefore, if the individual has a positive amount of initial assets or can incur some debt, there will be an initial phase during which he is not credit-constrained and this is followed by a phase in which he is. After this, the individual will start paying off his debt and save for the interval in life during which his earnings are low so that he is once again not credit-constrained during this third and final phase. Hence we can assert that if the individual is ever going to be credit constrained then it must be early on in life.

The typical lifetime plan then consists of the following three phases.

Phase 1 $(0, t_1)$
During this phase the following relations, derived from the first-order conditions, hold:

$$\left.\begin{array}{l} U_c = \lambda \\ V_h = \lambda w + q_2 \end{array}\right\} \Rightarrow wU_c \leqslant V_h, \qquad 0 \leqslant t < t_1, \qquad (6.15)$$

$$\frac{\dot{c}}{c} = \frac{r - \rho}{\varepsilon}, \qquad 0 \leqslant t < t_1, \qquad (6.16)$$

$$\frac{\dot{h}}{h} = \begin{cases} \dfrac{\rho - r + \theta}{\eta} & \text{if } q_2 = 0, \qquad (6.17) \\[2mm] 0 & \text{if } q_2 > 0. \qquad (6.18) \end{cases}$$

From a cursory look at (6.15)–(6.18), the following points are worth noting:

(i) The interest rate induces an early work effort and a postponement of consumption since savings increase which yield a return.
(ii) The subjective time-preference rate induces a postponement of work and a bringing forward of consumption since future work is more attractive compared to present work and present consumption is more attractive compared to future consumption.
(iii) The wage growth rate induces a non-negative relation between changes

in wages and changes in work. Optimality requires that the individual works harder when wages are high so that he will presently work less hard than in the future if wages are expected to rise.

When the wage rate is low, as at the beginning of life, the displeasure of work is not worthwhile so that the non-negativity constraint on work binds. The individual then starts economic life by not working at all. In response to rising wage rate, the individual will eventually enter the labour market. Consumption and work will take on interior values. In addition,

$$\dot{A} = rA + wh - c < 0, \quad 0 \leqslant t < t_1,$$
$$A(t) > \bar{A}(t), \quad 0 \leqslant t \leqslant t_1,$$
$$A(t_1) = \bar{A}(t_1)$$

and

$$\int_0^{t_1} c e^{-rt} \, dt = \int_0^{t_1} wh \, e^{-rt} \, dt + A_0 - \bar{A}(t_1) e^{-rt_1},$$

so that there is dissaving throughout this phase, but the debt limit does not bind.

Phase 2 (t_1, t_2)
The second phase is likely to occur fairly early on in life and is characterized by a limit on dissaving. The following equations hold through the phase:

$$U_c = \lambda, \quad t_1 \leqslant t < t_2,$$
$$V_h = \lambda w - \mu \alpha_2 w + q_2,$$
$$c = wh - \alpha_2 \bar{\theta} wh - \alpha_2 \frac{\dot{h}}{h} wh + r\alpha_1 + r\alpha_2 wh,$$

$$c = wh \left(1 - \alpha_2 \left(\bar{\theta} + \frac{\dot{h}}{h} - r \right) \right) + r\alpha_1, \qquad t_1 \leqslant t < t_2, \tag{6.19}$$

$$A(t) = \bar{A}(t), \quad t_1 \leqslant t \leqslant t_2,$$
$$\int_{t_1}^{t_2} c e^{-rt} \, dt = \int_{t_1}^{t_2} wh \, e^{-rt} \, dt + A(t_1) e^{-rt_1} - \bar{A}(t_2) e^{-rt_2}.$$

The separation of consumption and work plans, in the sense that consumption and work affect each other globally but not locally, is no longer possible because of the restriction on dissaving. From (6.19) it is apparent that consumption depends directly on w and $\bar{\theta}$ and is equal to current earnings, plus any further borrowing permitted by wage and work increases, less current interest payments.

Phase 3 (t_2, T)
When the wage rate begins to decline, the individual starts reducing work and may eventually choose to retire. During this phase, the individual first reduces his debt and then accumulates wealth for old age. Once again, consumption moves independently of the wage rate. In addition to the Phase 1 equations, (6.15)–(6.18), holding for all $t, t_2 \leqslant t \leqslant T$, these equations also hold:

$$\dot{A} = rA + wh - c > 0, \qquad t_2 \leqslant t \leqslant T,$$

$$A(t_2) = \bar{A}(t_2),$$

$$A(t) > \bar{A}(t), \qquad\qquad t_2 \leqslant t \leqslant T,$$

$$\int_{t_2}^{T} ce^{-rt}\, dt = \int_{t_2}^{T} wh\, e^{-rt}\, dt + \bar{A}(t_2)e^{-rt_2} - A(T)^{-rT}.$$

Comparative statics

We are now in a position to consider the following three propositions whose proofs are in the appendix to this chapter. We assume that c and h are continuous and differentiable in α_1, α_2 and A_0.

Proposition 6.1.   As a result of a slight increase in α_2,

(i) Work increases whenever it is carried out $(h > 0)$ during the initial unconstrained phase and consumption decreases throughout this phase.
(ii) The duration of the initial unconstrained phase is shortened.

Proposition 6.2.   As a result of a slight increase in α_1, (i) and (ii) as in Proposition 6.1 hold.

Propositions 6.3.   As a result of a slight decrease in A_0, (i) and (ii) as in Proposition 6.1 hold.

The propositions are illustrated in Figures 6.2 and 6.3. The broken lines in the figures trace out the individual's plan after the change in the relevant parameter. The figures illustrate the intuition behind the propositions: the individual accommodates an instantaneous change by spreading out his reaction to the exogenous change over all his choice variables and also over a longer period of time. Thus the whole of the consumption curve shifts down, as a result of an upward shift in the underlying work curve the entire earnings curve shifts up, and the credit constraint binds sooner.

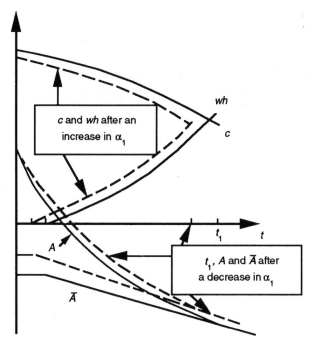

Figure 6.2 *Graphic illustration of Propositions 6.1–6.3.*

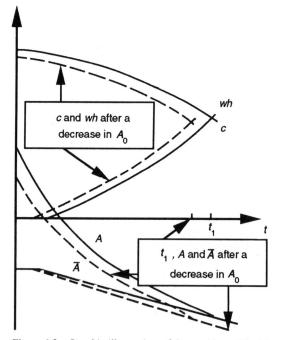

Figure 6.3 *Graphic illustration of Propositions 6.1–6.3.*

What we have is the result that a tightening of the credit constraint results in the individual consuming less and working more initially. Thus the individual is willing to bear greater displeasure of work in order to mitigate the effects of credit constraints on consumption. This result is encouraging in that by allowing for greater choice the burden of credit constraint can be spread over consumption and leisure. However, the analysis is based on a couple of strong assumptions so that the next task is to relax these in order to assess the role of work more critically. The assumptions are: (i) work is an unconstrained choice variable and (ii) the wage profile is independent of the work profile. We shall consider (i) immediately and tackle (ii) in the next chapter.

Work Constraints

First reconsider the analysis with the possibility of the work constraint $h(t) \leqslant \bar{h}(t)$ binding at some interval in life. The following propositions follow immediately.

Propositions 6.4–6.6. If there is the possibility of the work constraint binding, then each of the Propositions 6.1–6.3 will only be slightly modified to read:

(i) During the initial credit-unconstrained phase, consumption decreases throughout the phase and work increases whenever it is carried out $(0 < h < \bar{h})$.
(ii) The duration of the initial credit-unconstrained phase is shortened.

The incidence and duration of effective work constraints

Effective work constraints and the distribution of earnings over life are closely linked. Therefore, it is important to know the determinants of effective work constraints and this is accomplished by comparative statics exercises. But first we need some idea about the time-shape of $\bar{h}$.

Barro and Grossman (1976, pp. 45–6) and Ashenfelter and Ham (1979, pp. S110–11) assume that individuals anticipate future spells of the binding of the work constraint and go on to assume that

$$\bar{h}(t) = \bar{h}(0) \exp\left[\int_0^t v(\tau)\, d\tau\right], \qquad \frac{\dot{\bar{h}}}{\bar{h}} = v(t).$$

In order to concentrate on the interesting cases and also to simplify the analysis, we shall assume that

$$\frac{\dot{h}}{h} = \frac{\rho - r + \theta}{\eta} > \frac{\dot{\bar{h}}}{\bar{h}} = \bar{v} \qquad \text{and} \qquad h(0) < \bar{h}(0), \ \bar{v} \text{ a constant.}$$

As a result, as long as wages are low to begin with but rise rapidly and also decline rapidly later on in life, the following sequences of work over life will result:

first $0 \leqslant h < \bar{h}$, then $h = \bar{h}$, and finally $0 \leqslant h < \bar{h}$.

Comparative statics

First consider a slight decrease in initial assets, A_0.

Proposition 6.7.   If consumption and work are continuous and differentiable in initial assets and the individual is work-constrained for part of his life, then a decrease in initial assets increases the duration of the work-constrained interval.

(The proof of this proposition is based on that of Proposition 4.3 with the following addition: as the instantaneous utility function is strictly concave in consumption and work, each of these must be continuous.) The reasoning is simple: the wealth effect of a lower level of initial wealth raises initial work and as $\dot{h}/h$ is positive and unaltered, the work-constrained phase begins sooner. Thus the freedom to vary work and therefore mitigate the consequences of credit constraints for consumption purposes is the least for the less wealthy individuals. Such individuals plan to work harder so that the shortfall between h and $\bar{h}$ becomes less.

Another way in which the gap between h and $\bar{h}$ becomes narrower is a decrease in $\bar{h}(0)$.

Proposition 6.8.   If consumption and work are continuous and differentiable in $\bar{h}(0)$ and if the credit-constrained interval is such that it is a proper sub-interval of work-constrained interval then, as a result of a decrease in $\bar{h}(0)$, work increases whenever it is carried out $(0 < h < \bar{h})$ during the unconstrained phase and consumption decreases throughout this phase. The duration of this phase is also shortened.

One would naturally wish to know whether the above proposition also holds for those who are credit-constrained before they are work-constrained. The problem here is that whereas a change in $\bar{h}(0)$ will affect $h(t)$, it is not possible to sign this change in $h(t)$ during the intervals in which the individual is credit-constrained but not work-constrained. Hence it is difficult to deduce something resembling Proposition 6.7

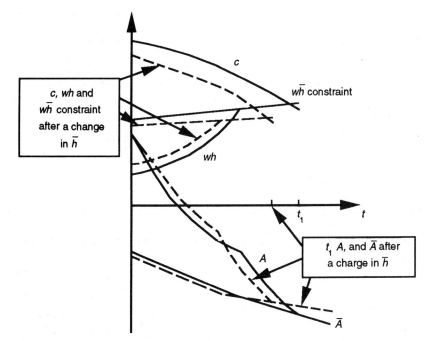

Figure 6.4   *Graphic illustration of Proposition 6.8.*

Proposition 6.8 is illustrated in Figure 6.4. Here, the change in the work constraint is represented by a downward shift in the earnings curve. An immediate consequence is that the segment of the $\bar{A}$ curve dependent on earnings shifts upwards. Once again, the reaction of the individual to increased work-constraining, and therefore also more credit-constraining, is (a) to shift the whole of the consumption curve downwards, (b) to shift, by working harder, the entire earnings curve upwards during the interval in which he can choose work freely, and (c) to bring forward t_1.

A Review

At this stage, a review is in order. In the situation in which work-leisure choice is ignored, if the individual anticipates earnings to increase and if credit constraints depend on current earnings, then he will plan to borrow but will not be able to borrow to the full; an uneven distribution of earnings over life causes credit constraints to bind and, as a result, matter for current consumption.

Allowing for work choice can make the distribution of earnings less uneven. This mitigates the effects of credit constraints on consumption. But work constraints can cancel out this mitigation. It depends on the shape of the work-constraint profile. We have taken it that as the wage profile is steep initially, so is the work profile. If the work-constraint profile is even steeper initially, then there is the real possibility that effective work constraints render the distribution of earnings even more disproportionate. Then credit constraints would bind more severely.

We have to explore this further. Clearly, we have concentrated on a work–leisure trade-off but, in a lifetime context, it is hard to ignore a work–training trade-off. One important difference between the two trade-offs is that whereas the work–leisure trade-off assumes a given wage profile, the work–training trade-off implies that the wage profile changes. This is because the wage rate reflects productivity which is determined by training which takes time. An increase in current work reduces current training time and hence reduces future wage rate. The upshot is that work choice is best viewed as job choice, each job being characterized by a job-entailed work and wage profile. It is to job choices, then, that we turn in the next chapter.

Appendix to Chapter 6

Proof of Proposition 6.1

1 (i) We will present the proof in three steps.
(a) During the first phase, upon differentiating, the following equations result:

$$\frac{\partial}{\partial t} \frac{\partial c}{\partial \alpha_2} \frac{r - \rho}{\varepsilon} \frac{\partial c}{\partial \alpha_2},$$

$$\frac{\partial}{\partial t} \frac{\partial h}{\partial \alpha_2} = \begin{cases} \dfrac{\rho - r + \theta}{\eta} \dfrac{\partial h}{\partial \alpha_2}, & \text{whenever } q_2 = 0, \\ 0, & \text{whenever } q_2 > 0. \end{cases}$$

Clearly, $\partial c / \partial \alpha_2$ and $\partial h / \partial \alpha_2$ cannot change sign. From the strict concavity of the utility function, c and h cannot remain unchanged if α_2 changes. But given our level of aggregation, and time-instantaneous separability, c and h are normal goods at each moment in time. Therefore either consumption increases throughout the first phase and work decreases whenever it is possible, or consumption decreases throughout and work increases whenever $h > 0$.

(b) Differentiating the debt limit we obtain that

$$\frac{\partial \bar{A}}{\partial \alpha_2} = wh + \alpha_2 w \frac{\partial h}{\partial \alpha_2}.$$

The first term on the right-hand side is positive but the second is negative whenever $\partial h / \partial \alpha_2 > 0$. Thus either $\partial \bar{A} / \partial \alpha_2 \leqslant 0$ or $\partial \bar{A} / \partial \alpha_2 > 0$.

(c) We now consider each of the possibilities obtained in (a) and (b) taken together. This results in four cases.

Case 1. Suppose $\partial \bar{A} / \partial \alpha_2 \leqslant 0$ and c increases while h decreases whenever $h > 0$. This case is then self-contradictory since for $\partial \bar{A} / \partial \alpha_2 \leqslant 0$ to be realized, we require h to increase.

Case 2. Suppose $\partial \bar{A} / \partial \alpha_2 \leqslant 0$ and c decreases while h increases whenever $h > 0$. This implies that $|\dot{A}|$ decreases throughout the first phase. With $\bar{A} / \partial \alpha_2 \leqslant 0$, however, it also means that positive savings will start taking place while $A > \bar{A}$. Clearly non-optimal.

Case 3. Suppose $\partial \bar{A} / \partial \alpha_2 > 0$ and c increases while h decreases whenever $h > 0$. This implies that $|\dot{A}|$ increases throughout the first phase. With $\partial \bar{A} / \partial \alpha_2 > 0$, however, it also means that the time taken for A to decrease from A_0 to $\bar{A}$ is reduced. But with c increased and h not increased,

$$c(t_1) > w(t_1) h(t_1) \left[1 - \alpha_2 \left(\theta + \frac{\dot{h}}{h} - r \right) \right] + r\alpha_1,$$

whatever the value of t_1 happens to be. This is clearly not optimal.

Case 4. Since none of the above are optimal strategies, it must follow that the remaining case, $\partial \bar{A} / \partial \alpha_2 > 0$ and c decreases while h increases whenever $h > 0$, must be the optimal reaction to an increase in α_2.

1 (ii) If t_1 is unchanged, then as c decreases and h has not decreased, it must follow that at this unchanged value of t_1,

$$c(t_1) < w(t_1) h(t_1) \left[1 - \alpha_2 \left(\theta + \frac{\dot{h}}{h} - r \right) \right] + r\alpha_1.$$

Thus t_1 must either increase or decrease. If t_1 increases then because $\dot{c}/c < 0$, $\dot{h}/h > 0$, $\dot{w}/w > 0$, the above inequality will be reinforced at the increased value of t_1. It therefore must follow that t_1 decreases so that the duration of the first phase is shorter.

Proof of Proposition 6.2

2 (i) Following the proof as in 1(i)(a) and replacing α_2 by α_1, we can deduce that either consumption increases throughout the first phase and

work decreases whenever possible, or consumption decreases throughout the first phase and work increases whenever $h > 0$.

(b) Differentiating the debt limit we obtain that

$$\frac{\partial \bar{A}}{\partial \alpha_1} = 1 + \alpha_2 w \frac{\partial h}{\partial \alpha_1}.$$

The second term on the right-hand side is negative whenever $\partial h/\partial \alpha_1 > 0$. Thus either $\partial \bar{A}/\partial \alpha_1 \leqslant 0$ or $\partial \bar{A}/\partial \alpha_1 > 0$.

(c) As 1(i)(c) with α_2 everywhere replaced by α_1.

2(ii) As 1(ii).

Proof of Proposition 6.3

3 (i)(a) Following the proof as in 1(i)(a) and replacing α_2 by A_0, we can deduce that either consumption increases throughout the first phase and work decreases whenever possible, or consumption decreases throughout the first phase and work increases whenever $h > 0$.

(b) Since $dA_0/dA_0 = 1$ and $\partial \bar{A}/\partial A_0 = \alpha_2 w(\partial h/\partial A_0)$, $\alpha_2 w(\partial h/\partial A_0) - 1$ can be positive if $\partial h/\partial A_0$ is negative. Thus either

$$\left(\alpha_2 w \frac{\partial h}{\partial A_0} - 1\right) \geqslant 0 \quad \text{or} \quad \left(\alpha_2 w \frac{\partial h}{\partial A_0} - 1\right) < 0.$$

(c) Case 1. Suppose $(\alpha_2 w(\partial h/\partial A_0) - 1) \geqslant 0$ and c increases while h decreases whenever $h > 0$. This case is self-contradictory following the reasoning of 1(i)(c) Case 1.

Case 2. Suppose $(\alpha_2 w(\partial h/\partial A_0) - 1) \geqslant 0$ and c decreases while h increases whenever $h > 0$. Non-optimal, following 1(i)(c) Case 2.

Case 3. Suppose $(\alpha_2 w(\partial h/\partial A_0) - 1) < 0$ and c increases while h decreases whenever $h > 0$. This case is not optimal following the reasoning of 1(i)(c) Case 3.

Case 4. Since none of the above are optimal strategies, it must follow that the remaining case, $(\alpha_2 w(\partial h/\partial A_0) - 1) < 0$ and c decreases while h increases whenever $h > 0$, must be the optimal reaction to a decrease in A_0.

3(ii) As 1(ii).

Proof of Proposition 6.4

4 (i)(a) Following the proof as in 1(i)(a) and replacing α_2 by $\bar{h}(0)$, we can deduce that either consumption increases throughout the first phase and work decreases whenever $0 < h < \bar{h}$ or consumption decreases throughout the first phase and work increases whenever $0 < h < \bar{h}$.

(b) $\partial \bar{A}/\partial \bar{h}(0) < 0$.

(c) We can now consider which of the two possibilities obtained in (a) holds.

First suppose that c increases throughout the first phase and h decreases whenever $0 < h < \bar{h}$. This implies that, given (b) above,

$$c(t_1) > w(t_1)\bar{h}(t_1)[1 - \alpha_2(\theta + v - r)] + r\alpha_1,$$

whatever the value of t_1 happens to be. This is clearly non-optimal. It must therefore follow that, c decreases while h increases whenever $0 < h < \bar{h}$, must be the optimal reaction to a decrease in $\bar{h}(0)$.

4 (ii) If t_1 is unchanged, then as c decreases and h has not decreased, it must follow that at this unchanged value of t_1,

$$c(t_1) < w(t_1)\bar{h}(t_1)[1 - \alpha_2(\theta + v - r)] + r\alpha_1.$$

Thus t_1 must either increase or decrease. If t_1 increases then because $\dot{c}/c < 0$, $\dot{h}/h > 0$, $\dot{w}/w > 0$, the above inequality will be reinforced at the increased value of t_1. It therefore must follow that t_1 decreases so that the duration of the first phase is shorter.

CHAPTER **7**

Labour Market Structure

In this chapter job choice is incorporated into the model. It will be assumed that work is job-entailed. This implies that the individual can only vary work by changing jobs. Earlier on it was noted that there is evidence to support the assumption that work is job-entailed. Since there is a work–training trade-off, the assumption of work being job-determined makes sense if it is thought that training is job-entailed. Certainly, early on in professional careers at least, employers require a lot of training leaving little choice of work. Training is expected to affect both the work profile and the wage profile over life, making them steeper. Individuals, therefore, have to take account of these shapes, which are expected to differ over jobs, when considering job choice. Account also has to be taken of the possibility that in a job with training, greater lifetime work may be carried out in order to extract the returns from training.

We begin by examining how, in theory, credit constraints affect job choices when jobs are characterized in the manner indicated above and then look at the empirical implications. Whatever econometric evidence there is turns out to be consistent with the theory. We then go on to examine the competing reasons found in the literature for the observed difference in shapes of earnings profiles over job sectors. It turns out that the view on earnings-profile difference which is sustained in an equilibrium set-up is our training-entailed one. We thus have an empirically consistent complete explanation for there being earnings profiles of different shapes and the way these are sustained in equilibrium with differing groups of workers allocating themselves to differing profiles. The role of credit constraints is central here. Finally, having introduced work into the analysis, we also take the opportunity to examine the consequences of a large unexpected change in work, such as unexpected unemployment.

Job Choice

There is now considerable evidence that can be related to binary job choice so that such a choice problem is quite a good starting point for analysis. It also brings into sharp focus the discrete feature of job choice, that is, the choice set has discrete alternatives instead of a continuum.

Consider then a choice between two jobs, job p entailing wage profile w^p and work profile $\bar{h}^p$, and job s being associated with w^s and $\bar{h}^s$. Anticipating, p will come to stand for a primary-sector job and s for a secondary-sector job. Thus the individual faces a choice between pairs of wage- and work-constraint profiles. The analysis is best carried out in a stepwise fashion and the interpretation given at appropriate stages.

Job choice: step 1

At the first step, assume that the $\bar{h}$ profiles are the same and w^p and w^s are such that

$$\int_0^T w^p(t)\bar{h}(t)e^{-rt}\, dt > \int_0^T w^s(t)\bar{h}(t)e^{-rt}\, dt.$$

Then, under the assumption of perfect credit markets and the assumption that $\bar{h}$ binds throughout life under both jobs, present-value considerations will dictate that $c^p(t)$, consumption associated with w^p, is greater than $c^s(t)$, consumption associated with w^s, for all t, so that job p will be chosen. We can then write that the individual will choose p if

$$((\text{PVY}_p - \text{PVY}_s) > 0, \tag{7.1}$$

where

$$\text{PVY}_i = \int_0^T y^i e^{-rt}\, dt \equiv \int_0^T w^i \bar{h} e^{-rt}\, dt, \qquad i = p,s.$$

Since under the perfect-credit-markets assumption the shape of the earnings profile is not a relevant consideration for making job choices, the first step isolates the role of present-value earnings in making such choices.

Job choice: step 2

At the second step we allow the work profile to differ over the two jobs. The specification of the work (and therefore also the wage) profile is motivated by the following comparison between an individual who leaves school immediately after completing the minimum amount of full-time education with an individual who stays on for further full-time education. The latter also undertakes a lengthy spell of further training after joining the labour force. As a result, the initial segments of the w and $\bar{h}$ profiles will show steep rises. As training decreases, the individual works more and with greater work experience comes greater work productivity so that both $\bar{h}$ and w profiles continue to rise. The former individual, on the other hand, faces flatter $\bar{h}$ and w profiles since there is little training involved and the nature of the job implies that work experience does not contribute a great deal to productivity. The wage and work profiles of the second individual start from below that of the first individual but are steeper and subsequently higher so that the earnings profiles of the individuals also follow the same pattern. These considerations, which also imply that present-value earnings for the former individual are less than for the latter, can be simply represented as follows:

$$w^{s}(0) > w^{p}(0), \quad \theta_s < \theta_p, \quad \bar{h}^{s}(0) > \bar{h}^{p}(0), \quad v_s < v_p,$$

$$\int_{0}^{T} w^{s}(t)\bar{h}^{s}(t)e^{-rt}\,\mathrm{d}t < \int_{0}^{T} w^{p}(t)\bar{h}^{p}(t)e^{-rt}\,\mathrm{d}t,$$

where

$$w^{s}(t) = w^{s}(0)e^{\theta_s t}, \quad w^{p}(t) = w^{p}(0)e^{\theta_p t}, \quad \bar{h}^{s}(t) = \bar{h}^{s}(0)e^{v_s t}, \quad \bar{h}^{p}(t) = \bar{h}^{p}(0)e^{v_p t},$$

and θ_s, θ_p, v_s and v_p are non-negative constants. Since work profiles differ between the two jobs, the job-choice criterion is best modelled in utility terms. Then let

$$J_c(i) = \int_{0}^{T} e^{-\rho t}U(c^{i})\,\mathrm{d}t \quad \text{and} \quad J_{\bar{h}}(i) = \int_{0}^{T} e^{-\rho t}V(\bar{h}^{i})\,\mathrm{d}t, \quad i = \text{p,s}$$

Then $[J_c(i) - J_{\bar{h}}(i)]$ is the lifetime utility that the individual would derive were he to choose job i. In deciding which job to choose, a given individual's decision will be dictated by the sign of

$$[J_c(\text{p}) - J_c(\text{s})] - [J_{\bar{h}}(\text{p}) - J_{\bar{h}}(\text{s})]. \tag{7.2}$$

Under the assumption of perfect credit markets, $c^p(t) > c^s(t)$ for all t so that $[J_c(p) - J_c(s)] > 0$. Were we to differentiate individuals by preference parameters (ε, η, ξ) only (introduced in Chapter 6), then the sign of $[J_c(p) - J_c(s)]$ would continue to remain positive for each of the individuals. But when we come to the $[J_{\bar{h}}(p) - J_{\bar{h}}(s)]$ segment of the lifetime utility difference between the two jobs, its sign is not clear-cut, for under the p job, the individual works less initially and more later on in life. Once the net disutility of working differentially is take into account, the sign of (7.2) can turn out to be negative for some individuals so that even under perfect credit markets, such individuals will choose the s job. For such a choice it is a necessary condition that $[J_{\bar{h}}(p) - J_{\bar{h}}(s)] > 0$, that is, there is greater disutility of work in the p job. In writing down the individual's choice criterion, we have to allow for this possibility. Accordingly:

choose p if $[J_c(p) - J_c(s)] - [J_{\bar{h}}(p) - J_{\bar{h}}(s)] > 0 \Rightarrow$

choose p if $[\text{PVY}_p - \text{PVY}_s] > C$ (7.3)

where

$$\text{PVY}_i = \int_0^T y^i e^{-rt}\, dt \equiv \int_0^T w^i \bar{h}^i e^{-rt}\, dt, \qquad i = p, s,$$

and C is a number that depends on the relative work structures. If C is positive when p is chosen it means that the wage profiles are such that any net utility of working differently in p jobs is more than compensated for by utility derivable from the extra consumption generated by the p wages. C will also depend on individual tastes, $C(\varepsilon, \eta, \xi)$, a higher ξ implying more disutility from work and hence larger C.

Job choice: step 3

At the third step, consider the situation in which the same job alternatives are there but in which there are credit constraints as well. The salient considerations involved in making the choice are represented by Figure 7.1. Under the steeper earnings profile, $\bar{A}$ is likely to be higher early on in life. If the individual is credit-constrained sufficiently early on, then there is a smaller debt to supplement early earned income which itself is smaller. Therefore, in such a situation, $c^p(0) < c^s(0)$. Of course, $c^p(t)$ will eventually exceed $c^s(t)$ as depicted in the figure, but the fact remains that the individual is prevented from smoothing out his consumption path. To the extent that this reduces $[J_c(p) - J_c(s)]$, given strict concavity, the individual will have less incentive for choosing the p job. Therefore, had he chosen the p job under the regime of perfect credit markets, whether or not he will

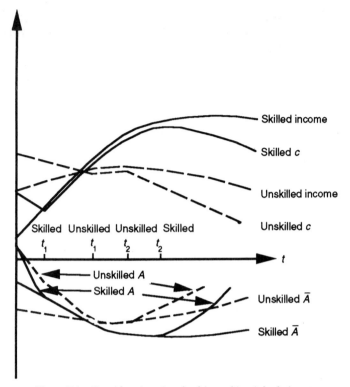

Figure 7.1 *Considerations involved in making job choices.*

continue to do so now will depend on the extent of effective credit-constraining and the magnitude of the difference between the two present-value earnings. The extent of effective credit-constraining will depend on the credit limit parameters and the steepness of the earnings profile, thus $C(\varepsilon, \eta, \xi, \bar{A}, \theta_p, v_p)$, $\partial C/\partial \bar{A} > 0$. From Proposition 6.3 it is clear that the less wealthy an individual is, the sooner he is credit-constrained, so that we may write $C(\varepsilon, \eta, \xi, \bar{A}, A_0, \theta_p, v_p)$, $\partial C/\partial A_0 < 0$. The individual's job-choice criterion now becomes:

$$\text{choose p if } [\text{PVY}_p - \text{PVY}_s] > C(\varepsilon, \eta, \xi, \bar{A}, A_0, \theta_p, v_p). \qquad (7.4)$$

Distribution of net worth

The implication of the foregoing analysis for the distribution of net worth is straightforward. The first step is to identify the credit-constrained individual who is indifferent between the two jobs. For this individual, the effectiveness of the credit constraint and the size of the present-value earnings compensation net of disutility of work must be in some balanced configuration. Since the present-value earnings compensation falls with A_0, the credit-constrained individual, with $A_0 = A_0^*$, who is indifferent between the two jobs, can be identified. Those individuals with $A_0 > A_0^*$ will prefer p jobs. Then the initial assets and welfare of the two individuals can be virtually equal but net worth,

$$A_0 + \int_0^T wh\, e^{-rt}\, dt,$$

can be highly unequal.

Empirical implications

Let us review the analysis carried out so far. There are two types of jobs, p and s, in which job p is characterized by greater present-value earnings and a steeper earnings profile than job s. Any given individual observes this employer-determined job and makes a choice that is determined in part by the severity of the credit constraint faced by the individual. Since there are no barriers of entry in each job market, individuals allocate themselves given their personal characteristics. Since the job choice is a free choice, there is no incentive to individuals to reallocate themselves and hence an equilibrium allocation is sustained. The presence of effective credit-constraining ensures that p jobs carry greater present-value earnings.

Much of the evidence that we can bring to bear is in the form of earnings equations and therefore the first step is to rewrite (7.4) in this form. Let

$$PVY_i = \int_0^T w^i(0)h^i(0)e^{\theta_i t}e^{v_i t}e^{-rt}\, dt \equiv \int_0^T y^i(0)e^{g_i t}e^{-rt}\, dt, \qquad i = p,s,$$

where $y^i(0)$ is the initial level of earnings in job type i and g_i is the growth rate of earnings. Then if T is ∞,

$$\int_0^\infty y^i(0)e^{g_i t}e^{-rt}\, dt = \frac{y^i(0)}{r - g_i}, \qquad i = p, s.$$

This is probably a good approximation since the consequence of replacing T by ∞ is lightly weighted for non-negligible values of $r(>g_i)$. Using these approximations for PVY_i we can write that

$$\ln\left(\frac{PVY_p}{PVY_s}\right) = \ln y^p(0) - \ln y^s(0) - \ln(r - g_p) + \ln(r - g_s)$$

$$= X(\beta_p - \beta_s) + (e_p - e_s) + \ln\left(\frac{r - g_s}{r - g_p}\right) \qquad (7.5)$$

by letting $\ln y^i(0) = X\beta_i + e_i$, $i = p, s$, where X is a vector of personal characteristics that predicts initial earnings with β_i coefficients and e_i is a normally distributed error representing unobserved characteristics affecting job i. Then the probability that the individual chooses job p is written as

pr(chooses p)

$$= \text{pr}\left\{ X(\beta_p - \beta_s) + (e_p - e_s) + \ln\left(\frac{r - g_s}{r - g_p}\right) > C(\varepsilon, \eta, \xi, \bar{A}, A_0, \theta_p, v_p) \right\}.$$

$$(7.6)$$

Evidence

One can estimate the above decision equation together with the two differing earnings equations to discover which individuals choose p jobs. But since we have merely asserted that p jobs can be distinguished from s jobs we need to check that the data confirms this distinction. Given that we do not know in advance if there is a p regime different from the s regime we have the problem of what is commonly known as unknown regimes. The econometric idea used to tackle this problem is to let the data speak by posing the question: do two earnings equations, one steep and the other flat, fit the given data set better than a single earnings equation? Formally, the answer can be executed by fitting two equations using maximum-likelihood techniques. At the same time, since it is not known *a priori* with which earnings equation to compare an individual, one can estimate the probit equation (7.6) which predicts regime or job-type attachment. Hence we have the task of estimation of an econometric model called an endogenous switching model with unknown regimes in which three equations, one probit and two earnings, are estimated simultaneously. Since the single-earnings-equation model is nested in the switching model, the hypothesis that the two-equation model fits the data significantly better than the single-equation model can be tested by comparing the log likelihood values for the two models. And if the single-equation model is rejected then the coefficients of the two earnings equations may be examined to see if they support the p and s sector dichotomy.

A complete switching model was estimated by Dickens and Lang (1985) using US data drawn from the 13th wave (1980) of the Panel Study of Income Dynamics. From the set of explanatory variables used, three stand out in the results: education, experience and a race dummy, race $= 1$ if non-white, $= 0$ if white. Their findings can be summarized as:

(1) A likelihood ratio test shows that two earnings equations fit the data much better than a single one.

(2) The p equation shows a rising earnings profile with the return to education at about 7% and the return to experience at about 1.5%. The s equation profile is completely flat.

(3) The s equation is almost everywhere below the p equation.

(4) The race coefficients are insignificant in each of the earnings equations.

(5) The estimate of the race coefficient in the probit equation is interesting. In the probit equation the coefficient of the race variable enters as $(\beta_{p,\,race} - \beta_{s,\,race})$. If race is not expected to affect to affect the C term in the probit equation (7.6), then the estimated coefficient, $(\widehat{\beta_{p,\,race} - \beta_{s,\,race}})$, should be equal to $(\hat{\beta}_{p,\,race} - \hat{\beta}_{s,\,race})$, the estimates, obtained from the earnings regressions, for the coefficients on race.

Dickens and Lang perform a test that rejects the hypothesis that $(\widehat{\beta_{p,\,race} - \beta_{s,\,race}}) = \hat{\beta}_{p,\,race} - \hat{\beta}_{s,\,race}$, that is, the estimated probit coefficient is significantly different from that predicted by the coefficients from the earnings regressions. In view of (4) it simply means that the race coefficient in the probit equation is significant. More generally, the result tells us that a variable like race affects the probability of being in a p job having taken into account the fact that such a variable may affect earnings in each job directly.

It is worth viewing the results (1)–(5) as a whole. (1) and (2) state that there are two earnings profiles, one steep and the other flat and, according to (3), the steep profile carries a sizeable lifetime earnings premium. The significance of (3) is that the model cannot be closed by appealing to the usual competitive forces since such forces would whittle down the premium. In fact, according to (4) and (5), it is the non-whites who do not compete away the earnings premium by moving into the p jobs. More generally, the identity of the individual matters in job allocation. It is also worth noting that Dickens and Lang ran through the econometrics with different data sets (1983 Current Population Survey) and also for different years (1973 and 1981 Current Population Survey) and reinforced the above findings (see Dickens and Lang, 1985b, 1987, 1988).

Interpretations

Our complete theoretical model is consistent with the full results of the econometric model. Thus, one way in which the dual job structure can be sustained is by an appeal to credit constraints such that at the margin there is a worker who is indifferent in utility terms between the two job types. Recalling that the $C(.)$ function is a compensating item, the extra lifetime earnings that just induces indifference between the two job types for the marginal individual, the compensating function of this marginal worker forms a threshold, $C^*(.)$, between the two sectors. Then workers with $C \leqslant C^*$ join the p sector and the others chooses the s sector. But by closing the model in this way there remains a causal indeterminate. It may also be recalled that the $C(.)$ function depends both on taste parameters (ε, η, ξ) and credit-constraint parameters $(\bar{A}, A_0, \theta_p, v_p)$. Then the result pertaining to race may be attributed to either of these parameter sets. That is, $\partial C(.)/\partial \xi$ $\partial \xi / \partial_{race} > 0$ as well as $\partial C(.)/\partial \bar{A} \; \partial \bar{A}/\partial_{race} > 0$ so that one could say that non-whites have a preference for s jobs because such jobs entail less lifetime work and/or non-whites are more severely credit-constrained. There is the problem of identifying the cause here. In such cases it is usual to resort to extraneous information. The kind of information one is looking for divides into two types: do non-whites have lower initial wealth and do non-whites face more severe credit constraints? Either would yield greater binding of credit constraints. On the first type there is well-documented evidence that non-whites are poorer. On the second type, whatever fragmentary evidence we have at hand suggests that non-whites are more severely credit-constrained than whites (e.g. Boczar, 1978). In view of this, it seems hardly plausible to think that non-whites have a preference for s jobs.

Dickens and Lang think that their results indicate that there is job-rationing: p jobs are rationed and there is a queue for such jobs with the order in the queue being partly determined by race. In other words, non-whites are discriminated against when seeking p jobs. But discrimination means non-economic barriers to p jobs and this seems incompatible with a tenet of neoclassical economics that competition would remove such a barrier. On the other hand a neoclassical explanation could rest on the hypothesis that if a queue for p jobs exists then p job employers can indulge in their taste for discrimination without affecting their profits adversely. But then one has to face the question of the queue existing there in the first place and proceed to appeal to a plausible argument for inflexible wages.

Labour Market Structures

First, a summary to set up the link between the previous section and this one. Empirical work yields the result that two earnings equations, one steep (with education and experience significant) and the other flat (with education and experience insignificant), provide a better fit to the data than a single equation. In addition, allocation of individuals to the two sectors is not random. Instead, personal characteristics, including seemingly unproductive ones, play a role. Now, whereas in the previous section an argument for such an equilibrium outcome was presented, in this section reasons for there being two differing earnings structures will be considered. The literature offers several reasons for this type of earnings-profile difference and we will be using the theoretical and empirical analysis carried out so far in evaluating them. It is important to check that the view on earnings-profile difference which stands out is consistent with the overall theoretical framework we have offered. In this way, we should obtain a better understanding of the structure of the labour market.

(i) On-the-job training

Job types
Assume that s jobs provide little training, being all work. On the other hand, p jobs involve both training (a good example is an apprenticeship or a junior slot) and work. Firms providing p jobs therefore sell training and in this respect are barely distinguishable from schools. The training can be formal (course work, seminars and classrooms) and/or informal (working under supervision). We now assume that the training is general in that it raises the individual's productivity by 100% in some other firms in the p sector besides the one providing it. This implies that if there is competition between firms then the worker can capture all the benefits of training. As a result, firms would be willing to provide such training only if the worker buys it by accepting a lower wage during the training period. There therefore results a negative correlation between the amount of training and the wage.

Individual behaviour
Turning to the behaviour of the individual, our formulation of his problem can be readily rewritten to accommodate this view of on-the-job training. Thus, the individual maximizes

$$\int_0^T e^{-\rho t}\{U(c) - V(\bar{h})\} \, dt$$

subject to

$$\dot{A} = rA + w(K)\bar{h} - c,$$

$$\dot{K} = n[\bar{I}K] - \delta K,$$

$$A_0 \geqslant 0 \quad \text{and} \quad A(T) = A_T,$$

$$A(t) \geqslant \bar{A}(t), \quad \bar{A}(t) = \alpha_1 + \alpha_2 w(t)h(t), \quad \alpha_1 \leqslant 0, \quad \alpha_2 \leqslant 0.$$

Here I is training time and, since it is firm-entailed, written as $\bar{I}$. Since $\bar{I}$ may interact with existing productive capital, K, to raise the flow, n, into K, n

is written as $n[\bar{I}K]$. And δK is exogenous depreciation of K. The individual's productive capital, in turn, raises the wage so that $w'(K) > 0$. The time-shape of $\bar{I}$ is likely to be such that training time is high at the beginning and low later on, so that time-shape of the wage profile is steep. Since $\bar{I}$ is firm-entailed, K is outside the individual's control once he chooses the firm and, as a result, w is outside his control as well. Then the analysis of individual behaviour that was carried out early on in this chapter goes through with an interpretation that encompasses on-the-job training. Of course, at some stage one should allow for I to be chosen by the individual.

Firm behaviour

Turning to the firms, in this set-up they are assumed to act passively in that they merely offer earnings profiles distinguished by the two elements of present-value earnings and steepness, it being understood that those firms which offer steep profiles offer training. Firms are profit maximizers and set the lifetime earnings they pay out to an individual equal to the lifetime productivity of the individual. There are assumed to be diminishing returns in each of the p and s sectors as well. The two sectors offer their respective profiles and let the individuals select.

Equilibrium

As the model stands, for the marginal worker to be indifferent between the two job types, the present-value lifetime earnings must equalize. This is awkward because it is inconsistent with the evidence at hand. One way out is to assume that earnings profiles are rigid so that there is a queue for jobs in the p sector which has greater present-value earnings. It also means that some individuals wish to train but cannot find the training facility. Note that the lifetime utility of the marginal worker is unequal in the two sectors. To tally with the evidence on race, we would also need to assume that whites are given preference over non-whites in selection for jobs in the p sector. An alternative way to ensure earnings premium in the p sector is to appeal to our model of credit-rationing. This is quite appealing because the lifetime utility of the marginal individual is the same in both sectors. To accommodate the result on race, we would need to assume that whites are less effectively credit-constrained than non-whites, most likely because they have greater initial wealth.

(ii) On-the-job training: education as a signal

Firm behaviour

It was implicitly assumed above that the firm knows the training cost of a given individual and adjusts the wage paid out accordingly. Thus someone with a high cost of training starts with a lower wage than someone with a low cost of training. Training costs depend on the trainability of an individual. However, trainability is an unobservable characteristic so that it becomes difficult for the firm to match wages and trainability. The firm could try to get at trainability by using screening devices but these are likely to involve substantial costs. On the other hand, the firm could use an observable proxy for trainability. Consider, therefore, education as a candidate for such a proxy. Clearly, education is a form of training and an individual's ability to absorb one type of training may indicate something about his ability to absorb another type. Good education performance could indicate that the potential worker has a measure of self-discipline and that he will be able to adjust to industrial discipline. It may then turn out that workers with the best education qualifications have the highest trainability and therefore the least training costs. In order to minimize training costs, the firms will offer less present-value earnings to workers with less education.

Individual behaviour
The individual will weigh up the costs and benefits of education. Those individuals with the least costs of education will acquire most education if they perceive there are greater returns to education.

Equilibrium
If education costs and training costs are, in fact, positively correlated, and credit markets are perfect, information equilibrium can be sustained. The p firms will be minimizing training costs, the individuals will be maximizing utility and those who are highly trainable will fill the training slots. The p firms will be correct in choosing on the basis of education and applicants will be correct in their decisions to acquire education. There is no tendency to change such an equilibrium outcome. Turning to the labour market structure, p jobs will be characterized by on-the job training imparted to educate workers and s jobs by little training for uneducated workers. Therefore, the underlying reason for allocation of workers to the two sectors is different learning abilities.

For there to be a present-value earnings differential between the two sectors it could, once again, be assumed that (a) earnings profiles are rigid so that there is a queue for jobs in the p sector with applicants being ranked according to education attainment. To explain the observation of non-whites in the s sector it has to be assumed that (b) given equal education, whites are given preference over non-whites in selection for p sector jobs.

Alternatively, we could appeal to our model with credit-rationing. Suppose that lenders, concerned about an individual's ability to repay a loan, lend according to the individual's choice of earnings profile. Thus all those who choose a steep earnings profile have greater access to credit than those who choose flat profiles. It would then appear that lenders lend according to trainability. But then there results the peculiar feature of equilibrium that since non-whites tend to choose flat earnings profiles, they are endowed with low trainability on average.

To get round this peculiar result we could assume that there is unequal wealth so that non-whites are more severely credit-constrained than whites. Then, even though each group may have the same trainability on average, non-whites will tend to choose flat earnings profiles. However, such credit-rationing is inconsistent with the theory of steep and flat earnings profile just presented. Recall that, in this theory, the information equilibrium that results from worker–employer interaction requires that those with the highest trainability have the least costs of education. If, however, effective credit-rationing is not according to trainability, then those with the highest trainability may not have the least costs of education if they face more credit-rationing. Employers in the p sector will then find that workers with equal education will have differing trainability, making education an unreliable predictor of trainability. Hence the information equilibrium will be damaged.

(iii) Delayed payment contracts and turnover costs

Job types
The two job types are differentiated by turnover costs: high and low. In the low-turnover sector, an individual can quit to move from one firm to another without penalty.

The firm
The firm in the high-turnover costs sector will wish to minimize turnover costs (hiring, firing, setting up a new worker, etc.). When hiring workers, the firm will give preference to those workers who are stayers or have a low propensity to quit. Accordingly, the firm will attempt to rank applicants by their quit propensities. However, the quit propensity of a worker is not observable. The firm can attempt to elicit these unobservable characteristics by the device of a steep earnings profile. Such a profile postpones reward for work so that there is an incentive to stay.

Individual behaviour
Consider the decision of the individual who has just completed full-time schooling and is choosing between two job types. Obviously, from what has

been stated so far, if he chooses a job in the low-turnover-costs sector, he may move from one firm to another whereas if he chooses a job in the high-turnover-costs sector, he stays with one firm through life. In making job choice, the individual will weigh up the relative utilities associated with each job type. Given credit constraints, there will be a trade-off between present-value earnings and steepness of earnings profiles.

Equilibrium
If credit markets are perfect, an information equilibrium can be sustained. If low-quit-propensity individuals choose steep earnings profiles for which they have an incentive and high-quit-propensity individuals choose flat profiles since they face a penalty if they choose steep profiles and then quit the firms will be minimizing costs and will not change their behaviour. Individuals, too, will be maximizing utility. For there to be a present-value-earnings differential between the two sectors assume (a) that earnings profiles are rigid, and to explain the concentration of non-whites in the s sector, assume that (b) given equally low quit propensities, whites are given preference over non-whites in selection for p sector jobs.

Unfortunately, if credit markets are imperfect, then the two problems of the previous labour-market-structure theory resurface. Either equilibrium is sustained but with the peculiar feature that non-whites are endowed with high-quit propensity on average or there is a mix-up of high-quit and low-quit individuals in the p sector which causes employers to revise their beliefs.

(iv) Delayed payment contracts and effort elicitation

Assume that the difference between the two job types arises from the technology associated with each job type. Some firms have technology which is conducive to piece rates, making it easy to monitor effort so that the firms can tie compensation to the quantity produced. In other firms, monitoring effort may be very difficult and devoting additional resources to supervision may prove to be too costly. Here there is a principal–agent problem.

The firm
Employers prefer workers not to shirk so that the contribution of the workers to output rises per given wage rate. In the firms in which monitoring work is costly, assume that a shirking worker can be caught by chance. Then the firm may be able to devise an incentive for individuals not to shirk by delaying payment. Anyone caught shirking is sacked and loses out since compensation for work has been shifted towards the end of the worker's career.

Individual behaviour

Once again, in making job choices, the individual will weigh up the relative utilities associated with each job type. Given credit constraints, there will be a trade-off between present-value earnings and steepness of earnings profiles.

Equilibrium

If credit markets are perfect, an information equilibrium can be sustained. Individuals with a low propensity to shirk will choose jobs with steep profiles in the p sector or the sector in which monitoring of effort is difficult. Individuals with a high propensity to shirk will risk a penalty if they choose the steep-profile jobs and therefore will tend to choose flat-profile jobs in the s sector in which effort is more easily monitored. Firms will, as a result, be obtaining maximum effort from workers and will adhere to their behaviour. The usual two assumptions are required to conform with the empirical evidence: (a) the earnings profiles are rigid so that present-value-earnings differential can persist and (b) given equally low propensity to shirk, whites are given preference over non-whites in selection for p sector jobs.

Once again, those two, by now familiar, problems re-emerge if credit markets are imperfect. Either equilibrium is sustained but with the peculiar feature that non-whites are endowed with a high propensity to shirk on average or there is a mix-up of low-shirk and high-shirk individuals in the p sector which causes employers to revise their beliefs.

Sections (iii) and (iv) above can be called the newer theories of dual labour markets and the reader is referred to Lazear (1981), Shapiro and Stiglitz (1984), Bulow and Summers (1986), and Hutchens (1986, 1987) for further details.

Assessment

An assessment of the various theories on steep and flat earnings profiles can now be made. The answer to the question 'Which of the theories is consistent with credit-rationing in a dual labour market equilibrium?' appears to depend on the assumptions made by any given theory on individual heterogeneity and observability.

Taking observability first, in the case in which individuals differ by only one characteristic (trainability, quit, or shirk) and credit-rationing is equal over minorities, an information equilibrium has a peculiar feature that the observed concentration of minorities in the secondary sector is endowed with an undesirable characteristic (low trainability, high quit, or high shirk). So either this feature is empirically false or the observed dichotomy in the labour market cannot arise through training, turnover or monitoring costs differences between firms. In the case in which individuals differ by another characteristic – minorities having less wealth – there is unequal credit-rationing. But then an information equilibrium breaks down because the p sector firms do not have a cheap and reliable way of distinguishing between individual workers.

Whereas trainability, quit and shirk are characteristics which are indeed difficult to observe, training imparted should not be. Then it is easy to think about an equilibrium in which:

(a) Jobs with steep earnings profiles are associated with on-the-job training. Individuals bear the cost of training and wages rise with absorbed training.
(b) Lenders lend according to ability to repay so that, *ceteris paribus*, those opting for jobs with training have greater credit than those without. Credit-rationing also implies that jobs with training carry a present-value-earnings premium.
(c) Non-whites have less wealth and therefore face greater effective credit-rationing. As a result, they tend to choose jobs without training.

Such a labour market structure has logical consistency. It rests on unequal opportunity sets facing individuals, the inequality arising from credit-market imperfections, in turn arising from information failures. Thus more importance is given to information problems there than to those in the labour market. But it simultaneously also provides a plausible explanation for the empirical evidence and a theoretical underpinning for the concept of dual labour markets.

Dynasties and Dual Labour Markets

We have, it appears, a credible framework in which credit-rationing and unequal wealth allocates minorities disproportionately more into the secondary sector. We now indicate briefly how our approach can provide theoretical underpinning for the more radical version of the dual labour market hypothesis where a dynasty is locked into secondary-sector employment.

Consider a credit-constrained dynasty and suppose it begins with low assets. It faces employment opportunities in both the primary and secondary sectors. Let A_0^1 denote the initial holdings of the first-generation individual and A_0^{1*} the threshold level at which he is indifferent between the two sectors. Suppose that $A_0^1 < A_0^{1*}$ so that he chooses a secondary-sector job. If he bequeaths such that $A_0^2 < A_0^{2*}$ then the second-generation individual will also choose a secondary-sector job. But previously in Chapter 5 we showed that $A_0^2 = A_0^3 = A_0^4 = \cdots$ so that all the individuals of the subsequent generations will seek employment in the secondary sector. It would be irresponsible to state that this analysis explains the situation of a lot of black dynasties in the USA, but the analysis is consistent with a broad empirical impression.

A dynasty may start in the secondary sector and subsequently make a transition into the primary sector. Suppose that $A_0^1 < A_0^{1*}$ but for some reason, perhaps altruism, the first-generation individual finds it worthwhile to 'bequeath' the dynasty into the primary sector so that $A_0^2 > A_0^{2*}$, and as argued in Chapter 5, $A_0^2 = A_0^3 = A_0^4 = \cdots$. This argument may be seen as being consistent with the experience of many of the Japanese and Chinese families in the United States. The Japanese and Chinese Americans started as porly paid unskilled workers in Hawaii's sugar plantations. Today, they are more highly over-represented in professions such as engineering and mathematics than Americans of any other racial groups. Of course, a dynasty that does not face any credit constraints may begin with primary-sector employment and remain in this sector for ever.

Our approach, by identifying a threshold level of assets and showing that this and initial assets are unchanged in the steady state, provides a self-contained choice-based theory which underpins even the most radical version of dual labour markets. It accomplishes this by simply deriving the implications of effective credit constraints.

Implications for the Unexpectedly Unemployed

Having introduced work into the analysis, it is clear that several interesting implications have emerged which in turn have generated rich analysis. We explore one more implication in which the individual reacts to a major unexpected change, namely change in employment status.

The general picture which has emerged so far is that individuals start work in different labour-market sectors, depending on the degree of credit-constraining that each individual faces. As they carry out their lifetime plans, they borrow in varying degrees so that after some time has elapsed, there will be borrowers with varying degrees of indebtedness. Now assume that there is an unexpected shock to the economy such that some individuals are unexpectedly unemployed. Then, at time $t = \tau$ there will be a cross-section of individuals who started work at $t = 0$, some of whom are unexpectedly unemployed and, therefore, about to revise their subsequent plans, and others who are able to proceed with their original plans. Of those individuals who are unexpectedly unemployed, there will be some who will have incurred debts of varying sizes, having first run down their initial assets.

For such individuals an unexpected change in $\bar{h}$ has two distinct effects. Firstly, the individual may view the future differently. However, if he thinks that he is temporarily unemployed, then he may view his future expectations of w and $\bar{h}$ to be unchanged so that he still has a motive for borrowing. Secondly, the borrowing conditions may alter. This arises because $A(\tau)$ may become less than $\bar{A}(\tau) = \alpha_1 + \alpha_2 w(\tau)\bar{h}(\tau)$, even if $A \geqslant \bar{A}$ just before $\bar{h}$ jumps down. Then the constraint $A \geqslant \bar{A}$ is violated. Once the lender perceives the change in the borrower's affairs, he attempts to minimize his losses and therefore attempts to affect the probability of bankruptcy. There are three possible courses of action: either the individual is declared bankrupt or his rate of borrowing is directly controlled or he is granted additional credit without any direct control on his rate of borrowing. The first course of action will be undertaken if the lender views the borrower's future earnings prospects to be extremely poor and there is no way in which the individual can reduce the debt while he is unemployed. In such an eventuality, the existing bankruptcy procedures are called into play. In contemplating the second course of action, the lender views the future earning prospect of the borrower to be good but does not wish to risk any additional funds. He may then grant a period of grace within which the individual must discharge his debt, and set a maximum limit on the rate of borrowing such that the debt does not grow faster than the interest charges. The problem can then be formulated as:

$$\text{Maximize} \int_\tau^T e^{-\rho t}(U(c) - V(h))\, dt$$

subject to

$$\dot{A} = rA + wh - c,$$

$$\dot{A} \geqslant rA \text{ whenever } A < 0,$$

$$h \geqslant 0, \qquad h \leqslant \bar{h},$$

and

$$A(\tau) < 0, \qquad A(T) \geqslant 0.$$

For simplicity, we have taken the period of grace to be the rest of lifetime, although in reality, it may be smaller. There is also a limit on borrowing, $\dot{A} \geqslant rA$, so that even if the individual believes that he is only temporarily unemployed, he cannot borrow further against his future income.

The individual will maximize

$$L = U(c) - V(h) + \lambda[rA + wh - c] + x[wh - c] + q_1[\bar{h} - h] + q_2[h]$$

whenever $A < 0$

and where x is such that $x \geqslant 0$, $(wh - c) \geqslant 0$, $x(wh - c) = 0$, and he will maximize

$$L = U(c) - V(h) + \lambda[rA + wh - c] + q_1[\bar{h} - h] + q_2[h]$$

subsequently when $A \geqslant 0$.

To start with, as $h = \bar{h}$ and the individual has a motive for borrowing, maximizing the first L will yield:

$$c = w\bar{h}, \quad \dot{A} = rA, \quad h = \bar{h} \quad \text{and} \quad A < 0.$$

Subsequently, $\bar{h}$ (and w) will jump up so that $h \leqslant \bar{h}$. This could imply that $0 > A > \alpha_1 + \alpha_2 wh$ but, given that $\dot{A} \geqslant rA$, $c = wh$. In other words, the net effect of being unexpectedly unemployed is that most of the credit facilities are withdrawn so that c is constrained for a period that is longer than the duration of temporary unemployment. But it is during this part of life that the individual would like to borrow further. Therefore, because of the initial downward jump in $\bar{h}$, the individual remains severely credit-constrained even when $\alpha_1 + \alpha_2 wh < A$. Thus a concentrated set-back is not insulated in its implications because he who violates $A \geqslant \bar{A}$ is penalized heavily.

Eventually, the individual will start saving for retirement so that, first, $\dot{A} \geqslant rA$ will cease to bind, and then, A will become positive. But, overall, the individual is left to contemplate a plan that involves severe credit-constraining initially just when he wishes to borrow. Thus some of the unexpectedly unemployed will join the poor as those individuals who are most likely to be credit-constrained.

Being unexpectedly unemployed, of course, alters the consumption profile. For comparison, consider the case where the unemployment is expected. In such an instance, the individual is able to smooth out his consumption path since income receipts are perfectly anticipated. Surveys have indicated that where unemployment is expected, savings are accumulated in advance of unemployment and dissaving and postponing payments are used to maintain the level of consumption (Cohen *et al.*, 1960; Lester, 1962). However, where unemployment occurs unexpectedly at time τ, consumption may jump down. The data of the original problem has changed so that the end point of the old consumption plan at τ may not necessarily coincide with the initial point of the new consumption plan. Further, if the individual is credit-constrained while he is unemployed, so that $c = w\bar{h}$, and he anticipates being employed in the near future so that h may jump, then c

may jump as well, as credit constraints prevent smoothing out of the discontinuity in h.

Thus far, we have assumed that the future expectations of the individual are, more or less, unaltered. Below, we outline a reason why this may not be so. Apart from the time translation, the individual who is unexpectedly unemployed is essentially in the same position that a credit-constrained individual was at time $t = 0$. He has used up his initial assets and credit facilities and acquired what we may loosely call 'human capital'. Suppose his human capital is not worthless in the sense that the firm that employed him is willing to re-employ him, after a lapse of time. In other words, he is merely temporarily unemployed. However, because of the credit constraints he faces, he will not be able to supplement his current consumption and thereby smooth out his consumption plan. Then the trade-off between smoothing out consumption and present-value earnings that we analysed previously applies here as well, so that he may be tempted to commence working immediately in a job that entails a flatter earnings profile and less earned income. Therefore, if the welfare costs of surviving temporary unemployment are heavy because of credit constraints, his job expectations may change from temporary unemployment followed by a return to the old job in the primary factor, to a new job offering less pay in the secondary sector.

Thurow has argued that if a worker in a primary sector becomes unemployed, he is not allowed to return to his old job.

To keep the training process going, employers will not allow the unemployed to bid back into his old job at lower wages.... Technically, the individuals have the necessary job skills, but they are frozen out of the market and thus do not represent an effective potential supply of labor. Their personal productivity and skills are irrelevant even though they exist. Similarly, manpower training programs report that they often have trouble placing trained workers since these workers are not allowed into jobs for which they have been trained.... Technically, the individual may possess the necessary skills, but institutionally speaking he does not.

(Thurow, 1975, pp. 85–86)

If the foregoing applies to the unemployed worker in the primary sector, then, in order to obtain another skilled job, he will need to retrain. The trade-off between smoothing consumption and present-value earnings will apply once again so that the individual's expectations may change from temporary unemployed, followed by a similar job in the primary sector, to a new job offering less present-value earnings in the secondary sector.

By now it should be clear that the changes in job expectations are a result of institutional arrangements for lending. The rules are such that the individual who has had the misfortune of being unemployed is not allowed 'another bite at the cherry'. If the individual were allowed further credit, then he would be able to ride out a temporary set-back, and then, secure a well-paid job. Consequently, he would also be able to discharge his debt easily.

Conclusion

To see the way in which this chapter fits in with the previous chapters recall that in Chapter 2 it was shown that the immediate implication of credit constraints is that the shape of the consumption profile is altered. In fact, over an interval of life, the shape could closely follow that of the earnings profile. In Chapter 3 it was shown that in order to compensate for this, the individual may choose a flatter earnings profile characterized by smaller present-value earnings.

There is the possibility, however, that the binding of credit constraints may be rendered less effective by allowing the individual greater choice. Accordingly, we explored the possibility that if there is concern for heirs then parents could be induced to choose bequests in order to weaken the effectiveness of credit constraints. Then, in Chapter 6, we examined the possibility that the individual can lessen the impact of credit constraints on consumption by working harder. In fact, if it is assumed that the wage profile is given and that work is an unconstrained choice variable, then the individual is able to alter the shape of the earnings profile by varying work and thereby weaken the impact of credit constraints on consumption. But once the possibility of a constraint on work effort is allowed for then the original effectiveness of credit constraints is more or less reinstated.

In this chapter we have looked at different types of lifetime work constraints. We have eased into this topic by arguing that within a lifetime context changes in work effort can change the wage rate and the way to take account of this is to take on board the idea of a lifetime work–training trade-off. Then if training is job-entailed work must be job-entailed as well, so that the analysis should embrace job choices. Work is still a choice but only to the extent that jobs are chosen, with different jobs entailing different wage and work profiles. We then demonstrated that job choice can be significantly influenced by credit constraints that an individual may face. In particular, if jobs can be divided into primary-sector and secondary-sector jobs then, *ceteris paribus*, an individual who faces greater effective credit-rationing is more likely to choose a secondary-sector job. Although the marginal individual is indifferent between the two job types since his welfare is the same in either sector, the present-value lifetime earnings are smaller in the secondary sector. Then there results a labour market structure which has empirical and logical consistency. It is characterized by jobs with steep earnings profiles being associated with on-the-job training with individuals bearing the cost of training, and jobs with flat earnings profiles being associated with little training. The labour market structure rests on unequal opportunity sets facing individuals, the inequality arising from credit-market imperfections, in turn arising from information failures. Alternative explanations for labour market structure were found either to have theoretical problems or to have problems in explaining empirical evidence. We also indicated how our explanation can form the basis for a theory in which a dynasty can come to be locked into secondary-sector jobs.

CHAPTER **8**

Housing Tenure Choice

So far, c, the rate of consumption, has been treated as scalar-valued. Although this is analytically convenient, at some stage we should make a distinction between durables and non-durables. This is because the acquisition, holding and disposition of durables is likely to be sensitive to liquidity constraints and will therefore influence the life-cycle plans of individuals.

Now buying a home is usually the largest investment an individual ever makes over his life cycle. Analytically, this is quite convenient for it enables us to abstract by ignoring other durables. Thus in this chapter the model is extended to incorporate housing. As the individual may then hold housing as well as financial assets, this incorporation enables us to consider assets-portfolio aspects of life-cycle planning and how the composition of the portfolio varies over individuals.

Another implication of incorporating housing into the model derives from the features characterizing the housing market. In a featureless housing market there is one price for housing services whereas, as will be shown, in real housing markets price varies over, for example, tenure type. It will be shown that individuals who hold a particular type of assets portfolio may consume cheaper housing services. The way this connects up with the analytical theme is that those who are credit-constrained may choose a different assets portfolio from those who are not. It may then easily turn out that credit-constrained individuals choose the more expensively priced housing. There are also implications for the choice of earnings profile.

Therefore, this chapter extends the analysis of the previous chapters by considering one more implication of credit constraints in a systematic way and connects this extension to the previous analysis by showing how it impinges on choices made in the earlier chapters. The upshot is that the previous results are considerably enriched. One result is worth stating straightaway. Low wealth can not only lead to low earnings and a secondary-sector trap, it may in addition lead to more expensive housing or a renting trap.

The Statement of the Problem

We begin by isolating the features of the housing market and reformulate the individual's basic intertemporal choice problem accordingly.

Housing stock and services

Following Muth (1960) and Olsen (1969), it is assumed that there is a homogeneous commodity called the flow of housing services, $g(t)$, which is obtainable from a stock of housing, $G(t)$. It is convenient to assume that $g(t)$ is proportional to $G(t)$, that is $g(t) = vG(t)$, where v is a proportionality factor. This is a standard assumption but it is perhaps more realistic to assume that v is a variable responding to the intensity with which the housing stock is used (Sweeny (1974) contains an interesting treatment of v). It is, nevertheless, assumed that v is a constant and it is also set equal to unity without any loss of generality.

Turning to depreciation of housing stock, this is not easy to define and is even harder to specify. Sweeny (1974), for example, has treated depreciation as an object of individuals' choice. However, for simplicity, endogenous depreciation will be ignored. Various other authors have used a variety of exogenous specifications for durables in general, such as constant evaporation depreciation, one-horse shay depreciation (loses life suddenly), non-constant depreciation for a fixed lifetime (e.g. Kleirman and Ophir, 1966; Parks, 1966; Levhari and Srinivasan, 1969; Swan, 1970). It is unlikely, however, that the qualitative results are sensitive to the exogenous form chosen, so the simplest one is adopted: G depreciates at the constant rate δ. Denoting additions to the housing stock by $I(t)$, $I(t) - \delta G(t)$ then represents net investment in the housing stock.

In accordance with casual empiricism, it is assumed that the individual obtains housing services by either renting privately or owning, but not both simultaneously.

The objective function

The instantaneous utility function is defined over $g(t)$, consumption of housing services, $x(t)$, all other consumption, and $h(t)$, proportion of time spent at work. To simplify matters it is assumed that $h(t) = \bar{h}(t)$, $\bar{h}(t)$ being given. Then the instantaneous utility function is $(U(x, g) + \text{constant})$. Since $U(x, g)$ is a monotonic transformation of $U(x, g) + \text{constant}$, maximization with respect to $U(x, g)$ alone will yield the same solution. It is assumed that U is strictly concave and that $U_x \to \infty$ as $x \to 0$, $U_x \to 0$ as $x \to \infty$, $U_g \to \infty$ as $g \to 0$ and $U_g \to 0$ as $g \to \infty$. These ensure that x and g are finite and positive. The individual's objective function then is:

$$\text{Maximize } J = \int_0^T e^{-\rho t} U(x, g) \, dt. \tag{8.1}$$

Mortgage limits

Let $M(t)$ represent the individual's mortgage at time t. The mortgage is secured on the house so that

$$M(t) \leqslant \sigma P_G G, \qquad 0 < \sigma < 1, \tag{8.2}$$

where $P_G G$ is the price per unit of housing stock at time t so that $P_G G$ is the current market value of the house, and σ is a constant.

The lending institution is also concerned about the individual's ability to service the mortgage and therefore limits M such that

$$M(t) \leqslant \overline{M}(t), \tag{8.3}$$

where $\overline{M}(t)$ represents the limit on M at time t. This $\overline{M}$ is determined by the individual's characteristics such as earned income. Equations (8.2) and (8.3) can be collapsed into one equation:

$$\overline{M}(t) \leqslant \min\left[\sigma P_G(t)G(t), \overline{M}(t)\right]. \tag{8.4}$$

Equation (8.4) says that the mortgage cannot exceed the minimum of the two limits.

Borrowing and lending rates

The tax systems of most countries drive a wedge between various borrowing and lending rates. Distinguishing between financial assets/liabilities, A, and mortgage debt, M, those features of the tax system that interest us here are the assymetric treatment of interest receipts and charges on A and tax relief on mortgage interest. Given the reasons of Chapter 4 and as interest on financial assets is taxable as a receipt but not deductible as an expense, it makes sense to assume that

$$r_1 < r_2, \tag{8.5}$$

where r_1 is the post-tax lending rate on A and r_2 is the borrowing rate. Further, because of tax relief,

$$r_M < r_2, \tag{8.6}$$

where r_M is the rate charged on outstanding mortgage, M. Because of differential market opportunities and imperfect information, r_1 is likely to vary over individuals but, in order to limit proliferation of analysable cases, it will be assumed, what appears to be the most common case, that

$$r_1 > r_M. \tag{8.7}$$

Evolution of assets

Over time, the individual's holdings of various stocks of assets will change. During owner-occupancy phases, their evolution can be usefully written as:

$$\dot{A} = r_1 A + y - x - P_G I - r_M M + m, \qquad A > 0, \tag{8.8}$$

$$\dot{A} = r_2 A + y - x - P_G I - r_M M + m, \qquad A < 0, \tag{8.9}$$

$$\dot{A} = y - x - P_G I - r_M M + m, \qquad A = 0, \tag{8.10}$$

$$\dot{G} = I - \delta G, \tag{8.11}$$

$$\dot{M} = m. \tag{8.12}$$

In the above equations, m denotes additions to mortgage debt.

Whenever the individual rents, he will neither have outstanding mortgage nor hold housing stock. In that case, there is only his stock of financial assets/liabilities which will evolve according to:

$$\dot{A} = r_1 A + y - x - pg, \qquad A > 0, \tag{8.13}$$

$$\dot{A} = r_2 A + y - x - pg, \qquad A < 0, \tag{8.14}$$

$$\dot{A} = y - x - pg, \qquad A = 0, \tag{8.15}$$

where p is the market rental per unit of g and the price of x has been set to equal unity.

In order to complete the characterization of the individual's lifetime budget, the starting and terminal values of A, G and M need to be specified. We will take the initial asset and debt position as given and impose the reasonable condition that the individual must die solvent. Thus:

$$A(0) = A_0, \ G(0) = G_0, \ M(0) = M_0, \ A_0 + P_G(0)G_0 - M_0 \geqslant 0, \quad (8.16)$$

$$A(T) + P_G(T)G(T) - M(T) \geqslant 0. \quad (8.17)$$

A_0, G_0 and M_0 are given constants and for the person who starts life by renting, G_0 and M_0 are zero. Equation (8.17) states that the net asset position of the individual at death-bed must be non-negative.

In order to complete the characterization of the individual's intertemporal problem we note that there is a limit on financial credit,

$$A \geqslant \bar{A} = \alpha_1 + \alpha_2 y. \quad (8.18)$$

The Solution

It shall be assumed, without any loss of generality, that the individual commences his lifetime plan by renting, switches to owning at time $t = t_1 > 0$, switches back to renting at time $t = t_2 > t_1$, switches back to owning at time $t = t_3 > t_2$ and so on. Of course it may turn out that either it is optimal for the individual to rent throughout life, in which case $t_1 \notin [0, T]$, or that it is optimal always to own, so that $t_1 = 0, t_2 \in [0, T]$. Identifying the last tenure phase with the last interval in the lifetime plan and working backwards from time T to the first tenure phase, which is the first interval, results rather naturally in a dynamic programming formulation of the problem. The actual maximization is carried out in a two-step procedure.

Firstly, fixing t_1

$$\text{Maximize } J = \int_0^{t_1} e^{-\rho t} U(x(t), g(t)) \, dt + W(A(t_1), t_1), \quad (8.19)$$

subject to (8.13)–(8.15) and (8.18), where

$$A(t_1^-) = A(t_1^+) + P_G(t_1^+)G(t_1^+) - M(t_1^+),$$

that is, at t_1 financial assets are converted into housing stock, mortgage debt and financial assets. $W(A(t_1), t_1)$ denotes the maximum of

$$\int_{t_1}^T e^{-\rho t} U(x(t), g(t)) \, dt$$

$$= \int_{t_1}^{t_2} e^{-\rho t} U(x(t), g(t)) \, dt + \int_{t_2}^{t_3} e^{-\rho t} U(x(t), g(t)) \, dt + \cdots,$$

subject to the owning constraints, (8.4), (8.8)–(8.12) and (8.18), during the periods $[t_1, t_2)$, $[t_3, t_4)$, ... and renting constraints during the periods $[t_2, t_3)$, $[t_4, t_5)$, ... and with $A(t_1)$ given. Secondly, denoting the maximum of J above by J^*, t_1 is varied at the second step to maximize $J^*(t_1)$.

Formally, at each t, $0 \leqslant t \leqslant t_1$, the individual maximizes $L = U(x, g) + \lambda_1 f + \mu[A - \bar{A}]$, where f is the right-hand side of (8.13)–(8.15). The first-order conditions are:

$$U_x = \lambda_1, \tag{8.20}$$

$$U_g = \lambda_1 p, \tag{8.21}$$

$$\lambda_1(t_1) = \frac{\partial W}{\partial A(t_1)} + \mu(t_1) \tag{8.22}$$

$$\left. \begin{array}{ll} \dot{\lambda}_1 = \lambda_1(\rho - r_1) - \mu, & A > 0, \\ \dot{\lambda}_1 = \lambda_1(\rho - r_2) - \mu, & A < 0, \\ \dot{\lambda}_1 \in [\lambda_1(\rho - r_2) - \mu, \lambda_1(\rho - r_1) - \mu], & A = 0. \end{array} \right\} \tag{8.23}$$

Defining

$$J^*(t_1) = \int_0^{t_1} e^{-\rho t} U(x^*(t), g^*(t)) \, dt,$$

t_1 is determined according to:

$$\frac{dJ^*(t_1)}{dt_1} + \frac{\partial W^*(A^*(t_1), t_1)}{\partial t_1} = 0 \Rightarrow t_1 \in [0, T], \tag{8.24}$$

$$\frac{dJ^*(t_1)}{dt_1} + \frac{\partial W^*(A^*(t_1), t_1)}{\partial t_1} < 0 \Rightarrow t_1 = 0, \tag{8.25}$$

$$\frac{dJ^*(t_1)}{dt_1} + \frac{\partial W^*(A^*(t_1), t_1)}{\partial t_1} > 0 \Rightarrow t_1 \notin [0, T]. \tag{8.26}$$

Here, x^*, g^* and $A^*(t_1)$ satisfy the optimality conditions (8.20)–(8.23).

As it is instructive to derive the optimality conditions during the phases the individual owns, let us consider the problem one interval further. Then, given $A(t_1^-) = A(t_1^+) + P_G(t_1^+)G(t_1^+) - M(t_1^+)$, the individual maximizes

$$\int_{t_1}^{t_2} e^{-\rho t} U(x(t), g(t)) \, dt + W(A(t_2), t_2)$$

subject to (8.4), (8.8)–(8.12) and (8.18). This is equivalent to maximizing at each t, $t_1 < t \leqslant t_2$, the expression,

$$L = U(x, g) + \lambda_1 k + \lambda_2[I - \delta G] + \lambda_3[m]$$
$$+ \mu[A - \bar{A}] + \zeta[\bar{M} - M] + \psi[\sigma P_G G - M],$$

where k is the right-hand side of (8.8)–(8.10). The first-order conditions are:

$$U_x = \lambda_1, \tag{8.27}$$

$$\lambda_1 = -\lambda_3, \text{ whenever } m \text{ does not jump}, \tag{8.28}$$

$$P_G\lambda_1 = \lambda_2, \text{ whenever } I \text{ does not jump}, \tag{8.29}$$

$$\begin{aligned}
\dot{\lambda}_1 &= \lambda_1(\rho - r_1) - \mu, & A &> 0, \\
\dot{\lambda}_1 &= \lambda_1(\rho - r_2) - \mu, & A &< 0, \\
\dot{\lambda}_1 &\in [\lambda_1(\rho - r_2) - \mu, \lambda_1(\rho - r_1) - \mu], & A &= 0,
\end{aligned} \tag{8.30}$$

$$\dot{\lambda}_2 = \lambda_2\rho + \lambda_2\delta - U_g - \sigma P_G\psi, \tag{8.31}$$

$$\dot{\lambda}_3 = \lambda_3\rho + \lambda_1 r_M + \zeta + \psi, \tag{8.32}$$

$$\lambda_1(t_2) = \frac{\partial W(A(t_2), t_2)}{\partial A(t_2)} + \mu(t_2), \tag{8.33}$$

$$\lambda_2(t_2) = P_G\frac{\partial W(A(t_2), t_2)}{\partial A(t_2)} + \delta P_G\psi(t_2), \tag{8.34}$$

$$\lambda_3(t_2) = \frac{-\partial W(A(t_2), t_2)}{\partial A(t_2)} - \zeta(t_2) - \psi(t_2), \tag{8.35}$$

where μ, ζ and ψ are such that

$$\begin{aligned}
\mu &\geq 0, \mu(A - \bar{A}) = 0 & &\text{for all } t, t_1 < t \leq t_2, \\
\zeta &\geq 0, \mu(\bar{M} - M) = 0 & &\text{for all } t, t_1 < t \leq t_2, \\
\psi &\geq 0, \psi(\sigma P_G G - M) = 0 & &\text{for all } t, t_1 < t \leq t_2.
\end{aligned}$$

Algebraic manipulation of (8.27)–(8.32) together with $\sigma = 1$ in (8.31) yields:

$$U_g = \lambda_1 P_G\left(r_M + \delta - \frac{\dot{P}_G}{P_G}\right), \qquad M = P_G G < \bar{M}, \qquad A > \bar{A}, \tag{8.36}$$

$$\lambda_1 P_G\left(r_1 + \delta - \frac{\dot{P}_G}{P_G}\right) > U_g > \lambda_1 P_G\left(r_M + \delta - \frac{\dot{P}_G}{P_G}\right), \tag{8.37}$$

$$M = P_G G = \bar{M}, \qquad A > 0, \qquad r_1 > r_M,$$

$$U_g = \lambda_1 P_G\left(r_1 + \delta - \frac{\dot{P}_G}{P_G}\right), \qquad M = \bar{M} < P_G G, \qquad A > 0. \tag{8.38}$$

When $M < \bar{M}$, $P_G G > M$ and $A > 0$, (8.27)–(8.32) imply that $r_1 = r_M$. But, since by assumption $r_1 > r_M$, the individual will never find it optimal to hold M such that $M < \overline{M}$ and $P_G G > M$.

$$\lambda_2 P_G\left(r_2 + \delta - \frac{\dot{P}_G}{P_G}\right) > U_g > \lambda_1 P_G\left(r_M + \delta - \frac{\dot{P}_G}{P_G}\right), \tag{8.39}$$

$$M = P_G G = \overline{M}, \qquad 0 > A > \overline{A}, \qquad r_2 > r_M.$$

$$U_g = \lambda_1 P_G\left(r_2 + \delta - \frac{\dot{P}_G}{P_G}\right), \qquad M = \overline{M} < P_G G, \qquad 0 > A > \overline{A}. \tag{8.40}$$

When $M < \overline{M}$, $P_G G > M$, $0 > A > \overline{A}$, (8.27)–(8.32) imply that $r_2 = r_M$. But, since by assumption $r_2 > r_M$, the individual will never find it optimal to hold M such that $M < \overline{M}$ and $P_G G > M$.

Analysis

Prices for housing services

As indicated earlier on, one implication of the features of the housing market is that there are different prices for the same housing services. We now turn to analysing these prices with a view to anticipating how, when taken together with (8.18) ($A \geqslant \overline{A}$), the individual's plans may be affected. We shall do this in two steps: first clarify the role of prices and at the second step analyse the implications of the binding of (8.18). Define:

$$P_M \equiv P_G\left(r_M + \delta - \frac{\dot{P}_G}{P_G}\right),$$

$$P_1 \equiv P_G\left(r_1 + \delta - \frac{\dot{P}_G}{P_G}\right),$$

$$P_2 \equiv P_G\left(r_2 + \delta - \frac{\dot{P}_G}{P_G}\right).$$

Then the first-order conditions, (8.20), (8.21), (8.27), (8.36) and (8.40) can be rewritten as:

while renting,
$$U_x = \lambda_1, \qquad U_g = \lambda_1 P;$$

while owning,
$$U_x = \lambda_1,$$

$$U_g = \lambda_1 P_M, \qquad \text{whenever } M < \overline{M}, \qquad P_G G = M,$$

$$\lambda_1 P_1 > U_g > \lambda_1 P_M, \qquad \text{whenever } M = \overline{M} = P_G G, \qquad A > 0,$$

$$\lambda_1 P_2 > U_g > \lambda_1 P_M, \qquad \text{whenever } M = \overline{M} = P_G G, \qquad A < 0,$$

$$U_g = \lambda_1 P_1, \qquad \text{whenever } M = \overline{M}, P_G G > M, \qquad A > 0,$$

$$U_g = \lambda_1 P_2, \qquad \text{whenever } M = \overline{M}, P_G G > M, \qquad A < 0.$$

Note that, in order to avoid tedious technicalities, σ in (8.4) has been set equal to unity. Except for some very old properties, 95% of mortgages are easy to obtain so that setting $\sigma = 1$ is no great departure from reality.

P_M is identified as the implicit rental per unit of housing services when the individual owns and is able to increase mortgage in order to purchase additional units of the housing stock. In a similar fashion, P_1 denotes the implicit marginal rental when he is not able to use additional mortgage in adding to his housing stock and has to employ his own funds which he could otherwise lend. Lastly, P_2 is the implicit marginal rental when he has to borrow from sources other than those granting mortgage in order to finance additions to his housing stock. The implicit average price of owning, of which we shall be making considerable use below, is then given by:

$$P_M, \text{ whenever } g < \bar{g},$$

$$\frac{(1 - b)(g - \bar{g})P_2 + b(g - \bar{g})P_1 + \bar{g}P_M}{g}, \; 0 < b < 1, \text{ whenever } g > \bar{g},$$

where $\bar{g}$ is the quantity of housing services attributable to the housing stock that is purchased with building society funds, $b(g - \bar{g})$ with his own funds and $(1 - b)(g - \bar{g})$ with funds borrowed from other sources.

In the interests of analytical tractability and ease of exposition, it will be assumed that P_G, P and y are constant over time. It is also assumed that the instantaneous utility function, $U(x, g)$, is additively separable and is written as

$$U(x, g) = \left(\frac{1}{1 - \varepsilon_x}\right)x^{1 - \varepsilon_x} + \zeta_g\left(\frac{1}{1 - \varepsilon_g}\right)g^{1 - \varepsilon_g},$$

where $\zeta_g > 0$, $-U_{xx}x/U_x = \varepsilon_x > 0$ and $-U_{gg}g/U_g = \varepsilon_g > 0$. The parameter ζ_g is a taste parameter that is larger for those who value housing services more highly.

Price stipulations

There are four different prices, P_M, P_1, P_2 and P, for housing services, g. It is probably true that P_M is the lowest and $P_2 > P_1$. There then remain three price stipulations:

$$P_2 > P_1 > P > P_M, \qquad (8.41)$$

$$P_2 > P > P_1 > P_M, \qquad (8.42)$$

$$P > P_2 > P_1 > P_M. \qquad (8.43)$$

Lifetime plans

Given the specification of the model, a wide variety of lifetime plans can result. As a consequence, general results are impossible to obtain. However, it is instructive to work with an example which serves to highlight the influence of prices on tenure choice over life. The example assumes $A > 0$, $b > 0$, $r_1 - \rho > 0$, and the price stipulation (8.41). Then (proofs are in the appendix to this chapter):

Propositions

  (i) If consumption and housing services are normal goods, then the individual will plan increasing x and non-decreasing g over life.

 (ii) Given the individual's optimal choice of x and g at any moment in time, the choice of tenure is then determined solely by the relative average prices of renting and owning.

(iii) A plan characterized by increasing x and non-decreasing g over life will also imply, for the owner-occupation alternative, a constant average price of g for $g < \bar{g}$ and a rising average price of g for $g > \bar{g}$.

Whenever $t_s \in [0, T]$, where t_s is the time at which the individual first switches from owning to renting,

(iv) $\dfrac{\partial t_s}{\partial \overline{M}} > 0$,

 (v) $\dfrac{\partial t_s}{\partial y} < 0$,

(vi) $\dfrac{\partial t}{\partial A_0} < 0$.

Lifetime renting
Consider the individual who starts life by renting. Then, according to (ii), the average price of renting for him must be less than that of owning. From (i), he will plan increasing consumption of x and g over life which, from (iii), immediately means that he will never own. Therefore he always rents and the reason is that in relation to the quantity of housing services that he plans to consume, the size of M is not large enough.

Owning followed by renting
Consider another similar individual but one who can borrow more such that, to start with, his optimal M is less than $\overline{M}$. Then, from (ii), he owns.

Following on from (i), mortgage debt rises over life and, in time, M equals $\overline{M}$. At this point, the marginal price jumps up from P_M to P_1. But although the marginal price of owning is above the market rental, the average price differential continues to be in favour of owning until t_s when the average prices equalize. At this stage he switches to renting and continues to do so for the rest of his life. Now consider (iv) which says that if the tenure profiles of two individuals who are alike in all respects except M are considered, then the one with the greater M will own for a longer period. The reason why more M means a longer owner-occupancy phase is that the net benefits of more M are concentrated within the owning interval in life whereas the individual finds it optimal to spread the resultant extra expenditure over the entire life. At a first glance, (v) appears somewhat at variance with casual empiricism for it says that the individual who earns more will rent for a longer period. The reason why this is so is because a larger y increases g, which pushes up the average implicit price of owning, given that the debt limit is fixed. The implication suggests that a closer look at how $\overline{M}$ is determined is warranted and it is reasonable to write that $\overline{M}$ is, in fact, often a multiple of current earned income:

$$\overline{M} = \beta y, \qquad \beta > 0. \tag{8.44}$$

Taking (8.44) into account means that high income earners can also have greater maximum mortgages, in which case it does not necessarily follow that they will rent for longer periods. A more precise answer depends on how $\overline{M}$ and y enter into the optimization problem and, more importantly, on the numerical value of β as a greater β implies more $\overline{M}$ given y. Then the balance between (iv) and (v) can be more accurately assessed. Turning to (vi), it is of interest to note that the individual with more initial assets, A_0, will rent for a longer period and the reason is the same as mentioned in the preceding paragraphs. It is worth noting that this result depends on the price stipulation (8.41).

In order to examine the plans of the borrower, consider the case in which $(P_G(0)G(0) - M(0)) > A_0$ so that he starts with negative A. He will then face the marginal price P_2. To see the effects of differential rates, r_1 and r_2, suppose momentarily that $r_2 = r_1$. Now let r_2 increase slightly such that $r_2 > r_1$. There will result an income effect and a substitution effect but it is well known that they are of the same sign for the borrower. Assuming x and g are normal, his consumption of each will decrease. Further, the average price of owner-occupied housing will also change. Overall, g must decrease, otherwise the individual will not satisfy his budget, but it is not possible to say, *a priori*, what happens to the price of owning.

The aforesaid suggests the following interesting possibility. Some individuals will start as owner-occupiers but will be neither lenders nor borrowers. With their financial asset position $A = 0$, at price P_1 they will desire to acquire more housing stock but in order to do so they will need to borrow, in which case P_2 will apply. But if P_2 is sufficiently higher than P_1 they may deem it desirable not to increase g. In such cases the initial phase will be characterized by $A = 0$ and $\dot{A} = 0$, all savings being used up to finance additions to the housing stock, until, when the relative average prices of tenure modes cross over, the switch to renting occurs.

It is worth gathering below those points emerging from the analysis which should be borne in mind when it comes to analysing the implications of the binding of the $A \geqslant \bar{A}$ constraint.

(a) Although the marginal and the average rental price, P, is the same for all individuals, the average implicit price of owning generally varies over individuals.
(b) This is primarily due to there being limits on maximum mortgages and differential interest rates.
(c) The presence of M and the differential interest rates make the personal characteristics of the individual determinants of the implicit average price and hence exert influence over tenure choice.
(d) Distinguishing individuals by initial wealth, one can think of the rich as being able to obtain a higher r_1 through better market opportunities and thus facing (8.41) and the poor as facing (8.42). Then both the extreme rich and the extreme poor are likely to rent more often.
(e) Even if every individual faces the same β, y (and therefore M), r_M, r_1 and r_2, the average prices of owning and, therefore duration of ownership, will be different across individuals if some other individual characteristic, such as A_0, is differentially distributed.
(f) Those who own do so because it is cheaper for them. The average implicit price in relation to the rental price is the only consideration in tenure choice.

The implications of the binding of the $A \geqslant \bar{A}$ constraint
Thus far, we have concentrated on the individual for whom the credit constraint is ineffective in order to concentrate on other features of the housing market. The optimal policy has involved switching according to the average price advantage. Therefore, whenever owning is cheaper, the individual owns. Then, under the price configuration $P > P_2 > P_1 > P_M$, the individual always owns. However, we now proceed to show that the implication of the binding of the $A \geqslant \bar{A}$ constraint is that the individual may choose to rent and that the price stipulation will be sustained in equilibrium.

Before going into details, it is worth stating the choice trade-off confronting the individual. On the one hand, owning is always attractive because of the relative price advantage. On the other hand, owning has the disadvantage that it interferes with the distribution of x and g that the individual plans over life because, if the individual cannot borrow freely, then his consumption of housing services is straightaway constrained.

First phase. In order to bring out the implications of the $A \geqslant \bar{A}$ constraint in greater detail, assume that the individual has no initial holding of the housing stock, $A(0) = 0$, $\alpha_1 = \alpha_2 = 0$ so that $\bar{A} = 0$ and $\bar{M}$ is 'not very large'. The individual will always find it cheaper to own; and let us suppose he starts by owning. However, from first-order conditions it is easy to deduce that

$$\frac{U_x}{U_g} < \frac{P_x}{P_1}, \qquad \text{if } A = \bar{A}.$$

Further, $\dot{A} = \dot{\bar{A}} = 0$ so that

$$I = \frac{y - x - r_M \bar{M}}{P_G}, \qquad \dot{G} = \frac{y - x - r_M \bar{M} - \delta G}{P_G}.$$

Therefore, I is constrained and G is not being accumulated rapidly. This together with the fact that $\dot{A} = 0$ and $A_0 = 0$ means that he will be consuming relatively small rates of g to begin with. The upshot is that over the early interval in life, the welfare of the individual can be less than that under renting. As switching is costless from one tenure to the other, he may begin life by renting. The price advantage of owning has to be balanced against the constrained consumption of housing services. It is interesting to note, that utilizing US panel data, Dynarski and Sheffrin (1985) find that transitory income plays an important role in financing down-payments in housing purchase.

Second phase. The individual begins life by renting and can carry on renting all through life if he so chooses. But while renting he can accumulate funds so that were he to switch to owning at some later stage, the loss in his welfare from constrained consumption while owning would be smaller. In other words, because the trade-off between smoothing of consumption and the price advantage always applies, saving up while renting is a sacrifice that yields price advantage in the future since it enables him to own later on in life. Therefore, the individual may be able to improve upon a plan of renting throughout life by saving up to own, while renting.

To see this more formally, examine the solution to the problem and, in particular, (8.24)–(8.26). Now (8.24) states that the individual switches to owning at time t_1 having started life by renting. At the switch point, the value of an extra unit of time spent renting is equal to the value of that time spent owning. Presumably, the individual found it optimal to save up to own while renting. However, if (8.26) holds, then the individual rents throughout life and so never switches to owning. The individual does not bother about saving up to own since the disutility of saving up outweighs the additional utility accruing as a result of owning at cheaper prices.

Third phase. In order to examine whether the individual re-switches to renting at some time $t = t_2$, assume that the individual has carried out the plan up to $t = t_1$, and inspect the rest of the lifetime problem. He maximizes

$$\int_{t_1}^{t_2} e^{-\rho t} U(x, g) \, dt + W(A(t_2), t_2) = V(t_2) + W(A(t_2), t_2)$$

subject to the owning constraints where

$$W(A(t_2), t_2) = \text{maximum of} \int_{t_2}^{T} e^{-\rho t} U(x, g) \, dt$$

and

$$A(T) \geqslant 0.$$

Examine first what is involved in owning right up to the end of life. Since the individual plans to save up initially to own, and since x and g are increasing over time, it must be true that $P_G G > \bar{M} \; \forall \, t > t_2$. But $A \geqslant \bar{A} \; \forall \, t$ so that as $\bar{A} = 0$, $A \geqslant 0$. Therefore, $A + P_G G - \bar{M} > 0 \; \forall \, t > t_2$. This certainly satisfies the terminal condition:

$$A(T) + P_G(T)G(T) - M(T) \geqslant 0, \tag{8.17}$$

but with strict inequality. However, it is clear that the individual can do better by satisfying (8.17) with strict equality. But as $A(T) \geqslant 0$, this requires the individual to reduce $(P_G(T)G(T) - M(T))$ from a positive value to zero, that is, run down his own equity in the house. Therefore, as $t \to T$, $P_G G \to \bar{M}$ is one possible strategy. But this involves the individual in reducing the consumption of g and increasing that of x as $t \to T$, possibly not the best of strategies as it prevents him from allocating his resources between x and g freely. In fact, diminishing marginal utility will imply that the individual would prefer to transfer expenditure from x to g. This can be accomplished if the individual were to re-switch, but obviously the consequent freedom to allocate his own equity between x and g freely requires buying housing services more expensively. Nevertheless,

$$\frac{\partial V(t_2)}{\partial t_2} = \frac{\partial W(A(t_2), t_2)}{\partial t_2},$$

$$\frac{\partial V(t)}{\partial t} < \frac{\partial W(A(t), t)}{\partial t}, \qquad t_2 < t < T,$$

is a possible outcome, implying that the individual will find it optimal to re-switch to renting at $t = t_2$ which is near the end of life.

A lifetime plan

The indirect utility functional can be written as

$$J^* = \max \int_0^T e^{-\rho t} U(x, g) \, dt = J^*(\lambda_1(0); \, A_0, A, \ldots)$$

and the individual chooses that $\lambda_1(0)$ which maximizes J. Given the values of all parameters, there are different values of $\lambda_1(0)$ that satisfy the first-order conditions. Thus $J^*(\lambda_1(0))$ warrants several possible paths of which only one is a mixed-tenure path displaying a turnpike type of property:

The initial renting phase

$$\frac{\dot{x}}{x} = \left(\frac{r_1 - \rho}{\varepsilon_x}\right), \qquad \frac{\dot{g}}{g} = \left(\frac{r_1 - \rho}{\varepsilon_g}\right),$$

$$A > 0, \qquad A > \bar{A}, \qquad M = 0.$$

The middle owning phase

$$A \geqslant 0, \qquad A \geqslant \bar{A}, \qquad M = \bar{M},$$

$$r_1 A + y = x + P_G I + r_M M.$$

The final renting phase

$$\frac{\dot{x}}{x} = \left(\frac{r_1 - \rho}{\varepsilon_x}\right), \qquad \frac{\dot{g}}{g} = \left(\frac{r_1 - \rho}{\varepsilon_g}\right),$$

$$\dot{A} < 0, \qquad A > \bar{A}, \qquad M = 0.$$

The extreme assumption of $\bar{A} = 0$ was made in order to bring into sharp focus the role of the constraint, $A \geqslant \bar{A}$. In fact, we can re-run through the arguments with the assumption $\alpha_2 = 0$, $\bar{A} = \alpha_1 < 0$ but close to zero for, by continuity, borrowing for house purchase is still desirable for small negative $\bar{A}$. The same three phases would be obtained, albeit with changes in the duration of each phase and also in rates of x and g. At the other extreme, where $\alpha_2 = 0$ and $\bar{A} = \alpha_1$ is sufficiently low that it never binds, it will be possible for the individual to own throughout life. For it is clearly possible for the individual to acquire the housing stock he demands at $t = 0$ without having to save up for it and also to satisfy the terminal constraint,

$A(T) = 0$, by continuing owning up to $t = T$ and then selling the entire housing stock at $t = T$ to pay off outstanding debts equal to the value of his own equity in housing. Therefore, there is no need for him to liquidate his own equity before T for consumption purposes.

A sufficiently low $\bar{A}$ at old age can encompass an annuity which converts equity in a house into an annuity with tenure until death. This eliminates a final renting phase. Bequests could also eliminate this phase. But it would depend on the value of $(P_G(T)G(T) - M(T))$, the parameters of the utility from bequest function, etc. For instance, smaller values of $(P_G(T)G(T) - M(T))$ and greater taste for bequests will postpone and perhaps even eliminate re-switching.

Distribution of ownership

To begin with, we shall persevere with the assumption $\alpha_2 = 0$, in order to concentrate on the role of $\bar{A}$ as a simple restriction on debt. Later on, we will allow for the possibility that $\alpha_2 < 0$.

For comparison consider (a) a 'poor' individual who faces stringent borrowing restrictions, has zero or little inheritance, and who therefore finds it optimal to rent throughout life; (b) an 'in-between' individual; and (c) a 'rich' individual who, because he faces no credit constraints and has a large inheritance, finds it optimal to own throughout life. Then,

(a) The 'poor' individual cannot take advantage of the price difference.
(b) The 'in-between' individual faces a constrained phase during which he cannot save or dissave in terms of financial assets.
(c) The 'rich' individual can take advantage of both the price difference and saving and dissaving opportunities.

In particular, note that whereas for the rich individual, I will respond freely to changes in P_G and r_1, for the in-between individual, I is constrained from above by income during the owning phase. Thus the main difference between the rich individual and the others is in the degree of choice over the composition of their assets portfolios.

It is important to realize that the classification, (a)–(c), is sensitive to the assumption $\rho < r_1$. In the case in which $\bar{A}$ does not bind, namely (c), the relative size of ρ and r_1 does not matter except to the extent that it alters the time profiles of x and g. The 'rich', who face no borrowing restrictions, will always own and hold portfolios of their choice irrespective of the size of the discount rate. For case (b), however, replacing $\rho < r_1$ with $\rho > r_1$ implies that as current consumption has greater weight, and as it is the saving-up process that enables the individual to become an owner-occupier, the individual will now find it difficult to save up for ownership. Therefore, if discount rates vary over the 'in-between' individuals, those with high discount rates for the future will, *ceteris paribus*, tend to choose renting throughout life and those with low discount rates will tend to choose a mixed-tenure path.

In writing down the classification (a)–(c), we had assumed that $\alpha_2 = 0$ in $\bar{A} = \alpha_1 + \alpha_2 y$. We now let $\alpha_2 < 0$ so that $\bar{A}(t)$ depends on current labour income. An increase in y can then have four effects: a higher y means lower $\bar{A}$ and a higher $\bar{M}$; a higher y also changes the rate of savings irrespective of its effect on x and g. The first two effects will certainly encourage owning. One suspects that savings will also increase immediately and this should be conducive to owning, but x and g are likely to rise and this would encourage renting. Clearly, the magnitude of each effect is important and this means that, for the first two effects, the numerical values of α_2 and β are crucial. If α_2 is sufficiently low and β is sufficiently high then the classification (a)–(c) can be seen to accord with low-, middle- and high-income earners respectively.

Equilibrium in the housing market with $P > P_2 > P_1 > P_M$

We now argue that the relation $P > P_2 > P_1 > P_M$ can be sustained. The explanation lies with the $A \geqslant \bar{A}$ constraint which acts as a barrier between tenure groups. Suppose $P < P_2$. Then every individual would want to rent and would be able to do so if there were no restrictions to rent at price P. Thus $P < P_2$ can be ruled out by an appeal to a kind of competitive force. But $P > P_2$ cannot be ruled out in this way. If there are some individuals who are in the position of neither holding nor having access to sufficient financial assets, and therefore having no option but to accept renting at P, then the price differential can be expected to prevail. The reasoning is that they are the very individuals who would have acted as a competitive force by moving across the tenures and thereby increased the number of owners and reduced the numbers of renters and hence reduced $P - P_2$. On the supply side, however, if the relative high rents imply that the return, $(P + \dot{P}_G / P_G - \delta)$, on a unit of housing is greater than r_2, then there is an incentive for landlords to expand their activities in the housing sector, causing P to fall. Thus, in order to maintain our hypothesis, we need to assume that the landlords have a limited access to funds too. Thus, it is the entry barriers of illiquidity that maintain the difference between P and P_2. Therefore, since the marginal owner faces P_2 and since we have argued that $P > P_2$, this suffices to show that $P > P_2 > P_1 > P_M$.

Choice of earnings profile

One way of connecting this chapter with the previous ones is by considering choice between steep and flat earnings profiles. Recall that previously we had identified for an individual, a threshold level of initial assets, A_0^*, at which he is indifferent between the two earnings profiles. The reason is that although a steep earnings profile entails greater present-value earnings, it may also steepen the consumption profile. Both these considerations influence individual welfare and are in balance at A_0^*.

The connection between the analysis of this chapter and A_0^* lies in consumption early on in life. To see this, consider a summary of the results of this chapter. Let P_c denote the price index for the aggregate composite consumption good c, aggregated over x and g. Then P_c for renters is greater than P_c for owners. Therefore, given the same resources, the individual who rents will consume less c than the individual who owns. Now consider the choice of earnings profile. Previously, a flat profile implied greater consumption early on in life compared to a steep profile. Now, a flat profile may further increase consumption early on in life by enabling acquisition of owner-occupied housing through the provision of greater mortgage and non-housing debt.

The threshold analysis is now richer although less precise. For someone who starts with low assets and faces stringent debt limits, a choice of renting and flat earnings profile is plausible. At the other extreme, someone with sufficient initial assets will choose owning and a steep earnings profile. In between these two extremes there are two threshold levels of initial assets since as assets increase the switch to owning from renting becomes attractive and also a steep earnings profile becomes relatively more attractive. The precise levels at which the switches take place are difficult to identify without specifying the sizes of $\bar{A}$, $\bar{M}$, $P - P_2$ and so on. Nevertheless, the following stylized example may prove to be instructive.

The individual with very low initial assets chooses a flat earnings profile and rents. A similar individual with greater initial assets also chooses a flat earnings profile, but owns. With greater assets, the price advantage of owning outweighs the disadvantage of reduced consumption of housing services since the credit constraint is now less severe. With even greater assets, another otherwise similar individual will rent but choose a steep earnings profile. The steep earnings profile reduces early consumption; greater initial assets enable an increase in early consumption to balance this and initial renting, although more expensive, increases consumption further. Finally, with sufficient initial assets, an otherwise similar individual will own and choose a steep earnings profile. It is worth remembering, however, that this is just an illustration of effects of changes in initial assets.

Evidence

It should be interesting to see how the existing evidence matches up with the model we have presented although there does not appear to be a great deal of hard econometric evidence that we can call upon.

One of the assumptions of the model is that an individual may be refused an adequate mortgage. Taken together with the imperfection in the non-mortgage credit market, it implies that he may not find it worthwhile to enter the owner-occupied sector. It should be interesting to see if there is any empirical support for such an outcome. To make the empirical connection, one could pose the following questions. Suppose an individual was picked at random, then what is the probability of that individual failing to get into the owner-occupation sector? If such a probability is significantly different from zero then it would be some support for the theoretical outcome.

In a paper containing econometric work on housing in the UK, King (1980) obtains probabilities which are not quite what we need but are nevertheless useful. Since the probabilities only indirectly relate to the ones we are thinking of, it is necessary to outline his method of obtaining them. King assumes that housing tenures in the UK can be grouped into three types: (1) owner-occupation, (2) subsidized rental and (3) unsubsidized furnished rental. He then makes a distinction between what households would like to obtain and what is actually observed. The difference arises because a household may not be able to obtain the tenure it wants. More formally, consider the probabilities q_{i1} and q_{i2}.

q_{ij} is defined as the probability of individual i being admitted into tenure type j conditional on requesting admission. A household may be observed in tenure 1 (owner-occupied) for two reasons. First, it chose tenure 1 and was admitted. Secondly, it chose tenure 2 (subsidised rental) and was refused admission into tenure 2 but admitted into tenure 1. Then P_{i1}, the probability of observing household in tenure 1, is

$$P_{i1} = \hat{P}q_{i1} + \hat{P}_{i2}(1 - q_{i2})q_{i1},$$

where $\hat{P}_{ij}$ is the probability that household i will choose tenure j. Similarly P_{i2}, the probability of observing the household in tenure 2, is

$$P_{i2} = \hat{P}_{i2}q_{i2} + \hat{P}_{i1}(1 - q_{i1})q_{i2}.$$

A household will only be observed in tenure 3 (unsubsidized furnished rental) if it is refused admission to both tenures 1 and 2:

$$P_{i3} = (1 - q_{i1})(1 - q_{i2}).$$

In order to obtain estimates of q_1 and q_2, King utilized FES (Family

Expenditure Survey) data. The FES data is a source of individual data with detailed information on incomes and expenditure though not on assets. His maximum-likelihood estimates are obtained on a subset (4238 households) of the full sample in which the head of the household was either in full-time employment or was self-employed. The estimates of the admission probabilities (q_1 and q_2) imply that the probability of a household being refused admission into tenure 1 is about 30% and of being refused admission into tenure 2 is about 18%.

While the results appear to provide support for our model, two points are worth noting. First, King assumed that q_1 and q_2 are the same for all households. This is not a good assumption in an empirical piece of work where it is very likely that these probabilities vary over households. But King goes on to state that 'Preliminary work on the question of rationing probabilities depending on household characteristics suggests that the admission probability into the owner-occupied sector is an increasing function of income, a phenomenon which reflects constraints in the capital market and the criteria used by building societies to ration mortgages' (King, 1980, pp. 156–7). Later we shall look at a study that considers this aspect of rationing. Secondly, it is worth repeating that his estimated probabilities relate to a refusal of entry into the owner-occupied sector whereas our outcome is such that the individual does not find it worthwhile to gain entry, given an inadequate mortgage. The connection between the two should be straightforward but is not there in any explicit form. This is because the two models have been developed separately.

We now consider evidence from a model that utilizes American data. Like King, Henderson and Ioannides (1986) treat the choice of tenure mode – whether to rent or own – and the housing-consumption decision as a joint decision and as arising from the same behavioural model. They differ from King in their analysis of the rationing function. King assumes that rationing does not depend on individual characteristics and is therefore purely random whereas Henderson and Ioannides are able to estimate a specific rationing function. Their function has as a dependent variable q, the probability that a family will be able to get a mortgage for a house purchase in the mortgage market. 'Exclusion from the market can occur because mortgage loan officers associate a high rate of default with a particular family, or because of discrimination. Loan officers might infer a high risk on the basis of age, sex, race, low education or low current income, controlling for socioeconomic characteristics. They might discriminate on the same basis' (Henderson and Ioannides, 1986, p. 233). The specific rationing function they work with is

$$q = f(\text{marital status, age, race, education, income}),$$

where f is the cumulative distribution function of the normal variable. Casual observation applied to the US institutional environment would lead one to expect that being married and also being white would raise the probability of obtaining a mortgage, as would higher values for age, education and income.

They estimate the parameters of the demand functions and the rationing function using maximum-likelihood methods. The data comes from the Annual Housing Survey for the United States for the year 1975. After deleting for missing values, the subsample they work with consists of 2663 observations – 2069 renters and 594 owners. As expected, the results show that increases in current income, education and age reduce the probability of being rationed. Similarly, being married and being white increase the probability of getting a mortgage.

We finally turn to a paper, Shah and Rees (1985), that exploits the idea that in a world with perfect markets the individual is anonymous whereas in an imperfect-markets economy the individual characteristics matter. In a perfect neoclassical world, housing-tenure allocation would be determined solely by relative prices so that the identity of the individual in the housing market is not important (and hence of no particular interest). In more detail, suppose the individual is a rational maximizing agent who chooses the housing alternative that is consistent with his plans of maximizing his lifetime utility. If it is assumed that taxes do not exist, that capital markets are perfect, and that at each moment for each mode demand equals supply in the neoclassical sense, then making some suitable stationarity assumption about intertemporal equilibrium, the individual will compare lifetime utility associated with owner-occupation with lifetime utility associated with private rental at the beginning of his life. It is clear that the individual will choose the lowest-priced alternative as that will yield the highest lifetime utility, but it is also apparent that in this perfect world relative prices will equalize so that the individual will be indifferent between renting and owning. But if capital markets are imperfect, that is, access to funds for owner-occupation varies from individual to individual, then the probability of securing this mode of tenure will depend on the ease with which funds are obtainable. This, in turn, will depend on the wealth position of the individual and also the manner in which lending institutions make lending decisions. For example, such lending decisions will depend on the characteristics of the individual such as current income, occupation status and marital status. Therefore, non-price individual characteristics will determine which individual gets the available mortgage loans and it follows that such characteristics will affect the probability of an individual being an owner-occupier.

For empirical verification a data set from the General Household Survey of 1973 was used. The results on influence of personal characteristics on the probability of owner-occupation relative to renting are as follows. As expected, an increase in income raises the probability of owner-occupation relative to renting. Age has the same effect, which is consistent with the view that individuals initially rent privately intending to switch to owner-occupation later on in life. Despite the small number of non-whites in the sample, being non-white decreases the probability of being in the owner-occupied sector. The married have a greater probability of being observed in the owner-occupied sector and this is consistent with the view that an engaged couple rents and saves to purchase a home after marriage.

The results discussed so far show the extent to which variables like income, age and race affect the probability of owner-occupation relative to private renting. Now in interpreting the effect of a difference in age it is assumed that all the other coefficients are unchanged. But this may not be entirely appropriate since the current picture of tenure distribution is, to some extent, influenced by past events. Thus although the results indicate that the young are disproportionately in the rental sector, it is not possible to say whether this is due to age effect associated with some form of life-cycle planning or the cohort effect in which the presence of intercohort differences would imply differing circumstances. The need for intercohort differences control can be met by good longitudinal data, but in its absence it is difficult to identify and correct for any possible differences that may exist between cohorts. However, at the very least, the sample can be stratified by age and the model can be estimated using each subsample separately. The results make interesting reading.

An increase in income increases the probability of owner-occupation in the younger (age < 30) group but does not affect the probability in the older (30–45) age group. This is consistent with the hypothesis that a young individual with a low wealth position is heavily dependent on the building-society mortgage (which is usually a multiple of current income) and with age he both saves and moves into a higher income bracket so that the mortgage inadequacy is reduced. Marriage has an uneven impact and the increase in the probability of owning for the young is twice that for the old. The race variable is insignificant for the younger age group.

Whatever evidence we have, therefore, is consistent with the prediction of the theoretical model that individual characteristics such as income, wealth and age influence the allocation of housing tenure and result in a turnpike-type life-cycle plan, for some individuals at least.

Conclusion

In previous chapters the consequences of credit constraints were analysed by working with a model that excluded consumer durables. Although analytically convenient, credit constraints impinge on durables in a different way than on non-durables. Therefore, in this chapter, the model was extended to incorporate durables. Such an incorporation alters the opportunity and choice sets of the individual and the simple task of this chapter has been to derive the implications of this alteration.

Actually, we begin by ignoring the credit constraint to show that the price for housing services varies by tenure type. Then those who own choose to do so because it is cheaper. The relative owner-occupation/renting price is the only consideration. Once we introduce credit constraints, however, the decision to own or rent depends on non-price considerations as well. For instance, given the same earnings profile, less wealthy individuals are more likely to choose to rent and hence purchase the same housing services at a higher price. If earnings-profile choice is allowed, a flat profile entails greater mortgage and other debt facilities earlier on in life and hence provides an additional incentive for choosing it. Of course, an individual may choose a flat profile and also renting if his asset position is low enough. Then we may observe the least wealthy both earning less over life and paying more for the same consumption bundle.

Recall that the overall theme of this monograph is to trace out the consequences of credit constraints for individual behaviour. Actually, in Chapters 5 and 7 we have been engaged in tracing out fairly far-reaching consequences. But a few results have been recurring. First, effective credit constraints have consequences in which the identity of the individual matters. Prices alone do not allocate housing tenure type, for instance. We have to ask who rents or owns. Second, the effectiveness of credit constraints depends on the individual's level of wealth. Those who have a high level of wealth escape credit constraints altogether. Therefore, if there was not an unequal distribution of wealth there would not be an unequal distribution of tenure type. Hence, the initial distribution of wealth does matter. Third, the partnership of wealth and credit constraints affects investment decisions via influence on consumption. A decrease in wealth shrinks the opportunity set of the individual and thereby alters the consumption profile and hence welfare. The individual then may react by reducing investment, that is, rent instead of own in order to mitigate the effects on consumption and welfare. Fourth, the individual can move out of the low-earnings-plus-expensive-renting trap, but the sacrifices are too great for those with low wealth. This is because low wealth plus credit constraints plus discrete alternatives puts a 'tight' lock on such traps. In other words, more tenure choices would make it easier to heave out of a trap and could become a viable policy alternative to evening the distribution of wealth or making credit markets more perfect.

Appendix to Chapter 8

This appendix contains the proofs of Propositions (i) and (v) in the text. Given that there are no transaction costs of switching, proof of (ii) is obvious. (iii) follows directly from the definition of average implicit price of owning. Proof of (vi) is identical to that of (v). Unlike the other propositions, (iv) is unsurprising and since its proof is tedious, it has been omitted.

Proof of Proposition (i)

I. During the owning phase,
(a) Over the interval $[0, \hat{t}]$,

$$\frac{U_x}{U_g} = \frac{1}{P_M}, \qquad M < \bar{M}, \qquad M = P_G G, \qquad 0 < t < \hat{t},$$

$$\frac{\dot{x}}{x} = \frac{r_1 - \rho}{\varepsilon_x}, \qquad \frac{\dot{g}}{g} = \frac{r_1 - \rho}{\varepsilon_g}.$$

(b) Over the interval $[\hat{t}, \hat{\hat{t}}]$,

$$\frac{1}{P_1} < \frac{U_x}{U_g} < \frac{1}{P_M}, \qquad M = \bar{M} = P_G G, \qquad \hat{t} < t < \hat{\hat{t}},$$

$$\frac{\dot{x}}{x} = \frac{r_1 - \rho}{\varepsilon_x}, \qquad \frac{\dot{g}}{g} = 0.$$

(c) Over the interval $[\hat{\hat{t}}, T]$,

$$\frac{U_x}{U_g} = \frac{1}{P_1}, \qquad M = \bar{M}, \qquad M < P_G G, \qquad \hat{\hat{t}} < t < T,$$

$$\frac{\dot{x}}{x} = \frac{r_1 - \rho}{\varepsilon_x}, \qquad \frac{\dot{g}}{g} = \frac{r_1 - \rho}{\varepsilon_g}.$$

II. During the renting phase,

$$\frac{U_x}{U_g} = \frac{1}{P} \ \forall t,$$

$$\frac{\dot{x}}{x} = \frac{r_1 - \rho}{\varepsilon_x}, \qquad \frac{\dot{g}}{g} = \frac{r_1 - \rho}{\varepsilon_g}.$$

III. If the individual switches from owning to renting at $t = t_s$ then:

$$U_x(t_s^-) = \lambda_1(t_s^-),$$
$$U_g(t_s) = \lambda_1(t_s)P_1,$$
$$U_x(t_s^+) = \lambda_1(t_s^+),$$
$$U_g(t_s^+) = \lambda_1(t_s^+)P.$$

Since λ_1 is continuous, x will be continuous at t_s but because $P_1 > P$, g will jump up at t_s. Therefore, given the price configuration and other assumptions, there are three types of lifetime plans: owning throughout, owning followed by renting, and renting throughout. I, II and III demonstrate that during each one of these plans, (i) holds.

Proof of Proposition (v)

This proof is presented in two steps. As a result of an increase in y, (a) x increases for all t, g never decreases and, in fact, increases during the intervals $[0, t]$, $[t, t_s]$ and $[t_s, T]$.

Proof of (a)
Utilizing the first order conditions, $U_x = \lambda_1$ and $\dot{\lambda}_1 = \lambda_1(\rho - r_1)$, differentiate and write:

$$\frac{\partial}{\partial t}\frac{\partial x}{\partial y} = \frac{(r_1 - \rho)}{\varepsilon_x}\frac{\partial x}{\partial y}, \qquad (8A.1)$$

which holds for all t as x is continuous and the first-order conditions always hold. Therefore, $\partial x/\partial y$ does not ever change sign.

Turning to changes in g as a result of an increase in y, we can carry out similar differentiation to that above and write:

$$\frac{\partial}{\partial t}\frac{\partial g}{\partial y} = \left(\frac{r_1 - \rho}{\varepsilon_g}\right)\frac{\partial g}{\partial y}, \qquad (8A.2)$$

which holds throughout the interval $[0, t]$, $[t, t_s]$, $[t_s, T]$. Over the interval $[0, t]$, g is constant since it is given by $g = \overline{M}/P_G$. Given (8A.1) and the specific form of the utility function, a change in y either increases $x(0)$ or decreases it. Suppose $x(0)$ falls. Then during $[0, t]$, from (8A.2) and the first-order condition that $U_x/U_g = 1/P_M$, g must be reduced as well. Similar arguments show that g must decrease during the intervals $[t, t_s]$ and $[t_s, T]$. As noted, g is constant over $[0, t]$. Therefore, if x is reduced, g does not ever increase, and decreases during some of the intervals. But this means that there will be income left over, unspent. Therefore, it must follow that as a result of an increase in y, $x(0)$ increases implying that x increases, and g never decreases and increases for some t.

(b) The individual switches earlier on in life.

Proof of (b)
Define g^1 to be such that $M = P_G G$ whenever $g = g^1$ and g^2 to be such that $(P_1 - P)(g^2 - g^1) + (P_M - P)g^1 = 0$ whenever $g = g^2$. Then it must follow that

$$(P_1 - P)(g - g^1) + (P_M - P)g^1 > 0 \quad \text{for } g > g^2. \qquad (8A.3)$$

From Proposition (ii), at $t = t_s$, $g = g^s$. From (8A.3), also at t_s,

$$(P_M - P)g^1 + (P_1 - P)(g^2 - g^1) = 0.$$

But since M, P_M, P_1 and P are all unaltered, the only change that needs to be considered is in g. But since g never decreases and increases during parts of the interval $[0, t_s]$, and is also continuous throughout this interval, it also follows that g^2 is attained sooner. Hence the individual will switch earlier on in life.

CHAPTER 9

Extensions and Implications

In this chapter, we explore the effects of credit constraints in other areas of economics. The idea is to show that credit constraints can have a wide-ranging influence. The chapter is organized around four topics.

In the first topic, the idea that if human capital affects an individual's work productivity then it should also affect his consumption efficiency is taken on board. It links with Chapter 3 where the analysis was organized around the premise that when choosing earnings profiles individuals anticipate that investment in human capital has a delayed effect on earnings. Use is made of the concept of a household production function and the topic links up with household economics.

When there is a temporary shock that induces a famine, the peasant near subsistence level has to forgo investment and even disinvest in order to ward off starvation. The idea here is that credit constraints can induce short-term planning at the expense of long-term gains. This topic links up with Chapter 7 where the analysis of unexpected short-term unemployment having permanent effects was considered.

The idea that credit constraints inhibit joining a club is explored in the next topic of self-employment. The requirement of set-up capital acts as an entrance fee. Four testable predictions are derived and evidence examined.

This topic links with Chapter 8 in which it was implicit that owner-occupied housing requires some down-payment.

Finally, in the fourth topic of relative deprivation, we show that a person can be deprived for part of his life if credit constraints bind. If there are no credit constraints then the person is either always deprived or never deprived. This topic also links with the previous chapter in which a mixed housing-tenure lifetime plan was analysed.

The four diverse topics have one thing in common: there is some evidence in support of each. Of course, more evidence would help. In addition, each topic is in need of further theoretical research.

Consumption Efficiency

The idea advanced in Chapter 3 was that credit constraints allied with low wealth induce sacrifice in consumption since the individual's consumption profile becomes constrained to follow the income profile. This depresses utility early on in life so that the individual has less incentive to invest in anything that tilts the earnings profile upwards. A good example of investment that is lowered is human-capital investment (education, health, etc.). An implicit assumption in the reasoning is that there is no connection between the stock of human capital and the level of consumption at any given time t. It is worth probing into this assumption's validity.

The reason for the connection between the stock of human capital and the level of consumption is essentially a simple one. Human capital cannot be separated from the individual. Then if human capital affects the individual's work productivity, it may also affect his consumption efficiency. If, in fact, there is a positive correlation between human capital and consumption efficiency then we may have underestimated the incentive to invest in human capital because the full return on an investment in human capital is the sum of increases in work productivity and consumption efficiency.

Work efficiency is best measured by the market wage, given a competitive environment. Consumption efficiency, however, is more difficult to measure since a corresponding market price may not exist. Consider a specific example. An individual may consume a home-cooked meal which is not bought and sold on the market. Here, a more able cook produces a more satisfying meal. More generally, a more educated person is more efficient at a number of activities – managing financial affairs, reading, searching for information, etc. – than a less educated individual. How does one measure the implied change in output or efficiency?

One approach is to work with shadow prices of non-market goods. This approach has been pioneered by Chicago economists (Michael, 1972;

Becker, 1975) and it is worth setting it out more formally. Consider the aggregate home-produced good, G, which may be simply called 'living' and which is produced with an aggregate market-purchased input, z_1, and a time input, z_2. We can then specify that

$$G = G(z_1, z_2, K),$$

where K stands for human capital. Now $G(\cdot)$ is homogeneous of degree one in z_1 and z_2. Assume that someone with more human capital is both exposed to a wider range of techniques for producing G and is also more proficient at using a given technique for producing G. Then $\partial G / \partial K > 0$.

Let q_1 and q_2 denote the market-determined prices for z_1 and z_2 respectively. Then, treating the efficient production problem as a cost-minimization problem, write:

$$\min_{z_1, z_2} \{q_1 z_1 + q_2 z_2 \mid G(z_1, z_2, K) \geqslant \bar{G}\},$$

where $q_1 z_1 + q_2 z_2$ measure the short-run cost of inputs, $\bar{G}$ stands for a given level of G, and $G \geqslant \bar{G}$ is the technological constraint. The (reduced form) cost function for producing $G = \bar{G}$ is given by

$$c(\bar{G}) = c(q_1, q_2, K, \bar{G}).$$

If G is homogeneous of degree one in z_1 and z_2 then the cost function may be written as

$$c(\bar{G}) = \pi(q_1, q_2, K)\bar{G},$$

where π may be interpreted as the shadow or implicit price of $\bar{G}$. Since $\partial c / \partial \bar{G} = \pi$, the shadow price has a marginal cost interpretation. But having imposed homogeneity on the cost function, π also has an average cost interpretation since $\pi = c/\bar{G}$. But π is also strictly increasing, concave and homogeneous of degree one in q_1 and q_2, and it is non-increasing in K. Then,

$$\frac{\partial c}{\partial K} = \bar{G}\,\frac{\partial \pi}{\partial K} \leqslant 0,$$

so that an increase in human capital tends to reduce the shadow price of G and hence the cost of producing G. In fact, an increase in human capital may be evaluated as either a reduction in the cost of achieving $G = \bar{G}$ or an increase in G, holding the levels of the factors of production, z_1 and z_2, constant.

The most direct test of the effect of human capital on efficiency would be to investigate output of G per unit of input. However, this approach is not feasible since we have not quantified, let alone identified, G. An indirect approach has to be employed, and for effecting that we need to look at the second stage of the optimization problem in which the individual minimizes the expenditure (or cost) of achieving a given utility level $U = \bar{U}$:

$$\min_{\bar{G}, x_1, x_2} \{\pi(q_1, q_2, K)\bar{G} + p_1 x_1 + p_2 x_2 \mid U(x_1, x_2, G) \geqslant \bar{U}\},$$

where U, the instantaneous utility function, is defined over G, x_1 and x_2. Here x_1 and x_2 are two market goods purchased for the direct utility they yield, and p_1 and p_2 are their respective prices. The resulting expenditure (or cost) function is

$$E = E(\pi(q_1, q_2, K)\bar{G}, p_1, p_2, \bar{U}) = Y \equiv q_1 z_1 + q_2 z_2 + p_1 x_1 + p_2 x_2.$$

Differentiating, we obtain

$$\frac{\partial E}{\partial \pi} \frac{\partial \pi}{\partial K} \, dK + \frac{\partial E}{\partial U} \, dU = dY.$$

Holding $dU = 0$,

$$dY = \frac{\partial E}{\partial K} \frac{\partial \pi}{\partial K} \, dK = G \frac{\partial \pi}{\partial K} \, dK.$$

Since $\partial \pi / \partial K \leqslant 0$, dY and dK are of opposite sign. The interpretation is that an individual with more human capital needs less income to achieve a given level of utility. The reason is, of course, that he is able to produce G more efficiently and hence needs less resources.

The empirical implication emanates from the increase in real income for the more educated individual. Accordingly, we would predict that the more educated individual behaves as if he had more real income, holding his actual income constant. The mechanics of testing this prediction is as follows. Suppose we estimate cross-sectional income–expenditure curves for (a) market goods and (b) services. The explanatory variables would be permanent money income (or a suitable proxy), education and other socioeconomic variables such as age, family size and geographical region. From such Engel curves one can infer the response of (a) market goods and (b) services to changes in income and education. From these observed income and education elasticities, an estimate of the magnitude and direction of the effect of education on non-market productivity can be computed; that is, knowing the magnitudes of the individual's response to changes in income and education, one can infer the corresponding change in income that would induce the observed response resulting from the education change. The individual is then said to behave as if his real income has changed by that corresponding amount, which is, in turn, attributed to education as its non-market efficiency effect. To take the above example, suppose it is discovered that individuals with greater income spend proportionately more of their total fixed expenditure on services and that, other things held constant including money income, individuals with greater education also spend proportionately more of this total fixed expenditure on services. Then, those with more education appear to behave as if they had more real income, despite the fact that their permanent money income is held constant. This, then, may be interpreted as evidence that the higher level of education enhances their consumption efficiency.

Actual evidence is quite sparse. However, Michael (1972) has assembled several pieces of evidence along the lines mentioned above and he concludes that, 'The findings from several bodies of cross-sectional data reveal that the education level does affect expenditure patterns and generally does so in the expected manner' (p. 5).

To see the implications for the analysis of this monograph, it is best to refer to Chapter 3 where it may be recalled that an individual faced two earnings-profile choices, y^f being flat and y^s steep. The steep profile was assumed to reflect greater investment in human capital and therefore carried greater earnings later on in life. In the presence of effective credit constraints, it was asserted that an earnings premium of a certain magnitude was necessary for an individual to be indifferent between the choice of the two profiles. If, on the other hand, education does raise consumption efficiency, then taking account of it would imply that the earnings premium required for an individual to be indifferent between the two profiles would be smaller in magnitude.

Famines and Starvation

Famines seem to keep on occurring. They are characterized by very low levels of consumption implying starvation and are clearly undesirable. In order to eradicate famines it helps to know what causes famines and in the literature two causes of famine have been identified: a supply-side cause in which there is a general reduction in food availability throughout the famine-affected region and a market-induced cause in which the available food in the region is unavailable to the starving in the sense that they cannot pay for it. The latter cause of famines has filtered through into the literature fairly recently. It may be called the exchange-entitlement view on famines and has been closely associated with the work of Sen (1977, 1981). The notion of exchange entitlements and its connection with the topic of famines can be explored with the help of our model of individual behaviour.

Accordingly, consider the version of our model in which the individual maximizes

$$\int_0^T e^{-\rho t}(U(c) - V(h))\, dt$$

subject to

$$\dot{A} = rA + wh - c, \qquad A(0) = A_0,$$

given

$$A(T) \geqslant 0.$$

If the individual works for the whole of the current period then he obtains w units of real consumption in the current period. So w is a measure of his contemporaneous exchange entitlement in which work is exchanged for consumption. The real wage, w, is of course the nominal wage, W, divided by the price level, P. The real exchange entitlement can then fall if the nominal wage falls or the price level rises or both. In connection with an application to famines, one can think of c as food and P as the price of food. Then h would stand for hired farm labour and W would denote the money payment made to the farm labourer for a unit of work carried out. The setting for famines would then be a monetized exchange economy in which either an increase in the nominal price of food or a decrease in the money wage rate would reduce the labourer's exchange entitlement.

Consider now an unexpected shock at time t_1 such that the real wage drops to $\tilde{w}$. Assume further that the shock is temporary so that it rises to its former level at time t_2. The reformulation of the individual's problem at time t_1 is

$$\text{Maximize} \int_0^T e^{-\rho t}(U(c) - V(h)) \, dt$$

subject to

$$\dot{A} = rA + \tilde{w}h - c, \qquad \tau_1 \leqslant \tau < \tau_2, \qquad A(\tau_1),$$

given

$$\dot{A} = rA + wh - c, \qquad \tau_2 \leqslant t \leqslant T, \qquad A_T \geqslant 0,$$

and where $(w - \tilde{w}) > 0$.

In a situation like this, the discontinuity in the real wage will not include a discontinuity in consumption. The consumption path will be given by

$$c(t) = c(\tau_1)e^{\dfrac{(r - \rho)t}{\varepsilon}} \qquad \text{if } U'(c) = c^{-\varepsilon}.$$

Work will be discontinuous however, jumping up at τ_2. The interesting point is that the individual can smooth out consumption so that the temporary fall in the exchange entitlement can be smoothed out. Hence, over the period $[\tau_1, \tau_2]$ starvation can be prevented.

Now suppose that there is a borrowing constraint,

$$A \geqslant \bar{A}$$

which may bind. If the borrowing constraint binds, then

$$c = r\bar{A} + \tilde{w}h - \dot{\bar{A}}.$$

There are several cases worth considering.

(i) The worst case from the individual's point of view is that in which the credit limit binds and the lender demands repayment of loans so that $\dot{\bar{A}} > 0$. Then the individual has to finance interest repayment and loan repayment from his money earnings. In connection with famines it means that if W has fallen, then after meeting the demands of the lender, there will be little left over for purchases of food. If P has risen instead, it means that the individual will be able to buy only a little of the now more expensive food. (ii) The second-worst case differs from (i) in that the lender may not demand repayment of loans so that $\dot{\bar{A}} = 0$. An alternative explanation for $\dot{\bar{A}} = 0$ is that many farm labourers are not deemed credit-worthy in the first place, so that $\bar{A} = 0 \; \forall \, t$.

Under both cases (i) and (ii) the individual can starve over the interval $[\tau_1, \tau_2]$. Hence, these cases capture the essential nature of famines for they yield a state of starvation as soon as the exchange entitlement drops. Underpinning this instance is a state of poverty, for implicit here is the assumption that rural peasants are normally at or just above subsistence level. Since this state of affairs is so well documented it is acceptable to go along with the assumption.

(iii) In this case, the individual's assets equal $\bar{A}$ but he is able to supplement consumption by borrowing, $\dot{\bar{A}} < 0$. One way this can happen is if the lender adheres to the rule $\bar{A} = \alpha \tilde{w}h$ and the individual increases work effort. Of course, working harder raises consumption more directly by raising $\tilde{w}h$.

(iv) The individual may have positive assets which he can run down to supplement consumption until he hits the credit limit. By eating into his capital, the individual may be able to prevent starvation. The individual has to forsake long-term planning and concentrate on instantaneous survival.

For case (iv) to be applicable to famines we need to consider instances in which those most affected by famines have some initial capital. Therefore, consider the example of the nomadic herdsmen of the Sahel who raise livestock and take it from one place to another for grazing. They regularly sell dairy products and occasionally sell cattle to buy grain from farmers. A drought could result in a decline in the renewable dairy-product output and also a decline in cattle output in terms of weight. If, in addition, the relative price of grain also rises, then the herdsmen suffer a real loss in exchange entitlements. Then the herdsmen are doubly vulnerable to starvation. Given the non-existence of credit markets, the herdsmen have no option but to eat into their livestock capital in order to avert starvation. Thus, in effect, they eat the seed-corn that would have generated future renewable output of dairy products.

Returning to the farm labourer–farmer example, it turns out that a few of the farm labourers have a little land and a couple of plough cattle. A famine would then result in a transfer of these assets from the farm labourers to farmers and larger landowners. Ghose (1982) documents some such evidence of transfers. He notes that in the aftermath of the Bengal famine of 1943, there was an increase both in landlessness and in inequality of the ownership distribution of land. The farm labourers who also owned little land were also those who suffered the worst losses. He documents similar observations concerning the loss of plough cattle. There was, then, a permanent increase in the inequality of distribution of productive assets resulting from temporary phenomenon of a famine.

It is worth summarizing the argument that famines may have a market explanation as opposed to a supply explanation. To start with, there is a distribution of exchange entitlements. Next, suppose that there is an exogenous shock such that relative prices and hence exchange entitlements are altered in such a way that those who have zero or low wealth and cannot borrow are the ones to be adversely affected. In the beginning, they may make up for the shortage in their purchasing power by running down whatever assets they may own. This is necessary to prevent starvation because the rural poor are usually near subsistence level. But, after that, malnutrition ensues and then starvation. It is worth emphasizing that there are usually two permanent consequences of a temporary famine: (a) redistribution of productive assets and (b) death. These consequences have a market explanation in that they emanate from a relative price change. By way of contrast, an absolute shortage of food would be a supply explanation.

Given the seriousness of famines, it is worth risking a brief discussion of policy. One solution would be to establish village-level grain reserves as an insurance against local crop failure. When localized famine is imminent, grain prices will rise and livestock prices will collapse. One way of pre-empting famine when such signs appear is to simply run down the reserves by increasing the purchasing power in the region by granting credit. This would help stabilize the price of grain and prevent, say, herdsmen from eating into their livestock capital.

One implication of the consequences of famines can be carried over to a situation that often occurs in industrialized economies. Often, in such economies, the process of economic growth is accompanied by structural changes. Some old industries are phased out and newer ones emerge. Such a change is accompanied by human capital becoming obsolete so that its productivity declines. One can think of this as a decline in the exchange entitlement of such labour. Like the herdsman in the Sahel, such an individual may have to run down his assets in order to retrain, a task which may not be worthwhile if his assets are meagre, he has limited access to credit, and there is considerable retraining involved. One way to check this out would be to examine people's occupations, a crude measure of human capital, both before and after a structural change. For instance, Nickell (1982) reports that each lengthy spell of unemployment which an individual suffers is associated with a significant fall in his position in the occupation hierarchy of some 3–6%. Of course, the reason for unemployment in Nickell's data set is unknown and there are many additional variables we would wish to hold constant. But although the empirical evidence that he reports may not quite match the experiment we have in mind, the method of investigation that we have outlined may be worth pursuing further.

Self-Employment

Self-employment has been receiving a great deal of attention recently. There are many reasons for this renewed interest, but perhaps the most important follows from the fact that self-employment is an alternative to paid employment and thereby broadens the choice facing both the potential entrant to the labour market and the unemployed. There are, of course, several important features of self-employment that distinguish it from paid employment, and it is worth considering them briefly. First, self-employment is generally regarded as being more risky than paid employment and, in fact, data sets show that the coefficient of variation of self-employment earnings is over three times that for paid employment (e.g. General Household Surveys for the UK). If individuals differ in their attitude to risk then, *ceteris paribus*, a less risk-averse individual is more likely to choose self-employment. Another important consideration in making a choice between self-employment and paid employment is the nature of the work involved. Two of the attractions of self-employment are thought to be flexibility associated with hours worked and the independence entailed. On the other hand, self-employment usually implies longer hours and greater responsibility so that it can be physically and mentally more demanding. Third, a self-employed person does better if he has a certain type of ability, call it entrepreneurial ability, which includes things like having good marketable ideas, knowledge of market gaps, managerial ability and so on.

However, the idea in this section is not to provide a comprehensive analysis of the self-employment decision but instead to see the way in which the method of analysis of the monograph can be applied to the topic of self-employment/paid-employment choice. Therefore, in what follows, we shall abstract from the above three considerations in order to concentrate on start-up capital. Self-employment usually requires substantial 'front-end' financial investment for inventories, equipment, or working capital. Start-up capital may be financed from gifts and inheritance, and it may also be patiently accumulated. Two other sources are loans and redundancy payments and we shall emphasize these in the following analysis. Consider, then, an individual who faces two options: employment or self-employment. The individual maximizes

$$V^i \equiv \int_0^T e^{-\rho t} U(c) \, dt, \qquad i = e, se,$$

where e denotes paid-employment and se denotes self-employment. Therefore, the objective function does not change with the employment status. Rather, the differences are captured in the constraints.

Employment option

The dynamic constraint in the employment option is the usual one:

$$\dot{A} = rA + y - c, \qquad A(0) = A_0, \text{ given} \qquad A(T) \geqslant 0.$$

We shall assume that the proportion of time devoted to work, denoted by h, is job-entailed and also that the individual may be unemployed. Then,

$$y(t) = \begin{cases} w(t)\bar{h}(t), & \text{if employed,} \\ b(t), & \text{if unemployed,} \end{cases}$$

where w is the wage rate per unit of time worked and b stands for unemployment benefits.

The Lagrangian for the problem is

$$L = U(c) + \lambda(rA + y - c)$$

and the necessary conditions for a maximum are

$$U_c = \lambda,$$
$$\dot{\lambda} = \lambda(\rho - r).$$

Assuming non-satiation so that $A(T) = 0$ and that the utility function has the simple form: $U(c) = \ln c + \text{constant}$, we can use the first-order conditions to derive

$$c(t) = c(0)e^{(r-\rho)t}$$

where

$$c(0) = \frac{\rho\left[\int_0^T y(t)e^{-rt}\,dt + A_0\right]}{[1 - e^{-\rho T}]} \equiv \frac{\rho\,[\text{PVY} + A_0]}{[1 - e^{-\rho T}]}.$$

It can then be written that

$$c(t) = c(0)(A_0, \text{PVY}, r, \rho, T)e^{(r-\rho)t}.$$

Since either an increase in A_0 or in PVY increases lifetime budget, it can be deduced in a straightforward manner that

$$\frac{\partial c(t)}{\partial A_0} = \frac{\partial c(0)e^{(r-\rho)t}}{\partial A_0} > 0, \qquad \frac{\partial c(t)}{\partial \text{PVY}} = \frac{\partial c(0)e^{(r-\rho)t}}{\partial \text{PVY}} > 0.$$

Turning to a change in the interest rate, $\partial c(0)/\partial r$ is indeterminate in sign, given opposite-signed income and substitution effects. However, if we assume that the individual is always a lender, then his lifetime budget increases so that total consumption over life will increase. We would then write the indirect utility function as,

$$V^e = V^e(A_0, \text{PVY}, r, \rho, T), \quad \frac{\partial V^e}{\partial A_0} > 0, \qquad \frac{\partial V^e}{\partial \text{PVY}} > 0, \qquad \frac{\partial V^e}{\partial r} > 0.$$

Self-employment option

Turning now to the self-employment option, assume that the enterprise can produce output Q, which requires the input of capital K. A functional form often used in the literature is $Q = \theta K^\alpha \varepsilon$, where θ is an index of entrepreneurial ability, ε is a log-normal disturbance, and $0 < \alpha < 1$ is a parameter of the production function. To keep matters simple, assume that the self-employed can arrange to rent capital K but that such an arrangement incurs transactions costs, $\gamma K, 0 < \gamma < 1$. The transactions costs are sunk costs, like an entrance fee to join a club. To keep matters simple, we shall assume that the self-employed do not add to the capital after the enterprise is under way. This is unrealistic but enables us to focus on the essentials without getting bogged down in accumulation specifications and the timing of switching into self-employment. But, at some stage, an extension in this direction is worth thinking about. On becoming self-employed, the individual's assets change discretely to $A - \gamma K \equiv a$. The dynamic constraint can be written as

$$\dot{a} = ra + Q(K) - rK - c, \qquad a_0 = A_0 - \gamma K, \qquad a_T \geqslant 0, \qquad a \geqslant \bar{a},$$

$\bar{a}$ being the credit limit. If $a < 0$, then ra is interest payment on personal loan and rK is interest payment on commercial loan. The capital constraint, $a \geqslant \bar{a}$, captures the feature that capital markets may provide too little capital to the self-employed, perhaps because of moral hazard and adverse selection problems.

The Lagrangian for the problem is

$$L = U(c) + \lambda(ra + Q(K) - rK - c) + \mu(a - \bar{a})$$

and the necessary conditions for an optimum are

$$U_c = \lambda, \qquad \dot{\lambda} = \lambda(\rho - r) - \mu, \qquad \mu \geqslant 0, \qquad \mu(a - \bar{a}) = 0.$$

If the credit constraint binds ($\mu > 0$, $a = \bar{a}$) and assuming for simplicity that $\dot{a} = 0$, consumption is given by

$$c = Q(K) - rK + r\bar{a}.$$

The indirect utility functional may be written as

$$V^{se} = V^{se}(A_0, \bar{a}, r, \rho, T), \qquad \frac{\partial V^{se}}{\partial A_0} > 0, \qquad \frac{\partial V^{se}}{\partial r} < 0.$$

The positive sign of $\partial V^{se}/\partial A_0$ comes about in a straightforward way since an increase in the overall budget must make the individual better off, given non-satiation. $\partial V^{se}/\partial r < 0$ is also straightforward to derive if it is assumed that when self-employed, the individual is always a borrower. Then, an increase in the interest rate reduces the overall budget and makes him worse off. The clear-cut nature of this result would dissolve if the individual, when self-employed, saved for some interval in life.

Employment/self-employment choice

We now examine the choice between employment and self-employment. To make the exposition easier, think of the individual at the margin, $V^{se} = V^e$.

Self-employment propensity and interest rate
First consider an increase in the interest rate, r. Recall that, if we maintain that when employed the individual is always a saver (so that $\partial V^e/\partial r > 0$) and when self-employed always a borrower (so that $\partial V^{se}/\partial r < 0$), then clearly $\partial(V^{se} - V^e)/\partial r < 0$, implying that an increase in the interest rate reduces the attractiveness of self-employment as opposed to employment. This result, based on strong assumptions, may not hold empirically since both the employee population and the self-employed population contain a mix of savers and borrowers. However, if switching from employment to

self-employment entails some capital investment, then proportionately more self-employment in a sample will be borrowers, so that $\partial(V^{se} - V^e)/\partial r < 0$ can be expected to hold in the data.

Self-employment propensity and initial assets
Turning to an increase in initial assets, A_0, we have the two derivatives: $\partial V^{se}/\partial A_0 > 0$ and $\partial V^e/\partial A_0 > 0$. However, there is a reason to think that $\partial V^{se}/\partial A_0$ is the larger of the two. Suppose in the employee option the individual is on the lending side of the credit market and in the self-employment option on the borrowing side and credit constrained. Then a slight increase in initial assets will raise consumption in both options but the utility gain in the self-employment option will be greater because of constrained consumption. In such a scenario we would expect $\partial(V^{se} - V^e)/\partial A_0 > 0$. Although it may appear that there is a great deal of simplification involved here, the argument goes though because self-employment involves capital investment in our model and hence the self-employed are more likely to be on the borrowing side of the credit market and, hence, more likely to be credit-constrained. Credit constraints can therefore form a 'barrier' to self-employment. An employee may switch to self-employment if only he can get his hands on enough capital. If credit markets are imperfect, however, then only the wealthy in such a class of otherwise similar individuals are likely to become self-employed.

Self-employment propensity and unemployment
Consider the marginal individual who chooses employment by tossing a coin, and suppose he then becomes unexpectedly unemployed. His current earnings, y, then get replaced by unemployment benefit, b, and he may also have to revise his future employee-earnings expectations downwards. Hence, his PVY falls so that, recalling $\partial V^e/\partial PVY > 0$, employment becomes less attractive. On the other hand, at the micro analytical level, V^{se} is unchanged. Hence $\partial(V^{se} - V^e)/\partial PVY < 0$ and we expect more unemployment to be associated with a greater tendency to self-employment. In this scenario, although the individual may choose self-employment, he prefers it over unemployment, but not over employment. Since he cannot find a job, his opportunity set shrinks and he chooses 'the lesser of the two evils'. It is in this sense that he gets 'pushed' into self-employment. If those who are prone to unemployment are also ill-equipped at self-employment, then the push may not be strong enough.

Self-employment propensity and redundancy payment
Having touched upon the 'barrier' to self-employment earlier on, it should be plausible to take it that the 'push' may not also be strong enough for

the intra-marginal employee who faces a severe credit constraint but who may be talented at self-employment. On the other hand, if unemployment is accompanied by redundancy payment, then although it will mitigate the decline in net worth accompanying unemployment, it will also erode the credit 'barrier'. We would then expect self-employment and redundancy payments to go together.

Evidence

The above capital-theoretic approach to employment/self-employment choice rests on binding credit constraints. Now if credit constraints are a permanent feature of the British economy, then the set of variables which we have isolated forms a long-run relationship. To estimate and test for the existence of such an equilibrium using time-series data, we have to take recourse to co-integration methods. The theory of co-integrated variables (Granger, 1986; Granger and Engle, 1987) allows the direct estimation and testing of the existence of the equilibrium relationship implied by economic theory.

In fact, Robson and Shah (1990) have utilized UK time-series data to examine the existence of the hypothetical relationship using co-integration techniques. They find that the set of variables forming the hypothesized relationship does form a co-integrating vector in the UK time-series data. The estimated equilibrium relationship also yields the following details.

(a) An increase in the real interest rate reduces self-employment. Typically, interest charges are cost items for geared self-employed, and for the credit-constrained self-employed an increase in such costs means a reduction in consumption.
(b) An increase in liquid assets raises self-employment. With binding constraints, wealth becomes an important determinant of self-employment.
(c) An increase in the unemployment–vacancies ratio increases self-employment, but the elasticity is negligible. Perhaps many of those who are prone to unemployment do not regard themselves as budding entrepreneurs.
(d) An increase in unemployment accompanied by redundancy payment increases self-employment further. Therefore, within the class of the unemployed, the 'push' into self-employment needs to be accompanied by an increase in wealth to surmount the 'credit barrier' to self-employment.

It is quite remarkable that the evidence accords with the theoretical predictions. It is remarkable because co-integration may be interpreted as a long-run relationship which holds except for a stationary disturbance term.

Relative Deprivation

The term 'deprivation' really means multi-dimensional poverty. Usually, an individual is understood to be deprived if, in addition to low earnings, he has poor housing, suffers a polluted environment, his working conditions are poor, his health is bad, and so on. An individual is relatively deprived if he does worse than the norm in the society on these multi-dimensional attributes. Common among sociologists, however, is another idea, that of 'social deprivation'. Its introduction to economists owes a lot to the work carried out by Townsend (1979) who surveyed the life-style of individuals and families living in the UK. Included in the survey were a dozen questions meant to measure activities, events, and so on (e.g. going on an annual holiday) which individuals normally carry out in society. Those who did not carry out the majority of these activities were classified as relatively deprived. Townsend's contribution was to make a connection between an unweighted index of relative deprivation and income. Specifically, he claimed to have identified a threshold level of income, 1.4 times the average social-benefits level, below which an individual was deprived. The either/or nature of this threshold meant that, just below the threshold, individuals suddenly stopped participating in social activities. It was the possibility of the existence of such a threshold that caught the attention of economists.

Townsend's work was scrutinized by both empiricists and theorists. Applied economists were uncomfortable with the list of twelve questions selected for measuring relative deprivation since a few of these were on activities not carried out by the majority in the sample (e.g. having a regular cooked breakfast). Moreover, some of the questions appeared to be of minor importance for relative deprivation (e.g. 'Do children in the family have birthday parties?'). Also, Townsend simply carried out a bivariate correlation between his relative-deprivation index and income, and so did not control for other factors such as tastes. Yet some of his questions were taste-based (e.g. 'Do you have a Sunday joint?'). More generally, there can be reasons other than income which could imply deprivation. In fact, Desai and Shah (1988) carried out a multivariate logit regression analysis in which the probability of each event was 'explained' by health status, family composition, education and wealth, as well as income. The most significant finding was that wealth was the most important determinant of activities, the *ceteris paribus* relationship being positive. Moreover, for several of the activities, income was not a significant determinant. It appears that the relative-deprivation threshold, if it exists, is more likely to be at some critical level of wealth.

For the theorist, the interesting question is the existence of the relative deprivation threshold. How can a particular level of wealth be significant? If all commodities were perfectly divisible and if the instantaneous utility function was differentiable, strictly concave and identical for all individuals, then consumption and wealth would have a smooth, continuous relationship. There is nothing here that gives a particular level of wealth any significance. However, suppose that there is an indivisible good z that takes the values 0 or 1, and let the instantaneous utility function be written as $U(c, z)$. As before, c is the continuously divisible aggregate consumption good whose price is normalized to one. Let p denote the price of z. Now consider the problem in which the individual maximizes

$$\int_0^T e^{-\rho t} U(c, z)\, dt$$

subject to

$$\int_0^T c(t) e^{-\rho t}\, dt + pz = \int_0^T e^{-\rho t} y(t)\, dt + A_0 \equiv \text{NW}.$$

If at $t = 0$ the individual purchases z then the indirect utility functional can be written as $V(\text{NW} - p, 1)$ and as $V(\text{NW}, 0)$ if he does not purchase z. Note that as yet a credit limit has not been brought into the problem, something that we shall consider after some preliminary analysis. Also note that both $V(\text{NW} - p, 1)$ and $V(\text{NW}, 0)$ are strictly concave. At low levels of net worth, say $\text{NW} < \text{NW}^*$, there is greater utility from devoting resources to consumption of c than from purchasing z so that $V(\text{NW}, 0) > V(\text{NW} - p, 1)$. At NW^*, utilities from the two alternatives are equal, $V(\text{NW}, 0) = V(\text{NW} - p, 1)$ so that the individual is indifferent between purchasing and not purchasing z. Finally, at high values of net worth, $\text{NW} > \text{NW}^*$, $V(\text{NW}, 0) < V(\text{NW} - p, 1)$ so that the individual purchases z at price p and spends the rest, $\text{NW} - p$, on consumption of c. The induced utility-of-net-worth function is sketched in Figure 9.1. It has a kink at NW^* which renders it non-concave. Note that the induced utility-of-net-worth function rises more steeply above the kink. This is because when some of the net worth is used up to purchase z, U_c becomes larger. As long as the two $V(\cdot)$ are strictly concave in NW, $V(\text{NW}, 0) > V(\text{NW} - p) \,\forall\, \text{NW} < \text{NW}^*$, $V(\text{NW}, 0) < V(\text{NW} - p, 1) \,\forall\, \text{NW} > \text{NW}^*$ and $p > 0$, there will result a kink in the induced utility-of-net-worth function, i.e. for any given individual the deprivation threshold is the level NW^* below which he chooses not to purchase z. The demand-for-z, $z(\text{NW})$ is such that

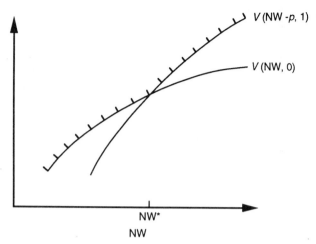

Figure 9.1 *Indirect utility functions.*

$z = 0 \; \forall \, NW < NW^*$ and $z = 1 \; \forall \, NW > NW^*$ and   it   is   sketched   in Figure 9.2.

Using the device of a lumpy good, we have thus obtained a rationale for the concept of deprivation threshold with the outcome that less wealthy individuals choose not to acquire z whereas wealthy individuals do. The intuitive argument is simple and rests on diminishing marginal utility of consuming c. If z is acquired, perhaps financed by borrowing, there is

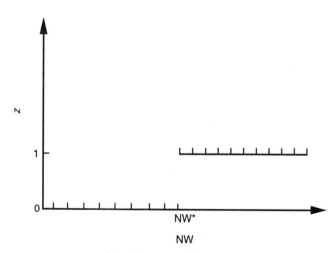

Figure 9.2 *The demand function for z.*

less NW left over for c. It then depends on the cost of acquiring z, that is, on p, and the size of NW, but given that U_c decreases with c, it may not be welfare-maximizing for the less wealthy to acquire z.

However, so far nothing in the argument has depended on credit constraints. It turns out that the effect of credit constraints is to further divide individuals who would have chosen to acquire z at $t = 0$ in the absence of credit constraints, into those that still do and those who may do so but at a later stage in life. The point of credit constraints is that either $A_0 - \bar{A} < pz$ so that it is impossible to acquire z at $t = 0$ or that after acquiring z there is little left over for initial consumption so that it is optimal for the individual to postpone the acquisition of z perhaps indefinitely. So the effect of credit constraints is to bring into the picture the category of individuals who are deprived for part of their lives – something which has been left out in the literature.

All this can be worked out formally but, before making the investment in formal analysis, we must examine the nature of z more closely for its plausibility. Actually, the good z can be either an indivisible good or a divisible good that entails a minimum resource cost (see Lewis and Ulph, 1988). As an example of the former, consider a car. While cars may be available at a whole range of different qualities and prices, there is an inescapable minimum resource cost of owning and running a car (maintenance, taxation charges, etc.). Then the price at which a car is available is bounded away from zero. As an example of the other type of z, consider holidays. Holidays are divisible but most people take a holiday of some minimum duration and/or distance from home. Here the technology for getting access to holidays has some increasing returns that operate like an indivisibility.

There may be quite a few divisible commodities with associated increasing returns. Suppose we focus on z_i, $i =$ health, education, housing; and suppose individuals perceive a range, $(0, \bar{z}_i)$, over which there are increasing returns. Then if prices, p_i, are fixed we can work out a prerequisite level of investment,

$$A^* = \sum_{i=1}^{3} p_i \bar{z}_i.$$

Those who make the investment achieve the needs and are non-deprived. This is probably what Sen (1983) has in mind when he views poverty as deprivation with respect to certain basic needs or capabilities, where it requires expenditure of a certain minimum amount to achieve these capabilities. If z_i are interpreted as social interaction goods such as holidays then it corresponds to what Townsend (1979) has in mind when he sees poverty as the inability to participate in certain forms of social interaction, where again it requires the outlay of some minimum amount in order to be able to participate. Therefore, we think that the good z is simply a lump-sum entrance fee which needs to be paid before functioning or participating in society.

One fruitful application of the above concept of z and the preceding analysis can be made to an identifiable section of a society. For example, consider why blacks appear not to participate in American society. Alternatively stated, consider why the life-styles of the white majority and the black minority differ considerably. One could test the explanation that the whites have support of more and better-quality education, access to superior health-care and owner-occupied housing in suburbia. First, one would examine simple averages of these investments and then work out the expenditure entailed for each group. The difference between the two expenditures should give an idea of the wealth the blacks would require in order to cross the threshold from one life-style to another.

Conclusion

In this chapter, four topics in economics have been considered to which the effects of credit constraints within a life-cycle setting can be applied. The results are briefly summarized as follows.

(1) There is some evidence that an increase in human capital raises consumption efficiency. If so, then ignoring this effect means that the value of human capital is underestimated. Then the earnings premium required for an individual to be indifferent between two earnings profiles or between primary- and secondary-sector jobs is overestimated.

(2) In a less developed, agricultural economy, suppose there is an exogenous shock such that relative prices and hence exchange entitlements are altered in such a way that those who have zero or low wealth and cannot borrow are the ones to be adversely affected. In the beginning, they may be able to smooth out consumption by running down whatever assets they may own. This initially prevents starvation of the rural poor who are usually near subsistence level. But after that, malnutrition ensues, and then starvation. One other consequence is that there takes place a redistribution of productive assets from the poor to the rich.

(3) Becoming self-employed requires set-up capital. This requirement acts like an entrance fee to a club. Then access to capital becomes an important determinant of self-employment. There are then four testable implications: (i) an increase in the interest rate, (ii) a decrease in initial assets, (iii) a reduction in unemployment, and (iv) a decrease in redundancy payment all decrease the propensity to self-employment. There is also evidence in support of these predictions.

(4) If, because of increasing returns, a minimum non-negative outlay on investment goods is required, then we can obtain a rationale for the concept of a deprivation threshold with the outcome that less wealthy individuals choose not to invest whereas wealthy individuals do. Here, the effect of credit constraints is to cause some investors to postpone investment.

Although the applications have been brief, they should have demonstrated that our understanding of each topic can be advanced by taking the possibility of binding credit constraints into consideration. There should also be considerable scope for research here. Moreover, there are other topics to which the effects of credit constraints within a life-cycle setting may be productively applied. Topics that immediately come to mind are: social-security wealth, the timing of bequests, and the peasant–landlord relationship in less developed countries. But there are more.

CHAPTER **10**

Conclusion

This monograph has featured intertemporal individual behaviour, thereby giving time a central role in the analysis. It has also incorporated more realistic assumptions which tally with optimizing behaviour.

Mathematical Method

All this has influenced the choice of analytical tools. As we have assumed throughout that point expectations are held with subjective certainty, explicit dynamic-programming techniques are not employed. Instead we have used optimal control theory in preference to the calculus of variations. Note that any problem which can be tackled by employing optimal control techniques is also capable of being treated by calculus of variations. However, the latter technique can be laborious whereas the ease and elegance with which the former method can be applied to inequality constraints explains our preference for it despite the intuitive appeal of the calculus of variations.

The Argument

The primary task of this monograph has been to trace out the consequences of credit constraints. These consequences can be structured into a long argument which is presented in a stepwise fashion below.

1 The microeconomics of the borrowing–lending relationship implies that in order to minimize defaults, lenders ration out funds and the allocation is according to the individual's characteristics, including earned income.

2 As a result, the utility-maximizing individual who plans consumption over life faces a sequence of debt limits.

3 Utility maximization yields an optimal time-shape for the consumption profile. In particular, given concavity, the individual will wish to smooth out consumption over life.

4 This means borrowing early on in life, if for example, the individual faces a steep earnings profile.

5 But if the credit constraint binds and the individual is unable to borrow then he is not able to trade-off current consumption for future consumption satisfactorily.

6 As a result, during a phase in his life, the shape of the earnings profile will influence the shape of the consumption profile. Current consumption will be strongly related to current earnings.

7 The comparative dynamics exercises show that the extent to which an individual is credit-constrained will depend on parameters like initial assets. Less initial assets means that the credit constraint will bind more stringently.

8 The result that, during the constrained phase changes in current earnings induce changes in current consumption and changes in future earnings do not affect current consumption, can be applied to a wide range of policy issues.

9 Returning to point 6, since the shape of the earnings profile influences the shape of the consumption profile, it also influences welfare. A steeper earnings profile holding present-value earnings constant means more constrained initial consumption and hence lower welfare.

10 Therefore, as both the present value and the shape of the earnings profile affect welfare, the individual will take both these features into account when making an earnings-profile choice in the first place.

11 The credit-constrained individual will consider the trade-off between the shape of an earnings profile and its present value and may choose a flatter earnings profile with a lower present value which would increase his consumption early on in life arising from greater initial earnings and a higher debt limit.

12 But the less severely an individual is credit-constrained, the less incentive there is for him to choose a given steeper earnings profile with lower present-value earnings. In particular, individuals with greater initial assets are less severely credit-constrained.

13 In fact there is a level of initial assets, A_0^*, at which the individual is indifferent between the two earnings profiles. At $A_0 < A_0^*$ he chooses the flat profile and at $A_0 > A_0^*$ he chooses the steep one.

14 It follows that large variations in present-value earnings can result from a small variation in initial assets around the threshold level, A_0^*.

15 If there are many earnings profiles differing in steepness and present-value earnings and ordered such that those with greater present-value earnings are steeper, then an increase in initial assets will be associated with step increases in present-value earnings.

16 Thus greater initial assets will be associated with greater present-value earnings, implying that absolute inequality in net worth will increase with initial assets.

17 Although the direct utility function is concave, the indirect utility function is not concave in A_0 if credit constraints bind and the individual faces a discrete choice set of earnings profiles. Then the shape of the indirect utility function around A_0^* implies that for an equal change in A_0, the individual's gain in utility exceeds the loss, thus providing him with an incentive to gamble.

18 But as the level of inheritance, A_0, received by the $(i + 1)$th generation depends on the bequests, A_T, made by the ith generation, then by introducing concern for the heir's welfare bequests may be treated as choice-determined so that the inheritance received is choice-determined as well. All the intragenerational consequences of credit constraints may then be re-examined to see if there are any changes.

19 First, since a tightening of the credit limit increases the marginal utility of bequests relative to the marginal utility of terminal consumption, parents of a dynasty facing more severe credit constraints bequeath more, thereby weakening the effectiveness of credit limits for their heirs.

20 However, if earnings choice is allowed for, then it is possible that such parents bequeath less because they choose a flatter earnings profile with less present-value earnings and therefore have less resources from which to bequeath.

21 But the very perception that the dynasty can be locked into choosing the flat earnings profile with less present-value earnings creates an additional incentive for bequests which could enable a dynasty to break out from a low-level earnings trap: the parents choose a lower present-value earnings profile. The subsequent generations also choose the higher present-value earnings profile because such a profile implies greater

bequests and also a more severe binding of credit limits, further implying greater bequests.

22 In fact, it can be shown that if the parameters facing a given dynasty are unchanged then the dynasty is characterized by every generation either (i) opting for the steep-earnings-profile option and passing on wealth which is greater than the threshold level or (ii) opting for the flat-earnings profile option and passing on wealth which is less than the threshold level.

23 Although a dynasty which starts with low wealth may be able to bequeath its way out of the flat-earnings-profile option, it seems most likely that it will get locked into dynastic poverty in the absence of any favourable exogenous shocks. A tight lock is placed by low wealth allied to credit constraints and discrete alternatives.

24 The binding of credit constraints may be rendered less effective by allowing for work–leisure choice. Since the shape of the earnings profile depends on the shape of the product of the wage rate and work, by working harder, the shape might be altered, borrowing reduced and greater credit made available.

25 In fact, if it is assumed that the wage profile is given and that work is an unconstrained choice variable, the individual is able to weaken the impact of credit constraints on consumption by bearing greater displeasure of work.

26 However, there is good evidence that work is job-entailed so that an individual may face binding work constraints. In that case, the above-mentioned mitigation of the impact of credit constraints cancels out. It depends on the shape of the work-constraint profile.

27 If the shape of the work-constraint profile is job-entailed then it is better to view work choice as job choice. Then by distinguishing jobs by training, we can introduce a work–training trade-off into the analysis in place of work–leisure trade-off.

28 If we assume that there are only two types of jobs – primary-sector jobs that entail a great deal of training and secondary-sector jobs that provide little or no training – then in our model of individual behaviour there will be choice over these two job types subject to credit constraints.

29 It turns out that this model is consistent with an equilibrium labour market structure in which there are these two sectors. It is also consistent with the econometric evidence at hand.

30 Making use of the concept of the threshold level of initial wealth, the model can be extended to explain why some dynasties that begin with zero or little wealth can get locked into secondary-sector employment.

31 Pursuing the theme of extending the implication of credit constraints in a systematic way, the model is next extended by making a distinction

between durables and non-durables. After all, acquisition, holding and disposition of durables is likely to be sensitive to credit constraints.

32 To simplify matters, only housing is incorporated into the model so that the individual can be viewed as holding a portfolio consisting of housing equity and financial assets.

33 It turns out that those who are severely credit-constrained may hold only financial assets whereas others may hold a portfolio consisting of both financial and housing assets.

34 But, given the character of the housing market which implies that the price of a unit of housing services varies with housing tenure, those who do not hold housing equity have, in fact, chosen to acquire more expensive housing.

35 It also follows that, given the same earnings profile, it is the less wealthy individuals who are more likely to choose to rent and hence purchase the same housing services more expensively.

36 But just as the possibility of constrained early consumption influences the choice of earnings profile, the possibility of expensive housing and hence a reduced aggregate consumption bundle also exerts an influence on earnings-profile choice.

37 It is then possible to have two extremes. At one end, an individual with a very low initial wealth and facing stringent credit constraints will earn less and pay more for the same consumption bundle. At the other end, an individual with enough wealth will earn more and pay less for the same consumption bundle.

We have concentrated on obtaining distributional results by employing comparative statics methods. This is accomplished by placing our model of individual behaviour in the setting of an economy in equilibrium. If the setting is unchanged then the comparative statics analysis can be employed in order to obtain results which are distributional in character provided the variables for the analysis are appropriately chosen. Thus, instead of analysing changes in the rate of interest, for instance, we have concentrated on individual characteristics such as initial assets.

Insights

One of the insights offered by the analysis is that credit constraints cause individual characteristics to matter for allocation of resources. In a world without credit constraints, allocation of credit is according to the price mechanism, that is, interest rate, and therefore the identity of the individual has no bearing on credit allocation. However, in a world in which the market fails to allocate credit by the interest-rate mechanism and there is effective rationing as demand exceeds supply, non-price characteristics have to be employed. Of course, these characteristics in turn affect allocation of other economic resources. To take an example, in a world without credit constraints the subjective discount rate does not matter in making choices over earnings profiles of varying degrees of steepness. But in a world with credit constraints, those with high discount rates are more likely to choose a flatter earnings profile carrying less present-value earnings.

The partnership of wealth and credit constraints

The individual characteristic that we have singled out is initial wealth. We have concluded that wealth confers a pecuniary advantage. In conferring this advantage, wealth and credit constraints work in partnership. To see this, consider the case in which individuals differ by wealth but credit markets are perfect. Then the consumption levels will vary over individuals but not the time-shape of the consumption profile. Nor will investment levels vary over individuals, and hence no individual will suffer a pecuniary disadvantage. Moreover, in the case in which everyone had great wealth there would be no effective credit-rationing and hence no inequality of pecuniary advantage. However, in the case in which there is unequal wealth and the same credit limits, there results unequal credit-rationing which implies unequal opportunity sets over individuals. This affects the choice of consumption over life such that those individuals who are more effectively credit-constrained choose a more uneven consumption profile. Such consumption losses reduce their lifetime welfare compared to a situation in which there is less effective credit-rationing. Even then, there need not result an investment disadvantage since investment can still be financed by making the necessary consumption sacrifices. However, if the consumption sacrifices are deemed heavy, then the individual may mitigate the adverse effect on lifetime welfare by reducing initial investment in human capital. The consumption sacrifices will be more costly to the less wealthy in utility terms if the less wealthy have no better access to credit than the wealthy and the utility function is strictly concave. It is strict concavity which makes a reduction in consumption progressively more painful and an increase in consumption progressively less pleasurable. Differing preference structures may partly explain why Japanese- and Chinese-born Americans invested heavily in education.

The partnership of wealth, credit constraints and discrete choice alternatives

The pecuniary disadvantage can become particularly acute when discrete

alternatives in investment choice are present. This is because the allocation
to an alternative is extremely rapid, and furthermore it is tight, so that it
can persist. For instance, when we consider choice over only two earnings
profiles, one steep and the other flat, all individuals have to allocate themselves to one of the two. With binding credit constraints, individuals have
no incentive to move from one profile to the other. So, any present-value
earnings difference between the two profiles does not get eroded. And, of
course, inequality of net worth will result and persist since the less wealthy
will choose flat profiles that carry less present-value earnings. Does the
tightness and persistence of such polarization endure if wealth is treated as
an object of choice? Actually when bequests are chosen it turns out that
parents bequeath either little or large amounts of wealth. But little wealth
is bequeathed if the child is expected to invest less in earnings and more
wealth is bequeathed if the child is expected to invest more in earnings. We
then have polarization in wealth and earnings that persists. In fact, such
polarization is attained within two generations and is tight in the sense that
the individual has to accumulate a discrete amount of wealth in order to
heave out from one extreme to the other.

Dynastic poverty

The results on acuteness, tightness and persistence of polarization that we
have obtained have enabled us to say something new and different about
poverty principally because the framework allows an analysis of choice and
lifetime poverty. Indeed, provided that the external environment is
undisturbed, we have an explanation for the transmission and persistence
of poverty from one generation to another. Our definition of dynastic
poverty is such that it implies that a dynasty is better off poor than rich,
given the opportunity set facing it. There is the opportunity to move out of
poverty but the sacrifices are too great to make it worthwhile, so poverty
is chosen. Dynastic poverty is then a permanent feature of an economy in
the sense that given no external disturbances, some dynasties choose
poverty. The result rests on the interaction between choice and unequal
intertemporal opportunity sets of a current generation arising from credit-
market imperfections, which provides no incentive for current generations
to improve the opportunity sets of future generations.

Within this dynastic framework, the analysis also encompasses outcomes
which are normally thought to lie outside mainstream theory. An example
is dual labour markets. The existing literature on dual labour markets posits
two types of jobs but the problem with the literature is that the allocation
between the two types is not specified, at least not in a non-arbitrary way.

Alternatively stated, the theoretical model is not satisfactorily closed. On the other hand, the analysis of this monograph provides a neat way of closing the model once a distribution of credit constraints is postulated over individuals. Then those facing more effective credit-rationing are more likely to choose secondary-sector jobs. Perhaps this serves as an illustration of the power of the existing neoclassical theory. The theory can be extended to obtain more realistic outcomes without sacrificing the assumption of rational individual behaviour.

The range of polarized outcomes

Like all theoretical economic models, this one is basically simple. But we have extended it by progressively altering the choice set. The result is that the framework has accommodated an outcome of polarization in which some individuals have little wealth, work in the badly paid secondary sector, rent more expensive housing and consume less, whereas others have more wealth, work in the better-paid primary sector, own cheaper housing and consume more. Such polarization also appears capable of being extended to a broader outcome of social deprivation which would rest on the partnership of the distribution of wealth, the distribution of credit constraints and discrete alternatives. However, once we extend the model to more dimensions of deprivation, mixed outcomes also become possible. But the power of the monograph remains since some dynasties choose to locate themselves at the extremes.

Of course, the greater the choice, the richer the outcomes. This is because in order to mitigate the effects of credit constraints individuals are able to adjust choice in some appropriate way. We have seen that the consequences are particularly interesting if there is an investment choice or two. This suggests that were we to allow for, say, investment in health, then the consequences could prove to be interesting. We should obtain mixed outcomes together with polarization. The reason why we have not made extensions in this direction is tractability. Although the basic model around which the economics is organized is quite simple, it has reached the stage where it becomes unmanageable if any more extensions are made. Generally speaking, it is undeniable that economic reality is greatly complicated but, in order to obtain results, theory has to be stylized. So there is admittedly a large gap between the model of this monograph and economic reality and hence practical policy. This raises the awkward question of the usefulness of economic theorizing. The answer probably lies in the power of the theory to pose awkward questions concerning the received economic wisdom and to generate insights. Then upon the results of theory, hunches about reality can be based.

The poverty of minorities

There is another way of looking at the monograph: the way a minority can become trapped in steady-state deprivation. After all, the outcome of polarization in which some individuals are deprived along many dimensions − wealth, earnings, work, housing, education and even social − matches the economic conditions of many minorities such as the blacks in the USA. According to our model, the present economic and social condition of the blacks in the United States is connected to the distribution of wealth and the allocation of credit that prevailed just after the civil war. The average black individual then had zero wealth and has since made relatively little progress compared to the spectacular progress of the white individual. This outcome is consistent with our theory although one cannot obtain a comprehensive picture of the blacks in the USA without referring to discrimination in various aspects of economic and social life. If one is sympathetic to a Rawlsian view (Rawls, 1972) then this becomes an extremely important subject in addition to being an interesting one.

A Final Word

One more paragraph. The fundamental driving force of this monograph is that opportunity sets are unequal. The inequality results when in the interaction between lenders and borrowers the interest-rate mechanism does not work to clear the credit market. To see what unequal opportunity sets imply, examine neoclassical economics. Its main weakness appears to be its neglect of wealth distribution. Here, the price mechanism clears all markets and the outcome is Pareto efficient no matter what the distribution of wealth. Then unequal wealth merely results in unequal consumption. However, we have shown that if we stay within a conventional neoclassical framework but take its logic a few steps further, then there must result market failure in credit in which case not only is the outcome Pareto inefficient, but it is such that there is an accentuation of consumption, investment and welfare if wealth is unequally distributed. So what causes wealth to be unequally distributed? It is history and the unequal use of wealth. Suppose in some distant past there was unequal distribution of wealth. Then the wealthy should have been able to let, via lending institutions, the poor use it for investment purposes. But when it comes to lending against human capital and the like, lenders do not find it worthwhile to perform this task so that the use of wealth remains unequal. Even so, individuals may attempt to acquire wealth by circumventing lenders, such as by gambling. But, as we have seen, such action simply accentuates wealth distribution. The action of gambling for investment purposes suggests that wealth may be a great opportunity for the deprived to break out of the multi-dimensional trap. But as long as credit constraints remain, current wealth distribution and hence history and therefore the systematic element in the distribution of wealth will continue to matter for the distribution of economic prizes.

Bibliography

Altonji, J. G. and Siow, A. (1987) 'Testing the response of consumption to income changes with (noisy) panel data', *Quarterly Journal of Economics*, **102**, 293–328.

Arrow, K. J. (1968), 'Optimal capital policy with irreversible investment', in J. N. Wolfe (ed.) *Value, Capital and Growth*, pp. 1–20, Edinburgh University Press (Edinburgh).

Ashenfelter, O. and Ham, J. (1979) 'Education, unemployment and earnings', *Journal of Political Economy*, **87**, No. 5, Part 2, October, S99–S116.

Atkinson, A. B. (1971) 'Capital taxes, the redistribution of wealth and individual savings', *Review of Economic Studies*, **38**, 209–228.

Barro, R. J. and Grossman H. I. (1976) *Money, Employment and Inflation*, Cambridge University Press (Cambridge).

Becker, G. S. (1975) *Human Capital* (2nd edn), National Bureau of Economic Research, New York.

Becker, G. S. and Tomes, N. (1979) 'An equilibrium theory of the distribution of income and intergenerational mobility', *Journal of Political Economy*, **87**, No. 6, December, 1153–1189.

Bellman, R. and Dreyfus, S. (1962) *Applied Dynamic Programming*, Princeton University Press, Princeton, N.J.

Bernanke, B. S. (1985) 'Adjustment costs, durables, and aggregate consumption', *Journal of Monetary Economics*, **15**, 41–68.

Bevan, D. L. (1979) 'Inheritance and the distribution of wealth', *Economica*, **46**, No. 184, November, 381–402.

Bird, R. C. and Bodkin, R. G. (1965) 'The national service life insurance dividend of 1950 and consumption: a further test of the "strict" permanent income hypothesis', *Journal of Political Economy*, **73**, No. 5, October, 499–515.

Blinder, A. S. (1974) *Toward an Economic Theory of Income Distribution*, The MIT Press (London).

Bliss, C. J. (1975) *Capital Theory and the Distribution of Income*, North-Holland (Amsterdam).

Boczar, G. E. (1978) 'Competition between banks and finance companies: A cross-section study of personal loan debtors', *Journal of Finance*, March, 245–258.

Bodkin, R. G. (1959) 'Windfall income and consumption', *American Economic Review*, **49**, September, 602–614.

Brumberg, R. L. (1956) 'An approximation to the aggregate savings function', *Economic Journal*, **66**, March, 66–72.

Bruno, M. (1967) 'Optimal accumulation in discrete capital models', in K. Shell (ed.) *Essays on the Theory of Optimal Economic Growth*, The MIT Press (London).

Bulow, J. I. and Summers, L. H. (1986) 'A theory of dual labor markets with application to industrial policy, discrimination, and Keynesian unemployment', *Journal of Labour Economics*, **4**, 376–414.

Campbell, J. Y. (1987) 'Does saving anticipate declining labour income? An alternative test of the permanent income hypothesis', *Econometrica*, **55**, 1249–1274.

Clarke, F. H. (1974) 'Necessary conditions for a general control problem', *International Symposium in the Calculus of Variations and Optimal Control*, Mathematical Research Center, University of Wisconsin: Academic Press.

Clarke, F. H. (1975a) 'Maximum principle with differentiability', *Bulletin of American Mathematical Society*, **81**, 1, 219–222.

Clarke, F. H. (1975b) 'The Euler–Lagrange inclusion', *Journal of Differential Equations*, **19**, 1, 80–90.

Cohen, W. J., Haber, W. and Mueller, E. (1960) 'The impact of unemployment in the 1958 recession', *Special Committee on Unemployment Problems*, U.S. Senate, Committee Print, June.

Deaton, A. S. (1972) 'Wealth effects on consumption in a modified life cycle model', *Review of Economic Studies*, **39**, 443–453.

Deaton, A. S. (1987) 'Life-cycle models for consumption: Is the evidence consistent with the theory?' in T. F. Bewley (ed.) *Advances in Econometrics*, Vol. II, North-Holland (Amsterdam).

Desai, M. J. and Shah, A. R. (1988), 'An econometric approach to the measurement of poverty', *Oxford Economic Papers*, **40**, 505–522.

Dickens, W. T. and Lang, K. (1985a) 'A test of dual labour market theory', *American Economic Review*, **75**, 792–805.

Dickens, W. T. and Lang, K. (1985b) 'Testing dual labour market theory: A reconsideration of the evidence', *NBER Working Paper*, No. 1670.

Dickens, W. T. and Lang, K. (1987) 'Where have all the good jobs gone?', in K. Lang and J. Leonard (eds) *Unemployment and the Structure of Labour Markets*, Basil Blackwell (Oxford).

Dickens, W. T. and Lang, K. (1988) 'Labour market segmentation and the union wage premium', *Review of Economics and Statistics*, **70**, 527–530.

Dreyfus, S. E. (1965) *Dynamic Programming and the Calculus of Variations*, Academic Press (New York).

Dynarski, M. and Sheffrin, S. M. (1985) 'Housing purchases and transitory income: A study with panel data', *The Review of Economics and Statistics*, **67**, 195–204.

Fisher, I. (1930) *The Theory of Interest*, Yale University Press (New Haven, Conn.).

Flavin, M. A. (1981) 'The adjustment of consumption to changing expectations about future income', *Journal of Political Economy*, **89**, 974–1009.

Flavin, M. A. (1985) 'Excess sensitivity of consumption to current income: Liquidity constraints or myopia?', *Canadian Journal of Economics*, **17**, 117–136.

Flemming, J. (1973) 'The consumption function when capital markets are imperfect', *Oxford Economic Papers*, **25**, 160–172.

Flemming, J. (1979) 'The effects of earnings inequality, imperfect capital markets, and dynastic altruism of the distribution of wealth in life cycle models', *Economica*, **46**, 363–380.

Friedman, M. (1957) *A Theory of the Consumption Function*, Princeton University Press, for NBER (Princeton, NJ).

Friedman, M. (1960) Comments in *Proceedings of the Conference on Consumption and Saving*, ed. by I. Friend and R. Jones, Philadelphia, Wharton School of Finance and Commerce, University of Pennsylvania.

Ghose, A. K. (1982) 'Food supply and starvation: A study of famines with reference to the Indian Sub-Continent', *Oxford Economic Papers*, July, 368–389.

Granger, C. W. J. (1986) 'Developments in the study of cointegrated economic variables', *Oxford Bulletin of Economics and Statistics*, **48**, 213–227.

Granger, C. W. J. and Engle, R. F. (1987) 'Cointegration and error correction: Representation, estimation and testing', *Econometrica*, **55**, 251–276.

Hadley, G. and Kemp, M. C. (1971) *Variational Methods in Economics*, North-Holland (Amsterdam).

Hall, R. E. (1978) 'Stochastic implications of the life cycle–permanent income hypothesis: Theory and evidence', *Journal of Political Economy*, **86**, 971–987.

Hall, R. E. and Miskin, F. S. (1982) 'The sensitivity of consumption to transitory income: Estimates from panel data on households', *Econometrica*, **50**, 461–481.

Ham, J. (1982) 'Estimation of a labor supply model with censoring due to unemployment and underemployment', *Review of Economic Studies*, **49**, 335–354.

Ham, J. (1986) 'Testing whether unemployment represents life-cycle labor supply behavior', *Review of Economic Studies*, **53**(4), 559–578.

Harberger, A. (1964) 'The measurement of waste', *American Economic Review*, **54**, 57–76.

Hayashi, F. (1982) 'The permanent income hypothesis: Estimation and testing by instrumental variables', *Journal of Political Economy*, **90**, 895–918.

Hayashi, F. (1985a) 'The effect of liquidity constraints on consumption: A cross-sectional analysis', *Quarterly Journal of Economics*, **100**, 183–206.

Hayashi, F. (1985b) 'The permanent income hypothesis and consumption durability: Analysis based on Japanese panel data', *Quarterly Journal of Economics*, **100**, 1083–1113.

Heckman, J. L. (1974) 'Life cycle consumption and labour supply: An explanation of the relationship between income and consumption over the life cycle', *American Economic Review*, **64**, March, 188–194.

Henderson, J. V. and Ioannides, Y. M. (1986) 'Tenure choice and the demand for housing', *Economica*, **53**, No. 210, May, 231–246.

Hestenes, M. R. (1966) *Calculus of Variations and Optimal Control Theory*, Wiley (New York).

Hirschleifer, J. (1958) 'On the theory of optimal investment decisions', *Journal of Political Economy*, 329–352.

Hirshleifer, J. (1970) *Investment, Interest and Capital*, Prentice-Hall (Englewood Cliffs, NJ).

Hutchens, R. (1986) 'Delayed payment contracts and a firm's propensity to hire older workers', *Journal of Labor Economics*, **4**, 439–457.

Hutchens, R. (1987) 'A test of Lazear's theory of delayed payment contracts', *Journal of Labor Economics*, **5**, S153–S170.

Jaffee, D. W. and Russell, T. (1976) 'Imperfect information and credit rationing', *Quarterly Journal of Economics*, **90**, 651–660.

King, M. A. (1980) 'An econometric model of tenure choice and demand for housing as a joint decision', *Journal of Public Economics*, **14**, 137–159.

Kleirman, E. and Ophir, T. (1966) 'The durability of durable goods', *Review of Economic Studies*, **33**, April, 165–178.

Laitner, J. P. (1979) 'Bequests, golden-age capital accumulation and government debt', *Economica*, **46**, No. 184, November, 403–414.

Lazear, E. (1981) 'Agency, earnings profiles, productivity, and hours restrictions', *American Economic Review*, **71**, September, 606–620.

Lee, T. H. (1975) 'More on windfall in income and consumption', *Journal of Political Economy*, **83**, April, 407–418.

Lester, R. A. (1962) *The Economics of Unemployment Compensation*, Princeton University Press, (Princeton, NJ).

Levhari, D. and Sheshinski, E. (1972) 'Lifetime excess burden of a tax', *Journal of Political Economy*, **80**, 139–147.

Levhari, D. and Srinivasan, T. N. (1969) 'Durability of consumption goods: Competition versus monopoly', *American Economic Review*, **59**, March, 102–107.

Lewis, G. and Ulph, D. (1988) 'Poverty, inequality and welfare', *Economic Journal (Supplement)*, **98**, No. 390, March, 117–131.

Lundberg, S. (1985) 'Tied wage–hours offers and the endogeneity of wages', *Review of Economics and Statistics*, **67**, August, 405–410.

Mariger, R. P. (1987) 'A life-cycle consumption model with liquidity constraints: Theory and empirical results', *Econometrica*, **55**, 533–557.

Michael, R. (1987) *The Effect of Education on Efficiency in Consumption* (New York).

Mirrlees, J. A. (1971) 'An exploration in the theory of optimum income taxation', *Review of Economic Studies*, **38**, 175–208.

Modigliani, F. and Ando, A. (1957) 'Tests of the life-cycle hypothesis of savings', *Oxford University Institute of Economics and Statistics Bulletin*, **19**, May, 99–124.

Modigliani, F. and Ando, A. (1963) 'The "life-cycle" hypothesis of savings', *American Economic Review*, **53**, March, 55–84.

Modigliani, F. and Brumberg, R. (1954) 'Utility analysis and consumption function: An interpretation of cross-section data', in K. Kurihara (ed.) *Post-Keynesian Economics*, pp. 388–436, Rutgers University Press (Brunswick, NJ).

Moffitt, R. (1984) 'The estimation of a joint wage–hour labor supply model', *Journal of Labor Economics*, **2**, October, 550–566.

Muellbauer, J. (1983) 'Surprises in the consumption function', *Economic Journal*, **93**, Supplement, 34–49.

Murphy, K. and Topel, R. (1987) 'Unemployment, risk and earnings;

Testing for equalising wage differences in the labor market', in K. Lang and J. Leonard (eds) *Unemployment and the Structure of Labour Markets*, Basil Blackwell (Oxford).

Muth, R. F. (1960) 'The demand for non-farm housing', in A. C. Harberger (ed.) *The Demand for Durable Goods* (Chicago).

Nickell, S. J. (1976) 'Wage structures and quit rates', *International Economic Review*, **17**, No. 1, February, 191–203.

Nickell, S. J. (1982) 'The determinants of occupational success in Britain', *Review of Economic Studies*, **49**, 43–53.

Olsen, E. O. (1969) 'A competitive theory of the housing market', *American Economic Review*, **59**, September, 612–622.

Parks, R. W. (1966) 'The demand for consumers' durable: A utility maximisation approach', paper presented at the Winter meeting of the *Econometric Society*, December, 1966.

Pontryagin, L. S., Boltyankii, V. G., Gamkrelidze, R. V. and Mischenko, E. F. (1962) *The Mathematical Theory of Optimal Processes*, Interscience (New York).

Ramsey, F. (1928) 'A mathematical theory of saving', *Economic Journal*, **38**, December, 543–559.

Rawls, J. (1972) *A Theory of Justice*, Clarendon Press (Oxford).

Robson, M. T. and Shah, A. R. (1990) 'A capital-theoretic approach to self-employment in the UK', *Mimeo*.

Sen, A. K. (1977) 'Starvation and exchange entitlements: A general approach and its application to the Great Bengal Famine', *Cambridge Journal of Economics*, **1**, 33–59.

Sen, A. K. (1981) *Poverty and Famines: An Essay on Entitlement and Depreviation*, Clarendon Press, Oxord.

Sen, A. K. (1983) 'Poor, relatively speaking', *Oxford Economic Papers*, **35**, 153–169.

Shah, A. R. (1980) 'Keynesian multipliers in temporary equilibrium with consumer credit rationing', *Journal of Economic Theory*, **22**, No. 1, February, 107–112.

Shah, A. R. (1981) 'Imperfections in the capital markets and consumer behaviour', *Southern Economic Journal*, **47**, April, 1032–1045.

Shah, A. R. (1983) 'The size of the lifetime excess burden of a tax', *European Economic Review*, **20**, 1–11.

Shah, A. R. (1990) 'Credit rationing within a life-cycle context', *Mimeo*.

Shah, A. R. and Rees, H. (1985) 'The distribution of housing tenure in Britain', *Manchester School*, **58**, September, 296–314.

Shapiro, C. and Stiglitz, J. E. (1984) 'Equilibrium unemployment as a worker discipline device' *American Economic Review*, **74**, June, 433–444.

Shapiro, M. D. (1984) 'The permanent income hypothesis and the real-interest rate: Some evidence from panel data', *Economics Letters*, **14**, 93–100.

Shell, K. (1967) Preface in *Essays on the Theory of Optimal Economic Growth*, ed. K. Shell, MIT Press, (London).

Shorrocks, A. F. (1979) 'On the structure of intergenerational transfers between families', *Economica*, **46**, 415–426.

Swan, P. L. (1970) 'Durability of consumption of goods', *American Economic Review*, **60**, December, 884–894.

Sweeny, J. L. (1974) 'Housing unit maintenance and the mode of tenure', *Journal of Economic Theory*, **16**, 111–138.

Thurow, L. C. (1975) *Generating Inequality*, Basic Books (New York).

Tobin, J. and Dolde, W. (1971) 'Wealth, liquidity and consumption', in *Federal Reserve Bank of Boston, Consumer Spending and Monetary Policy: The Linkages*, Boston.

Townsend, P. (1979) *Poverty in the United Kingdom*, Penguin (London).

Varian, H. R. (1974) 'Inequality and the motive for bequests', unpublished, Massachusetts Institute of Technology, November.

Wales, T. J. and Woodland, A. D. (1976) 'Estimation of household utility functions and labor supply response', *International Economic Review*, **17**, 397–410.

Wales, T. J. and Woodland, A. D. (1979) 'Labour supply and progressive taxes', *Review of Economic Studies*, **46**, 437–468.

Wan, J. Y. (Jr.) (1971) *Economic Growth*, Harcourt Brace Jovanovich (New York).

Watkins, T. (1977) 'Borrowing–lending interest rate differentials and the time allocation of consumption', *Southern Economic Journal*, **43**, January, 1233–1242.

Weiss, Y. (1972) 'On the optimal pattern of labour supply', *Economic Journal*, **82**, December, 1293–1315.

Willis, R. J. and Rosen, S. (1979) 'Education and self-selection', *Journal of Political Economy*, **87**, S7–S38.

Wise, D. A. (1975) 'Academic achievement and job performance', *American Economic Review*, **65**, No. 3, March, 350–366.

Wiseman, C. (1975) 'Windfalls and consumption under a borrowing constraint', *Review of Economics and Statistics*, **57**, May, 181–184.

Yaari, M. E. (1964) 'On the consumer's lifetime allocation process', *International Economic Review*, **5**, 304–317.

Zbalza, A. (1979) 'The determinants of teacher supply', *Review of Economic Studies*, **46**, No. 142, January, 131–148.

Author Index

Altonji, J. G., 46
Ando, A., 17
Arrow, K. J., 16, 17
Ashenfelter, O., 95
Atkinson, A. B., 17

Barro, R. J., 95
Becker, G. S., 72, 152
Bellman, R., 15, 16
Bernanke, B. S., 45
Bevan, D. L., 72
Bird, R. C., 44
Blinder, A. S., 17, 18, 31
Bliss, C. J., 3
Boczar, G. E., 110
Bodkin, R. G., 44
Brumberg, R. L., 17
Bruno, M., 17
Bulow, J. I., 116

Campbell, J. Y., 45
Clarke, F. H., 63
Cohen, W. J., 120

Deaton, A. S., 17, 44

Desai, M. J., 164
Dickens, W. T., 108–109
Dolde, W., 63
Dreyfus, S. E., 15, 16
Dynarski, M., 136

Engle, R. F., 163

Fisher, I., 17
Flavin, M. A., 45
Flemming, J., 63, 72
Freidman, M., 17, 44

Ghose, A. K., 157
Granger, C. W. J., 163
Grossman, H. I., 95

Haber, W., 120
Hadley, G., 16
Hall, R. E., 45
Ham, J., 87, 95
Harberger, A., 35
Hayashi, F., 45, 46
Heckman, J. L., 18
Henderson, J. V., 143–144

Hestenes, M. R., 15
Hirschleifer, J., 63
Hutchens, R., 116

Ioannides, Y. M., 143–144

Jaffe, D. W., 6

Kemp, M. C., 16
King, M. A., 142–143
Kleirman, E., 125

Laitner, J. P., 72
Lang, K., 108–109
Lazear, E., 116
Lee, T. H., 44
Lester, R. A., 120
Levhari, D., 35, 125
Lewis, G., 167
Lundberg, S., 87

Mariger, R. P., 46
Michael, R., 151, 154
Mirrlees, J. A., 16
Mishkin, F. S., 45
Modigliani, F., 17
Moffitt, R., 87
Muellbauer, J., 45
Mueller, E., 120
Murphy, K., 86
Muth, R. F., 125

Nickell, S. J., 158

Olsen, E. O., 125
Ophir, T., 125

Parks, R. W., 125
Pontryagin, L. S., 15, 16, 17

Ramsey, F., 17
Rawls, J., 178
Rees, H., 144–145

Robson, M. T., 163
Rosen, S., 31, 56
Russell, T., 6

Sen, A. K., 154, 167
Shah, A. R., 22, 35, 45, 70 144–145, 163, 164
Shapiro, C., 116
Shapiro, M. D., 46
Sheffrin, S. M., 136
Shell, K., 16
Sheshinski, E., 35
Shorrocks, A. F., 72
Siow, A., 46
Srinivasan, T. N., 125
Stiglitz, J. E., 116
Summers, L. H., 116
Swan, P. L., 125
Sweeny, J. L., 125

Thurow, L. C., 121
Tobin, J., 63
Tomes, N., 72
Topel, R., 86
Townsend, P., 164, 167

Ulph, D., 167

Varian, H. R., 27

Wales, T. J., 87
Wan, J. Y. (Jr), 17
Watkins, T., 63
Weiss, Y., 17
Willis, R. J., 31, 56
Wise, D. A., 31
Wiseman, C., 44
Woodland, A. D., 87

Yaari, M. E., 17

Zbalza, A., 31

Subject Index

Arrow–Debreu economy, 2–3, 9
Asymmetric information, 8, 11

Bankruptcy, 119
Bequests, 13, 18, 27, 28, 71–84, 122, 139, 159, 169, 172, 176
Borrowing–lending relationship, 3–10, 119–22, 156, 171, 178

Calculus of variations, 15–17, 170
Capabilities, 167
Capital,
  human, 13, 14, 54–55, 60, 83, 121, 150–154, 168, 175, 178
  livestock, 156–157
  set-up, 14, 150, 159–164, 168
Choice,
  discrete alternatives, 50, 62, 83, 84, 146, 165–169, 172, 175–176, 177
  earnings profiles, 50, 54–60, 72, 78–83, 102–118, 141, 146, 171–172
  sets, 71, 85, 95, 177
Co-integration methods, 163
Collateral, 23

Comparative statics, 12, 18, 28–31, 46, 66–68, 69, 73–74, 89, 93–94, 96–97, 160–162, 174
Consumption efficiency, 150, 151–154, 168
Consumption–housing trade off, 135–139, 141, 146
Consumption function, 20, 42, 45
Co-state variables, 17
Cost functions, 152–153
Credit constraints, 3–10
Credit constraint,
  intergenerational consequences, 13, 15, 71–84, 117–118, 172, 176
  phases, 22, 24, 28–30, 33, 36, 73–74, 92, 95–96, 136–139, 156, 162
  simulations of phases, 31–33, 36–41, 53–54, 57–59, 74–75
Credit market failure, 3–12, 178
Credit rationing,
  evidence, 44–46
  rule, 10–11, 22–23, 140

Default incentives, 3–12, 22
Default propensities, 10

Distribution,
  home-ownership, 139–140, 146
  income, 13, 27, 59–60, 107
  land, 157, 168
  net worth and wealth, 51, 59–60,
    106–107, 172, 176, 178–179
Dual labour markets, 13, 14, 102–103,
  107, 109, 111–118, 121, 122, 168, 173,
  176–177
Durables, 124–125, 145–146, 167, 174
Dynastic poverty, 82–84, 117–118, 123,
  172–173, 176–177

Earnings equations, 107–110
Education, 104, 109, 111, 113–114,
  152–154, 167–168, 175, 178
Engle curve, 153
Equilibrium,
  general, 17, 18
  housing market, 140, 144
  inefficient, 7
  information, 114–116
  job-training model, 111–114, 117
  labour market, 107, 173
  rationing, 7–8, 10, 11
  single-contract, 6, 8
  steady-state, 72, 118
  temporary, 9
Ethnic minorities, 83, 109, 112–118,
  143–145, 168, 175, 178
Exchange entitlements, 154–158, 168
Exponential distribution, 7
Euler–Lagrange equation, 17

Famines, 14, 150, 154–158, 168

Gambles and gambling, 51, 61–62, 79–82,
  84, 172, 178

Housing investment, 125, 132, 135–136,
  139, 146
Housing services prices, 124–125, 128,
  131–136, 140, 144, 146, 174
Housing tenture choice theory, 14,
  124–140, 151, 174
Housing trap, 124, 146

Imperfect information, 3–12, 112–117
Inequality constraints, 17, 24, 170
Inheritance, See bequests
Interest rates divergence, 63–70, 127
Intertemporal consumption substition, 35,
  41, 43, 68

Jaffee–Russell model, 3–12
Job types, See dual labour markets

Kuhn–Tucker conditions, 16

Life-cycle hypothesis, 17–19, 45–46

Maximum likelihood estimates, 108,
  143–144
Maximum principle, 16–17, 64
Moral hazard, 8, 11
Mortgage limits, 126, 134, 140–146

Optimal control theory, 15–17, 64, 170
Opportunity sets, 51, 61–62, 117, 123, 127,
  146, 162, 176, 178–179

Pareto distribution, 7
Pastoralists, 156–158
Pensions, 44, 169
Permanent income hypothesis, 17–18
Phase diagrams, 17, 66–68
Polarized outcomes, 176–178
Portfolio choice, 14, 124, 139, 174
Poverty, 13, 83–84, 120, 135, 139, 156,
  164–169, 176, 178–179
Primary sector jobs, See dual labour
  markets
Principal-agent problem, 115
Probit equation, 108–109

Quit propensities, 113–114, 116–117

Redundancy, 159–164, 168
Relative deprivation, 14, 151, 164–169,
  177–178
Retirement, 19, 93, 120
Risk classes, 10–11, 22

Secondary sector jobs, See dual labour
  markets
Self-employment, 14, 143, 151, 158–164,
  168
Shirk propensities, 115–117
Simulations, 31–33, 36–41, 46, 52–59,
  74–75, 78
Social deprivation, See relative deprivation
Starvation, See famines

Tastes,
  housing, 132
  work, 89, 105
Tax,
  income, 45
  interest, 35–36
  lifetime excess burden, 34–41, 46
  relief, 127
  temporary, 42–43, 46

Threshold level,
  assets, 13, 59–62, 79–83, 106–107,
    117–118, 141, 165–169, 172,
    173
  lifestyle, 168
Trainability propensities, 112–114,
    116–117
Training,
  costs, 112–114, 117
  job-entailed, 102, 111–113, 122,
    173
  life-time profile, 86, 98, 104–106

Unemployment, 86, 103, 118–122, 151,
    158, 162–163, 168
Unselfish behaviour, 2, 46, 118

Wage,
  adjustment, 86–87
  life-time profile, 89, 91, 98, 102
Walras' law, 9
Windfall income, 43, 46, 61, 136
Work,
  constraints, 85–86, 89–90, 95–97, 98,
    103–106, 122, 173
  effort, 115–116
  job-entailed, 85–86, 98, 102, 117, 122,
    173
  life-time profile, 86, 93–94, 102,
    103–106, 118
Work-leisure trade-off, 13, 18, 85–98, 173
Work-training trade-off, 13, 98, 102, 122,
    173